PURSUING INTELLIGENCE

REAL AND ARTIFICIAL

R. S. Eisenhour

First Edition

NEWMAN SPRINGS PUBLISHING
320 Broad Street
Red Bank, NJ 07701

First originally published by Newman Springs Publishing 2025

ISBN 979-8-89308-208-1 (Paperback)
ISBN 979-8-89308-209-8 (Digital)

Printed in the United States of America

PREFACE

When one enlists the use of artificial intelligence (AI), one tends to assume that it establishes credibility for the resulting decision or action. Based on experience as an engineer and inventor, it is irresponsible to accept the trustworthiness of AI devices without confirmation. One class of AI devices simply executes techniques or approaches prescribed by its designers. It is the designer's intelligence and corresponding credibility that is to some extent imparted to the device. The AI device simply provides a means to express it. To illustrate, in the 1600s, it was considered an intelligent position to believe that Earth is at the center of the solar system. Suppose we build an artificially intelligent device that abides that concept. As part of a modern class, students ask our AI device about this topic and submit this answer to their teacher. The students cite the authority of an AI device as a means to defend their position. Upon review, the teacher objects to the reply and states that their answer is erroneous and not intelligent. Had this response occurred in the 1600s, it would be judged as intelligent and correct. This fallacious dynamic does not necessarily require an "expert AI device"; it can arise from trust in any "credible authority" on any topic. This point reveals the situational nature of intelligence recognition, which calls into question what intelligence actually is. How is it that a once intelligent response is later judged as foolish and vice versa?

Conventionally, intelligence is a specialized ability. Any ability requires an opportunity to be displayed for the purpose of recognition. Reactions to the environment are opportunities for intelligence demonstrations. This means that, at first, the environment needs to be perceived. Our five senses enable us to observe our environment. Our human abilities to perceive and react are enhanced and extended through the use of tools or machines. Our tool set has matured through time and has become quite sophisticated. Machines (hardware) can mimic sight with cameras, hearing with microphones, touch with pressure and temperature sensors, and smell or taste with gas and chemical analyzers. Optical tools enable object observations that are much smaller, much farther away, and in different wavelengths of light than our eyes can readily discern. Colossal machines can move objects that we couldn't even budge, and we move at high speeds en route to far away destinations that are not even possible with our limbs. We are able to flip switches on and off at incredible rates of at least a few billions of times per second with computerized tools. This may seem excessive, but it is this binary "on and off" or "yes and no" capability that is vital in decision-making. The hardware used for intelligence demonstration by humans and by machines is similar in nature (perhaps because of our intent to extend our senses) and differ primarily in proficiency. This serves as a starting point for a popular hypothesis that humans and machines each have potential to act intelligently.

Intelligent behavior includes the action of translating observations into perceptions that then give rise to making a response. At first, observations have to be interpreted. Preconceived ideas or templates are compared to the incoming information to associate it with meaning. When the incoming information fits a preconceived template, it is "activated" and associated responses follow, like answering a familiar question. This combination of preconceived templates (perceptions) and connected responses are commonplace and may be the result of training or referred to as instincts. For example, a loud noise incites the flight of birds from an otherwise safe location. It is natural to jump up and move away from any object that causes pain (i.e., sharp or hot objects). These mechanisms are ingrained (learned deeply) and do not require conscious effort to decide what to do. Similar intelligent behaviors are demonstrated in a variety of familiar machine-based control systems in our lives. Among those are a building's temperature control, alarm clocks, timers, and television-show recording systems to cite a few examples. These control systems unburden us from the tasks of condition monitoring and the requirement to intervene during chore execution. For example, when the home's temperature sensor (thermostat) indicates a level that is preconceived as becoming too warm, the air-conditioner is activated. It does not require someone feeling too warm to activate it. Similarly, we don't have to turn the power off to an automatic garage door opener to avoid slamming the door into the ground and breaking it. It is managed by a control system that slows the speed as the door approaches the end of travel. The fact is that, these dedicated systems are frequently more diligent, attentive, and better at the task than we would be with conscious effort. These control systems are designed to react to perceptions (inputs) and make responses (outputs) in an approach not unlike how humans often display intelligence when familiar circumstances are encountered.

In the case of unfamiliar situations, a preconceived interpretation template and its associated response do not exist. This deficiency requires a learning function to develop the interpretation and response connection. In such a case, it is necessary to translate observations into an interpretation. If a response mechanism is not connected to the interpretation, training has to be done. This is a dynamic situation that likely requires response preparation, rather than simply using an existing one. For example, if one wishes to play music with an instrument, there is a need to learn how to read music. The observation of musical notes on a page needs to be interpreted and connected to finger actions (and possibly other complex moves), which need to be trained. The refinement of the performance response can occur in stages laced with deviations from the ideal intent. As the corrections of those deviations become ingrained, proficiency develops. Ultimately, the situation matures with a strong template that simply recognizes written music and connects that interpretation to automatic refined physical action.

Decisions present another opportunity to display intelligence. In common practice, the interpretation and response actions are executed in reverse order. Candidate responses are offered, and their potential impact requires interpretation. This requires recognition of the consequences of each response choice to aid in the decision. Similarly in the world of AI, the training of the device involves guessing and checking the results. The guesses are refined to improve the result suitability. A land-navigation system is an example of this type of decision-making. An iterative (trial and error) evaluation of multiple road combinations to reach a destination in the least amount of time is reviewed by an internal simulation. In this way, the imagined resulting condition is interpreted for each response option. Since the calculation of travel time through knowledge of distance and legal speed along each path is very good, the recommended path selection can be quite proficient. However, if the information used in the simulation is faulty, the recommendation may be considered foolish as it directs one to a dead end (i.e., some roads are closed).

The latter point shows that the mechanisms leading to a response may earn labels ranging from genius to fool. Thus, the response proficiency follows from the use of intelligence mechanisms that interpret the circumstance and select the pertinent resources in forming or choosing a response. It is these mechanisms that support the ambitious goal of teaching intelligence to a device (AI). By extension, there is no reason to think that we cannot teach the human population how to be more intelligent by cultivating the use of those mechanisms. This book will explore the essence of intelligence with the aim of augmenting intelligent behavior and ideally discarding unintelligent behavior in humans and machines. If successful, not only knowledge can be taught but intelligence as well.

CHAPTER 1

PREPARATION

Common sense suggests that misunderstandings make intelligent responses highly unlikely. If an artificially intelligent device fails to recognize a command properly, it will not deliver an appropriate response. When we misread a question on a test, we will likely fail to provide the correct answer. In this way, a demonstration of intelligence is highly dependent on communication proficiency. As in any communication activity, the development of the thinking shared in this book has the potential to be misunderstood. As a means to mitigate this risk, this chapter is intended to prepare a shared foundational understanding regarding intelligence in a manner that enables improved communication proficiency throughout the remainder of the text. To that end, an awareness of our training and cultural backgrounds will need to be shared to expand our communication potential.

In some cultures, the responsibility to communicate resides with the speaker. This is how we interacted with our earliest computing machines. Early artificial intelligence devices required the speaker to make their intent very clear. This occurred through delivery of specific key words (i.e., patterns in punch cards) with correct spelling and syntax to the device in order to access its designed responses. In these situations, the requirements of the listener (computer) had to be served by the speaker (programmer), or no suitable response was made. From this inflexible position, a machine or person with a similar mindset does not carry communication responsibility. In other cultures, the listener has the responsibility to grasp the meaning and intent of the speaker. Thus, the demands on the discipline of the speaker are relaxed a bit as the listener assumes a measure of responsibility in the communication process. For example, a spell-checking aid shows how a device can participate in anticipating the typist's intent. As an example from interpersonal human interaction, this scenario provides a communication advantage as each participant projects expectations into the conversation. Many times we know what is going to be asked, and even complete the thought for someone else to expedite the information flow. It is as if we have already had the conversation while we are listening. When the context or train of thought is shared, the communication becomes highly proficient. One of my favorite experiences that revealed this occurred in Japan as I conducted some technical training for a group of engineers. A skilled translator was assigned to assist me. Naturally, questions and explanations were quite demanding for my translator, who happily had a technical background and was very helpful. After one of my sessions, an engineer approached me with a desire to discuss more advanced aspects of my work. At that time, his English language skill was very weak, and my Japanese was horribly deficient for a detailed technical discussion, so my translator remained to support us. I began writing equations on the board, and my new friend pointed to the parameters that were unclear to him. I was able to clarify their definitions and meanings, and he would then add to the equations himself, and I would challenge him similarly. This exchange continued very satisfactorily for quite some time. Then suddenly my translator had a problem.

He exclaimed, "How can the two of you possibly communicate so well? My English proficiency is at least twice his, and you didn't even need me for this!"

Each of us was amazed by his correct observation. Through the years, my inquisitive new friend's English skills grew stronger, and we stayed in touch. We would often recount this experience and how a shared heart (his words) transcended the language barrier. It was the similarity of our interpretation of the topic that facilitated our success.

Imagine a medical doctor explaining a new medication to a colleague and again to a child. In order to be effective, the doctor's choice of words, content, and style needs to be adapted to the recipient of the information. This adjustment is based on the listener's background and the speaker's intent to expand the recipient's ability to interpret information related to this medicine. To serve this and future situations, let us define an interpretation framework as the structure (or perhaps template) that is used to classify and organize observations and information. The basic concept of an interpretation framework should be familiar to us considering that we have all at some point been required to search for something. During the quest, the characteristics of what we are seeking are compared to observations to interpret their relevance. The doctor's communication challenge is to add characteristics to the recipient's interpretation framework. The doctor's colleague has a medical education and has prescribed similar medications. This suggests a largely shared interpretation framework that has perhaps 95 percent of everything already known going into the conversation. This means that the colleague is able to relate to almost all of the content that will be shared and may anticipate large parts of the conversation. This individual will appreciate grasping how this medication differs from others and its relative benefits and risks. On the other hand, the child has a very basic idea of what medicines are and what they can do. Obviously, this suggests an interpretation framework that is not at all ready to have a technical conversation. The doctor elects to share relatable clinical stories of success when patients used this new medicine with the child. The child's interpretation framework can be grown from a background of knowing what being sick is like by linking particular symptoms to this candidate remedy. It would be silly to suggest to the child that this new medicine is similar to another one with a complicated name, yet it is a great choice of content for a colleague. Effective communication comes from building on the interpretation framework that is already in place for the listener.

If the circumstance of the listener is not addressed adequately, communication can fail. As noted before, early artificially intelligence devices that had a limited vocabulary could only be related to with key words or instructions from specific forms of information. If a request is made of such a device neglecting the communication parameters, there will not be any useful response from it. This is a stark example of how not matching the content to the recipient's interpretation framework results in failure. Similar to the device, we possess interpretation frameworks that have been imparted to us, such as language among many others. In human practice, the failures to communicate happen in varying degrees. This is due to a partial matching of the speaker's expressed content to the listener's interpretation framework. Naturally, this inefficiency is something we wish to avoid from our very beginning as children.

We start life with embedded innate "wiring" that allows us to contend with many critical challenges (i.e., digesting food and breathing) that does not require us to be trained to function proficiently. For other challenges, we need to be trained and instructed to become proficient. Other people, as individuals or organizations, feed us literally and figuratively while serving as examples of how to interpret and contend with these challenges. Let's call those people teachers for the sake of simplicity. One task of a teacher, for example, is to grow and impart an interpretation framework to their students. We have grade levels in school that in some way are indicative of the maturity of this process. Each grade level has criteria that are to be met by the student that become increasingly more sophisticated and dependent on aptitude developed in the earlier grades. This follows from the educator's efforts to associate the biological age to the grade requirements that strike a good balance between the content limits of being too trivial and being overwhelming for the student population as whole. This suggests that the instruction content has a sort of bounded continuum that depends on the student's ability to contend with it. When the content is outside of the boundaries, the teacher's lessons are a poor match to the student's needs, and the learning experience is hampered. To avoid this loss, tutors and advanced classes are often provided to compensate for an individual's interpretation framework maturity mismatch. This education construct provides a specific example of a communication exercise that warrants some reflection related to keeping content inside of healthy boundaries.

It is highly likely that we have all experienced responses, given or received, that have been too much or too little. Even in the same circumstance, some complain about too much information while others object to the brevity of the content. In general, a response can range from complete neglect to near insatiable obsession with too much information. Somewhere between neglect and obsession is what I will call a plateau in which suitable responses exist. Communication effectiveness can be interpreted with this scheme. An example comes from conversations that take too long. A simple polite greeting with a neighbor may lead to an excessive and lengthy disclosure of the family's situation and cause the conversation to fall off the cliff. There is some degree of discomfort and awkwardness afterward. Prior to going too far, there is a sweet spot that would be judged to be quite satisfactory to close the conversation. Further, to completely ignore or neglect the conversation opportunity would also be unsatisfactory. In the dating process, some contact between dates may be appreciated (not neglected), but excessive stalking types of intrusions take the situation over the cliff. Beyond communication, there are other responses that follow the plateau-cliff principle. A plateau is bounded by at least one cliff, depending on the nature of the challenge for which the response is being made. One cliff may exist at the edge of neglect; and the other, at the edge of obsession. A successful athlete cannot neglect training, and yet training without giving the body a chance to recover and rebuild is detrimental. This overtraining cliff is an example of a circumstance where the good behavior is taken too far and has become harmful. Suppose a person has a tendency to eat too much and may have passed over the cliff to a level that is unfavorable to their well-being. However, eating is essential and cannot be neglected—this is another cliff. Time-allocation management is another place where plateaus and cliffs can be found. For example, one may have the interest and capacity to work at a job nearly every day for all waking hours. This cliff of obsession may have a variety of consequences, one of which is burnout after a few months or years. In such a case, the outside-of-work relationships and responsibilities tend to be neglected and have fallen off their own cliffs, which suggest that some minimum amount of time needs to be spent to maintain them. The discipline to balance time allocation to keep multiple concerns or interests on their plateaus is important to avoid performance loss in them. Single-cliff situations exist as well. A casual drinker may have a cliff at a few drinks, before it becomes too much, and having no drinks is also satisfactory. The dangerous "location" of a cliff for an addict may be anything beyond abstinence—a very narrow plateau (complete neglect is required and is not a cliff).

The plateau-cliff principle plays out in building task proficiency as has been indirectly identified by business consultants Ken Blanchard and Paul Hersey (1977) in their Situational Leadership Models. Their models identify development levels, or stages, of task proficiency and link them to leadership behaviors that help facilitate growing competency accordingly. In their approach, the leadership or coaching needs of an individual are classified into four separate development levels as part of an interpretation framework. Their models can generally be applied to any task. At the highest level, called D4, the individual is essentially a self-sufficient expert that does not require direction or leadership support to complete the task. This enables full delegation of the task of concern to that person. Similarly, a highly developed artificially intelligent device could have tasks delegated to it without intervention. This mature condition is easy to manage, basically delegate. However, when a person or device is not mature, it is important to support their needs and not jump ahead of them by assuming competency that is not yet developed. For example, an erroneous full-competency assumption presents a communication cliff of neglect for the individual. If the maturity is underestimated by the leader, a communication cliff of "too much information" is experienced. The leadership models identify behaviors that provide an appropriate level of support and direction to a person or perhaps an artificially intelligent device that depends on their task-performance maturity. These models essentially establish a communication plateau for each development level. For example, because of the risk of damage or injury, it is unwise to completely delegate the driving of a vehicle to an inexperienced driver, who may need support and direction to help them to grow their competency. From an emotional perspective, it can be very scary to be thrown into a task with no idea of how to proceed. (What am I supposed to do?) This sets a person up at the cliff of neglect, and leadership attention is needed. By contrast, it may be quite insulting to be given detailed instructions for a task in which one has mastery. (Why are you talking down to me?) This cliff is one that some call micromanagement in which too much information and oversight from a leader is provided. A review of the consultant's development levels can help us acknowledge or interpret the growth status in ourselves and those that we support. With this insight, we can deal with each other more effectively (stay away from the cliffs). One key point is that these models are task specific. For instance, one might be a high-level automotive mechanic that can be left alone to fix a vehicle and yet needs detailed instructions and supervision to bake a cake. In other words, an expert label for all tasks is not earned simply because one task is mastered.

The first development level is called D1, which is for a person that lacks skills and competence for the task at hand. This is familiar when one is trying something for the first time (new job, etc.). The leadership required to grow D1 individuals (or devices) is highly directive. The leader interprets each challenge and strengthens the connection of that interpretation to the appropriate responses that are provided to the individual. In order to improve your sense of this, suppose I ask you to retrieve my glasses in a fictitious task. I might tell you that they are on my desk. If this is all that I provided, I have assumed a number of things about your ability to complete the task. You must favorably answer the following questions for yourself (and many others actually). Do you know what glasses are? Do you know what makes my glasses distinct from other glasses? Do you have sufficient knowledge about my desk? Do you know how to locate my desk? Are you physically able to get to my desk? If I described my glasses in great detail (to distinguish them from other glasses on my desk) and told you where my desk is located, and then give you the key to my office and the best way to get to my desk, I would be giving high direction to you to complete the task. Your lack of experience is being addressed by my detailed instructions and would serve your needs at this immature task development level of D1, and the cliff of neglect is avoided. As another example, suppose we create a driving aid that alerts the driver to nearby obstacles. The use of radar and rules to manage alerts has to be developed in detail. Thus, we train recognition of the vehicle-to-obstacle's distance to trigger the responses. At the D1 level, the act of giving the device (or person) the rules and interpretations assigns meaning to observations. Those details lead to the subsequent actions (perhaps also taught) that ensure successful task completion. When the details have been explained and ideally learned, the competency has grown, and the device or individual progresses to the next development level called D2.

In the D2 development level, the individual has some competency but frequently needs direction particularly when new aspects of a task are encountered that requires additional training to deal with their unique gaps in the D1 learning process. The individual at this level knows enough to ask relevant questions and to receive coaching during the process of securing what they know. Often, a person has already developed a logic structure in dealing with similar tasks and will likely attempt to apply it to this new situation. Those familiar logic structures are incorporated into the newly formed interpretation framework through ongoing questions and experiences with support from a leader or coach. Various components of the task have their own communication plateaus and cliffs. For example, the individual may receive subtask direction as an insult to their intelligence or feel lost without enough information. As a D2, if I asked you to retrieve my glasses, you would have some questions for me: Are they in your office? If so, where are they in your office? I can ignore those questions and place our communication over the cliff of neglect and hope you can figure it out. I can also answer in great detail what an office is and that it contains a brown desk that has four legs and three drawers. This detail could make you feel that I think you are stupid and don't have a working knowledge of a typical office space. However, if my "plateau" answers are sufficient, you can proceed successfully unless we missed something. In such as case, suppose you return with the wrong glasses, then we should have shared the answer to "What do they look like?" and not assumed that only one pair of glasses was on my desk. This refinement stage can be very frustrating. The supervisor or coach and the individual are both eager to move out of this stage. Each person wants the individual to perform without error and certainly not experience a task-completion failure. Further, each of them would like to dispense with the tedious, time-consuming detailed instructions. In a relatable D2 experience in a new job, one might come home from a bad day and say that I screwed up again. I forgot or I don't remember ever being told how to handle what happened. The boss seemed busy and I didn't want to look stupid, so I didn't ask for help. These discouraging experiences may cause persons to give up on the task and never move on to competency. This is the hardest phase of growing task maturity, and perseverance is essential in this development level. The demands on coping skills and patience that deal with failure are shared by the coach and the individual. Should either one give up, success is forfeited. In the case of an artificially intelligent device, the device is just as happy failing as it is succeeding and will not cease to participate. It is the teacher that might lose motivation.

The third development level, D3, identifies an individual that is able to answer many of the pertinent questions for themselves related to the task. The individual can navigate the task with very little direction and largely contend with incidental details independently. The individual is an expert in training, as experience is gained and remembered for the assigned task. Their approaches may be effective but not necessarily efficient or refined, kind of like the early stages of learning to walk. For this stage, external intervention is supportive of the approaches already learned for the purpose of fine-tuning, reinforcement, clarification, and mastery. For an artificially intelligent device, this expertise is task specific and matures to autonomy as the level is completed. At this level from the glasses-retrieval example, I ask you to collect my glasses, and you usually succeed. One day, you return and tell me that my office is locked and you cannot retrieve them. You explain that you asked the secretary to gain access, but my consent was required. Since you literally failed to open the door, I might feel justified in explaining the details of how a door and lock mechanism works. It is highly likely that this needless detailed information would be insulting to you, given that you successfully used several doors to find the one in my office. This would (obviously) be over the cliff of too much information regardless of how pertinent it seems. It would be much better if I sent a consent note with you or gave you my key.

The fourth development level, D4, permits full delegation of tasks to the individual. Leadership and coaching intervention is minimal. Only a rough idea of the task is all that is necessary to trigger successful action. The related interpretation framework at this level is extensive and is simply activated rather than explained. From an artificially intelligent device's perspective, it is left alone to run through its processes without ongoing maintenance. For example, a calculator that finds the values of trigonometric functions is trusted to complete the task without confirmation or adjustments. The task is fully delegated. Successful self-guided behavior is indicative of maturity in this level for a specific task for an individual or a device.

In the glasses-retrieval example, despite ample directions given to the D1-level individual, there are still many assumed competencies that come into play. Imagine how tedious the training task would be if explanation of how to get up from a chair, move to the door, how to open it and close it en route to getting the glasses was required. Thus, it is desirable to skip the excessive subtask-direction burden as much as possible. Clearly, this burden can largely be avoided with a sufficiently competent person. This is the reason behind an employer's job-interviewing process that favorably considers candidates based on their demonstrated competencies (education and experience). A candidate that has already performed the same job elsewhere, hopefully, can adapt quickly and not require excessive management attention and resources for direction or support. Similarly in professional sports, the top college athletes are likely to be successful professionals since a good portion of their development is already in place. Awareness of these development levels can help coaches or supervisors maintain reasonable expectations and offer appropriate support. Further, the individuals in training can acknowledge their need for patience as they manage their own expectations. Together, the frustration that follows when expectations are not met can be reduced. In effect, they can maintain a healthy plateau throughout the learning process.

The content of this book is intended to build on the reader's existing interpretation frameworks and not fall off a communication cliff in the effort to expand them. The interpretation framework being built involves a multitude of contributing concepts. Strictly speaking, these concepts are actually interpretation frameworks that are part of a larger overall interpretation framework. For some individuals, a given concept is already secure when it follows from recognition of similar experiences and education (a shared interpretation framework), while for others, analogies are helpful in making new concepts relatable to familiar observations that enable borrowing an existing interpretation framework for a new purpose. Because of differing needs on the part of various readers, it is hoped that the analogies achieve or strengthen the understanding of the concepts without being over the cliff. When a concept is a bit more complex, it may be required to develop its interpretation framework in stages to expedite effective communication later. Such a case follows:

Later in this book, some technical information will be shared that does not fit well into most reader's existing interpretation frameworks because of a lack of familiarity. If the mismatch is too large, a failure to communicate may happen, much like an early artificially intelligent device fails to comprehend when an improper syntax is used. To help mitigate this risk, growth of the reader's existing interpretation framework is pursued to a point of readiness for a future technical discussion. This attempt will serve as an example of the process of generating shared interpretation frameworks. To start, let's imagine an empty bucket that has a dime-sized hole near its base. The bucket is positioned under a water faucet that can be used to fill the bucket. The intent of this image is to help us clearly share a starting point for the conversation. If this situation or background is not relatable, the discussions that develop from here will fail. However, if we are on the same page, we can share interpretive awareness of this situation and ensure a growth of mutual understanding. Now, let us imagine that water flow from the faucet is a trickle, just a few drops per second. Would one expect the bucket to fill up eventually? It will not. The hole in the bucket is large enough to release the water that enters. Imagine if the faucet is turned to a high water-flow condition. The leak cannot keep up with the incoming water flow rate, and eventually, the bucket will overflow. The change in the level of water in the bucket follows from the flow-rate difference between the leak and the faucet. Let's call the difference the net flow rate (faucet minus the leak). To secure this concept of the net flow rate, what does it mean when the net flow rate is zero? It means that the water flowing from the faucet into the bucket exactly matches the flow that is being leaked out. With this, what happens to the level of water in the bucket over time? It stays the same. This situation of balance is called equilibrium. This circumstance for the bucket's water level can be described by a first-order differential equation. Depending on the reader's interpretation framework, the first-order-differential-equation description may or may not be familiar and, in the latter case, may be a bit intimidating. Yet the concept is likely clear regardless of using the fancy name for it, and that is what really matters. The equation describes that the rate of change of the bucket's water level depends on the net flow rate. In practice, the bucket can be filled to a desired level quickly with a high faucet flow rate, and then the faucet is set to match the leak flow rate to maintain that level. It is not important to write the equation, but the grasp of the concept of an interaction between the net flow rate and the bucket's water level is what is important. To reiterate, when the flow rates match, a water level change does not happen. If this equilibrium condition is not met, the bucket eventually overflows or it empties. This nature is common in many circumstances. It even can be used to explain why we take out the trash so that it does not accumulate and overflow in our homes. An example of a common error for interpreting these circumstances is thinking that a single faucet flow-rate setting corresponds to the bucket's standing water level—it does not. This might have its roots in the familiar volume control of an audio system in which sound level directly depends on a knob's position. If this misinterpretation can now be avoided by the reader, the interpretation framework growth was successful. Now let's use the interpretation framework to help secure it.

In another familiar first-order-differential-equation situation, consider an air conditioner in a building on a hot summer day. If the air conditioner is not providing cool air at a sufficient rate, the room temperature rises toward the outside temperature. If the air conditioner is too strong or operates too long, the room temperature may become too cool. The net rate of heat exchange influences the change in temperature of the room. Typically, the system is turned off when it starts to overcool the room and is later reactivated in order to keep the room from becoming too warm. This interrupted cooling operation basically compensates for the heat gained from the outside (sun load and temperature) conditions, accomplishing equilibrium at or near a comfortable room temperature. (Similarly, the water faucet could be turned off and on to keep the water level in the leaky bucket near a target level.) Through the awareness of these rate-based influences, the reader's interpretation framework is capable of correctly recognizing those situations. It does not matter if the concept was new or not, if the interpretation framework has been sufficiently prepared for future use.

Let's reflect on the interpretation framework growth process in the discussion so far. Familiar experiences were shared, or at least some that were easily imagined. These familiar circumstances were altered, and expected results were shared. Then the results and causes were explored and interpreted. This was the new part, but it wasn't really that new—the reader likely already had a sense of the reasons. This means that the interpretation framework was ready to be built upon, perhaps like the doctor's colleague with 95 percent of the content already in place. This incremental development mimics the education process that has grade levels and prerequisite classes. The student's incomplete interpretation frameworks have to be refined to a sufficient level to enable success with higher levels of connected information. For example, in early elementary school, a student was asked what the distance around a circle was called and replied "perimeter" rather than the expected response, "circumference." The student did not interpret the circle as a special case with its own unique name for the distance around the figure. This somewhat small flaw or lack of completeness in the interpretation framework of the student resulted in a failure. Interpretation flaws undermine the chance to make an intelligent response in the case of human beings, and this extends to artificially intelligent devices as well. If a person or device is to be considered intelligent, interpretation proficiency will play a central role.

Among the flaws that plague the interpretation function are thought poisons that arise from inappropriate internalized beliefs. These belief systems are a special form of an interpretation framework that creates what is often called a biased mindset. These beliefs serve as a means to make sense of (or reject) new or old information. Suppose a person is told they are not good at mathematics from an early age. Perhaps a computational failure was met with such strong disapproval, the person feared trying again and, subsequently, did not refine the needed skills to excel. Perhaps expectations were lowered by a comment that "Everyone in our family struggles with math—it is just the way we are." This person is set up with a limiting mindset or a preconceived idea that mathematical proficiency is out of reach. This type of poisonous mind food can come in many forms in almost any aspect of life. Labeling and discouragement can be taken in by an individual to create limiting behaviors and manifest in subpar intelligent responses with a lack of proficiency. Here are examples:

- You are too slow.
- You are impatient and careless.
- You are too fat.
- You are too thin.
- You cannot do it.
- It is too difficult for you.
- You aren't smart enough.
- You aren't that athletic.
- Of course you can't, it is normal for someone like you.
- Everyone else is better than you.
- You always choke.
- Can't you see the obvious?

- You should already know this.
- You are too short.
- You are too tall.
- You can't improve on this; it is perfect.
- You will never ___.
- You always do ___.
- You don't ever ___.
- We have always done it this way, accept it.
- You should do it that way.
- You disappoint me.
- No one else could do it.
- Don't reinvent the wheel.
- Don't insult me with your stupid questions.
- You are hopeless.
- You will never learn.
- How dare you question me?
- And on it goes…

Hopefully, as you read the extensive list of poisonous crap, you moved from "That sounds familiar, I've heard this before," to "This is getting ridiculous and almost preposterous." In fact, it is preposterous. A large enough dose of this nonsense at once forces recognition; and it makes the stench overwhelming, repulsive, and ridiculous. Unfortunately, it seems that small and frequently repeated doses of thought poisons are readily ingested by most of us by not acknowledging it for what it is. We then internalize the corresponding limiting mindsets and expectations and live by them. When we encounter a situation, we tend to use the biased interpretation from the poisonous mindset to formulate our response:

- I won't answer this question because I am not good with this topic…
- I won't try since others that are smarter have failed to do it…
- Oh, I am too fast and too slow at the same time? Perhaps I should not move at all…

These poisonous beliefs should have no place in an intelligent being (artificial or otherwise). As humans, we need to clean this out of our thinking. One tactic to purge the poison is to end its influence. First, the person recognizes that they have owned or accepted the harmful belief, which has been true, at least to them, at some level. Next, a decision is made that the belief will not be true from now on—it is disowned. For example: "At that time (perhaps in childhood), I was not able. From now, I am able, if I choose to try." As an inventor: "Yes, no one has done this before, including me. Other's failures are not relevant to my attempts. My skill set and experiences are unique to me and may enable my success." The key point, by whatever means, is to dismiss the poison and act as if it was *never* ingested. The dismissal is important. If it is not dismissed, there is a risk of adversely reacting to the poison beyond the obvious limitations of accepting it:

Some particularly strong people can treat the thought poison as motivational fuel to prove them all wrong. Let us call this thought poison defiant-poison. The negative label expressed in the poison is summarily rejected in such a way that it alters one's thinking to consider the label as an inherent weakness that must not be exposed. Defiant-poison reactions can include overcompensation by obsessing about defeating the label and disproportionately seeking opportunities to demonstrate how the label is untrue. Some coaches can exploit defiant-poison to motivate athletes to higher levels of performance when nothing is ever good enough for them. The athlete bearing this mindset is in a perpetual condition of shortfall and will continue to strive for more and more, never being satisfied. If fully poisoned, a person will try to prove oneself in situations that really don't require it. These people have become enslaved to the idea of resisting the original poison. If insecurity exists about one's abilities, the person may needlessly take or steal credit for an accomplishment or undermine someone else's work that eclipses theirs. The poison or defiant poison may be counterproductive to goal achievement by adding potentially off-task behavior (and possible neglect of other important things). For example, a player on a team may be poisoned and distracted with a fear of making a mistake in a key moment and fail.

A player with defiant-poison wants to be a star and competes against a teammate for individual glory in a key moment and disrupts the team's effort. It would be healthier to be driven by clear goals and to perfect the means to reach them. Ideally, the goal alone is worthwhile, and this value motivates improvement to that end. It appears that in human experience, the thought poisons undermine efficient progress to our goals since they force additional agendas and related consequences in the process of their pursuit. Thus, it is appropriate to build an artificially intelligent device or a human mindset that is goal focused and not poisoned.

Thought poisons can be created by the cliffs of the plateau-cliff scenario. Suppose a person is subjected to daily bombardment with negative comments about performance or appearance. This situation is like being pushed toward a "not good enough" cliff. This exposure can work one to the cliff's edge of accepting that thought poison or rejecting it by ingesting a defiant poison. Another reaction is to elect to completely ignore this barrage to avoid the hurtful comments. They are not acknowledged. With this ongoing daily "training," one may learn to regard all feedback as unwarranted criticism. This endangers the person to falling off the plateau from the cliff of neglecting to hear constructive advice. Perhaps some well-meaning supportive people may try to help them, but the feedback is perceived as more unwanted criticism and is ignored. It is like being wounded and not allowing treatment because that hurts too. As a result, there is no inclination to test new situations to see if what has been habitually believed truly matches reality. If the over-the-cliff condition were recognized, kind intervention (on the plateau) might be accepted.

Beyond the poisonous thoughts, other thought pollution includes distractions and entertaining irrelevant thoughts. The competition for our attention can have its origins internally and externally. This observation has given rise to the following construct called thought-space that is characterized by conscious directed attention and focus. For example, academic situations often have one topic being discussed in detail and reside in this thought-space. Control of the thought-space takes discipline and can be challenging to a student. The attention span of the student body may be varied, which causes some to tune out at least intermittently during a discussion. Causes may be that the burden to focus becomes too much or judgments of value creep into the thinking (I will never use this) or simple distractions enter into the situation (i.e., hunger). A highly disciplined mind can defend the thought-space from distraction and hold a focus on a goal or task by entertaining only relevant thoughts and questions. This does not mean that only simple thoughts are in this space. In fact, relevant complex thoughts can fill this space and enable high performance because of wide and deep consideration. Thought pollution intrusions into this space by inefficient, off-task, or simply irrelevant thoughts have many sources. The sources can be emotional. They may be paradigm based. They may come from regrets or worries. They could be physiological. They could be social. They could be environmental. They could be psychological. They could come from competing goals. They could come from time constraints. They could be financial. They could be political. They can come from ingrained limiting thinking habits (poisons). They can originate in a recent intense experience. They can come from task-execution struggles. In summary, our thought-space is under siege by almost everything we encounter or have ever encountered. An artificially intelligent device can be designed to keep the thought-space on task. Humans tend to struggle with keeping focus, but we have some powerful tools that help us independently accomplish tasks regardless of the condition of clutter in our thought-space. These tools take the form of habits.

Habits do not depend on an awareness or special attention to perform them. As an example, mechanical-like ingrained habits demonstrated by a skilled typist, musician, or in a baseball pitcher's throwing motion do not consume conscious attention for their intricate coordinated actions. However, when a habit is developed, thought-space is occupied in the process of practicing and embedding the techniques. For example, a musician learns to read music and consciously controls physical actions to make the sounds until it becomes automatic. The habit-training process can be interpreted using the development levels. For instance, high direction is needed at the beginning (D1 and D2) to recognize what is to be accomplished and a means to do it. This is a thought-space intensive phase of building a habit. Since the learning process of habit formation is full of shortcomings, there is considerable exposure risk to thought pollution that can start a destructive cascade of distractions. External poisoning from the "support" of others can generate thought pollution distractions through the threat of social consequences and possible attacks on self-esteem. Internally, an interpretation of a shortfall may be extrapolated to other failure expectations in various aspects of life (creating a failure bias). In the process of cultivating habits, a good coach can help secure the desired habits without adding external thought pollution to the process. Once some degree of mastery is achieved for the chosen automatic reaction, the connection of triggers to these learned actions develops proficiency (D3) through practice. At this level, the thought-space resources are mostly dedicated to dealing with inefficiencies in habit execution. As those inefficiencies diminish, the related thought-space activity also wanes. When the refined responses (D4) achieve statistical reliability, confidence and trust in the habit grows, this signals that the embedding process is completed. In this state, the habit is triggered, and the response follows without much directed attention.

The point of statistical reliability is a very important one. It suggests that the habit delivers the desired response most of the time, but not necessarily always. An inability to recognize habit maturity in this way may risk future performance in the event of a failure. Any lapse can trigger a resetting of the habit's learning process to the earlier development levels as in the following example from golf: The habit of a good swing has been trained for an amateur golfer. The habitual golf swing effectively delivers almost all of the time. If the swing produces an errant shot, the swing habit may come into question. In such a case, thoughts of corrective actions to avoid another swing error often enter the thought-space (perhaps they are offered by someone trying to "help"). This challenges the habit itself and can serve to restart the habit-learning process and harmfully fill the thought-space. To make matters worse, a potentially overwhelming flood of distractions can fill the thought-space related to the failed action. The poor ball position and environmental distractions such as lakes, trees, wind, rain, and noises can become objects of attention. Past experiences may also flood one's thoughts as well:

> Last time this happened…
> I always mess up like this…
> It is impossible from here…
> Look how well my friends did…
> I don't want to fail in front of them…
> Everyone is watching me…
> I lost my composure, and I am embarrassed…
> I hate how my opponent looks down on my play…
> I can't win now…
> I disappointed my partner or team…

In this condition, the thought-space is full of many off-task distractions and threatens the good swing habit's use in the future. The fact is that a swing error had a physical consequence (i.e., the ball is behind a tree), and anything beyond that is a choice. If the reaction to the error is allowed to destroy the confidence in the swing habit, new actions are attempted that are not refined, which typically forfeits high performance. Thus, it is better to recognize that a momentary failure is somewhat rare and keep the otherwise reliable habit without adding the mental burden of thought-space disruption. It has been noted that some successful athletes have a short memory of their failures and rebound from them to have great success. In effect, they trust the habits formed in their training and do not question or abandon them when failure happens. This discipline to preserve their habits protects their thought-space and avoids potentially harmful intervention that would replace a good habit with unproven responses. It is a little ironic that the most intelligent response is to ignore or forget consequences when dealing with mature habits.

An artificially intelligent device should not have this problem with distractions. However, the hardwired automatic responses that habits represent are terrific for a device as well. This translates to stand-alone functions that get triggered and deliver well-rehearsed results (i.e., an event-based software program). For example, the event of clicking on an icon in a display is similar to this, since action isn't triggered until the click happens. Just like a good habit, a dependable action follows when triggered. The need to interpret information in the computer's thought-space (i.e., a sequential software program) is unnecessary since the interpretations are already decided in the form of triggers and automatic responses. A trivial physical example could be simply maintaining the temperature in a room. A mechanism senses the room temperature and will activate the air conditioner or heater as needed. An analog sensor (like a thermostat) continuously monitors the condition and will make a preplanned action if the sensor indicates a need to do so. In effect, the sensor's condition pushes the button to activate the air conditioner or to turn on the heater without "thinking." This function is just like the habitual tasks we perform without thinking.

In the next chapter, we will begin building a novel-interpretation framework for intelligence itself. The existing intelligence interpretations leverage the same observations that the new framework will. Thus their perspective is extremely helpful in the identification of important observations. However, conventional interpretations tend to establish paradigms that may distort the observations. This means that some testing may be required to remove that distortion. By analogy, we see the same landscape and may interpret the Earth to be flat, but through testing, we find it is not. The idea that the Earth is flat serves as critical evidence of the existence of the landscape observation. After correction, that pure observation is no longer distorted by an assumption of flatness. It is the fresh comprehension of fundamental observations that enables creativity, novelty, and growth.

CHAPTER 2

REACHING FOR INTELLIGENCE

It has been common practice for active individuals of uncommon ability to generate knowledge, solve difficult problems, and demonstrate exceptional skills. They often teach, coach, lecture, and publish as a means to share their findings and their techniques with others. The masses can then mimic or duplicate their accomplishments via memorization and training through rote process standardization. An intelligent pupil that fully grasps the related content can not only duplicate previous success but also build upon it to create new knowledge and even higher achievement. Those individual's intelligence skills or their use of them appear to be exceptional compared to the rest of us. Perhaps their skills could be trained or shared as a means to expand our collective intellectual capability. If this can be accomplished, we may be able to harness the nature of intelligence much like we have done with recorded knowledge. Thus, we could elevate a previously incapable person to a high-functioning expert and similarly create truly intelligent devices. To that end, we need to clarify and define the nature of intelligence and its attributes in order to impart those attributes to devices and to humans. Let us explore the conventional thinking related to the concept of intelligence as a reasonable place to begin.

First, we turn to the dictionary. Intelligence is "an ability to learn facts and skills and to apply them, especially when it is highly developed" (Encarta). Intelligence is "an inborn quickness of understanding and adaptability to relatively new situations or information" (Webster). *Webster's New Lexicon Dictionary* adds the ability to perceive logical relationships to the definition in the process of solving problems and responding to new situations. Moreover, this word is a noun, which objectifies it and makes it something that can be recognized. Since "ability" is central to the definitions, it is important to note that ability requires demonstration in order to be recognized. For example, addressing a challenge or solving a problem can enable these "ability" demonstrations. In this way, a challenge is required for a display of intelligence and, therefore, is a key to recognition of it. In addition, the definitions are vague concerning demonstration proficiency. What does "a highly developed skill application" or "quickness of understanding" really mean, since it implies a judgment against an unknown performance baseline level? Perhaps this relative proficiency element is evident when we examine intelligence testing that purports to generate an intelligence ranking.

Standardized intelligence testing establishes a grading scale based on an exam that is frequently used to label people as intelligent or perhaps not. This potentially creates a means to judge the relative proficiency of intelligence demonstrations through responses to questions. Conventional testing contains exam questions that have correct answers that are directly aimed at detecting knowledge through an ability to apply or, at least, recall information. In intelligence testing, it is assumed that the questions are able to detect intelligence. If the questions are somehow inappropriate, the merit of the test (as with any test) is diminished. A test subject that can recognize patterns, analogies, associations, or relationships will tend to do well in intelligence testing. The ability or tendency to project valid assumptions into unfamiliar circumstances also tends to be rewarded in these tests, as long as the subject jumps to the same conclusions as the question's creator. Some questions ask for a prediction of an unknown extension of a pattern. Suppose the question designer decides that the pattern of a short list of numbers is increasing by a common increment (i.e., 2, 4, ____). A test subject will be rewarded with a correct answer if that same logic is used (2, 4, and

6). Yet this logic choice is an assumption by the tester that it is the only answer. Sometimes more obscure relationships or patterns can be recognized than the tester expects [i.e., 2, 4, 16 (the next number in the series is the square of the preceding number) or perhaps 2, 4, 8 (the next number is double the previous number)], and any alternative response is considered to be incorrect without cause. Regardless, these types of test questions are largely aimed at revealing an ability to hypothesize relationships or expectations based on existing information. The breadth of the ability to do this in a variety of circumstances is needed to gain high test-score achievement. This creates an unavoidable bias that dictates the relative importance of the tested circumstances (domain and count of the questions). To exaggerate, if there is only one math question and ninety-nine word-association questions, word-association aptitude will be rewarded, and proficiency with mathematics is nearly irrelevant. What should that mix be? I don't think there is an answer that can be responsibly defended. Perhaps each question's domain identifies a type of specialized intelligence. This concept of intelligence partitioning has already been explored in the field of psychology.

Psychologist H. Gardner (1983) recognizes eight separate types of intelligence and possibly more. Each of these types emphasizes "ability" and the "ease" of the demonstration. This is consistent with contents of the definitions that carry a proficiency comparison to a vague baseline level of performance. A short description of these intelligence types follows:

The first type is called linguistic, which is described as a high level of an individual's ability of "self-expression" and to easily grasp the viewpoint of others. The second type is logic, which is the ability to manage math and logic with ease. Kinesthetic intelligence is the third type, which relates to the ease of bodily expression, for example an athletic performance. The fourth type is spatial or visual intelligence, which is having the ability to create, imagine, and draw images. The fifth is musical intelligence, which is expressed by an ability to listen to sounds and identify patterns with ease. The sixth type is interpersonal intelligence, which at least in part includes the ability to recognize skills and qualities in others and easily bring them out (like a leader). Intrapersonal intelligence (seventh type) is expressed in someone that is self-reflecting and able to know personal limitations. Finally (eighth type), a naturalist's intelligence displays an understanding of living things and has sensitivity to the natural world. In summary, the intelligence types recognize opportunities to reveal high proficiency that might be judged as intelligent based on the uncommon ability and ease of the demonstration.

One could argue that a person highly skilled in a given intelligence type exhibits ability and ease. Thus, greater skill leads to a corresponding greater intelligence impression due to the proficiency recognition. In a similar manner, the use of tools can artificially enhance the ability and ease to execute a task. This proficiency connection leads to an analogy that intelligence skills and tool choices have a similar nature. For example, a poor tool choice and poor intelligence skills will underperform relative to the recognition of ability and ease. With this conceptual latitude, let us introduce a fictitious intelligence type for the task of driving nails that has visible physical mechanisms related to the resulting proficiency. The ability and ease to accomplish this task remains consistent with H. Gardner's style, despite its pure physical nature. For example, attempting to drive a nail with a bare hand will result in low proficiency since the "ability and ease" is not demonstrated. Thus, that "tool" choice resource is considered lacking in intelligence. By contrast, if a hammer is used, the nail-driving intelligence is remarkably improved, since a nail can be successfully driven in a reasonable amount of time. By extension, a genius in this intelligence type uses a nail gun, by demonstrating greater ease than using a hammer. The value of this intelligence-tool analogy as it relates to the nature of intelligence begs an investigation into the nature of tools. Ideally, we will find similarities and exceptions from intelligence-to-tool comparisons as a means to further our understanding. The exceptions can help guide us to further investigation, and the similarities enable us to secure our understanding, which would fulfill the function of an ideal analogy.

Tools primarily serve two roles: First, tools can help us perceive the environment. Microscopes and telescopes are certainly among those tools as an example. Our place in the universe and the causes of disease were much better understood through the use of these tools. Second, our tools can help us contend with our environment. For example, we may wish to cross the ocean and elect to use a boat or an airplane to respond to that environmental challenge. As time has progressed, our perceptions and interpretations of the environment have grown and so have our skills to leverage a variety of technologies to respond to the opportunities that they present (i.e., synchronous orbit communication satellites). Tools, by nature, can help us compensate for a lack of skill, gaps in perceptions, and lapses in judgment. In short, they can make us more effective and proficient. Following the analogy from an intelligence perspective, one could postulate that there are resources that are dedicated to perceiving and interpreting as well as making a response. The specialized perception or interpretation mechanism for the musical intelligence type may very well be a great example of this. The kinesthetic intelligence type recognizes exceptional ability to respond physically. The fact that there are specialized distinct functional separations in the variety of intelligence types implies that there may be an array of possible resources (skills) that reside in either of these two classifications or roles.

The subjective judgment of what level of ability and ease is exceptional, and therefore, intelligent in the intelligence types is problematic because of its vagueness. In practice, we have a sense of relative intelligence in that some responses are less clever than others. In this way, we are able to recognize uncommon and exceptional performance and label it as intelligent. Similarly, we know when one tool works better than another. For example, prior to the invention of the nail gun, the hammer was proficiently used to drive nails and is a clever tool. It could meet the nail-driving challenge. The advent of the nail gun does not diminish the capability of the hammer to deliver results. It is its new and uncommon level of proficiency that gains our admiration and alters the subjective judgment to perhaps downgrade the hammer's perception. Does this imply that the choice to use the hammer to drive nails is suddenly not intelligent, when it was intelligent in the past? If the answer is no, it suggests that the pertinence or effectiveness of a tool choice dictates its intelligence value. Further, the merit or proficiency of the response is the result of those tool choices. This leads to a hypothesis: *An intelligent action serves to select and utilize resources that may deliver differing levels of proficiency to accomplish a task.* With this I am proposing, that relative response proficiency is not part of the nature of intelligence, it is just a consequence of it.

Now let us entertain the premise that relative proficiency is not a requisite defining characteristic of intelligence. Conventionally, it is unnatural to judge a slow, clumsy yet effective response as intelligent when it is compared to a successful response that is faster and much more elegant. For us, it may be difficult to separate the ingrained "ability and ease" from our consideration, but this separation naturally happens during the development of an artificially intelligent device. A machine that can complete a given task clearly demonstrates the "ability" to do the task and the "ease" of doing it has little meaning. This renders those tempting subjective intelligence type qualifiers to be nearly irrelevant. Additionally, proficiency perception usually has an element of response speed to it. A computer's hardware can be upgraded to provide faster response speeds and falsely give the impression of proficiency while using somewhat inept software/logic approaches. Thus, the development of artificial intelligence (AI) depends on intelligent functions and does not rely on proficiency assessments. Research for artificial intelligence has identified a variety of intelligence functions that may be utilized to address challenges, which are labeled as tribes.

There are five predominant tribes, or paradigms, in the AI technical arena of how to "think" in problem-solving and in dealing with the environment (Pedro Domingos, *The Master Algorithm: How the Quest for the Ultimate Learning Machine Will Remake Our World* [New York: Basic Books, 2015]). The reasons for the multiple paradigms are that their individual appropriateness is circumstance specific: one paradigm may work better or at least faster than the others. The paradigms are personified and perhaps oversimplified for the purpose of explanation in the following discussion. Each paradigm (or representative) has its own unique interpretation framework. Our ability to connect our interpretation framework to theirs will strengthen our grasp of each one's merits and limitations. In fact, the style used to describe them can enable us to see them in ourselves and others. In effect, this makes the tribes a simple way to label and organize the major thinking approaches that are part of intelligent life.

The symbolists use inverse deduction based on philosophy to guide their thinking. In other words, the symbolist uses previously learned paradigms that are used for interpretation and to deliver a connected response. This style of thinking has its roots in theoretical ideas or belief systems to craft reactions and to form interpretations. This can be the domain of philosophy, religion, politics and virtually any other ideology. In essence, any new information is filtered by the rules and assumptions in an interpretation framework that reflects their ideology. The symbolists tend to act as if their insight is correct. In the absence of statistical evidence or a rigorous proof to support their position, their confidence is derived from faith or arrogance. A symbolist tends to hold to their beliefs despite compelling evidence to the contrary. For example, some symbolists believed that the Earth is the center of the universe and that it is shaped like a table with dangerous edges for quite some time in our history.

The symbolists use theories and beliefs from this paradigm as a means to deal with unknown circumstances through extrapolation. In the field of physics, Sir Isaac Newton's theoretical concepts that explain how objects move (i.e., behave) guided the selection of attributes for an experimental Earth-based investigation that confirmed them. The theory was also used to explain observations of celestial motion. The evidence of the theory's correctness was very strong, and it was relabeled as the laws of motion. Our initial reach into outer space was enabled by our confidence that our calculations based on those laws were applicable in dealing with that unknown environment. Similarly, analogies in the form of myths (i.e., the sun being lifted from the Earth and carried across the sky by a chariot) are sometimes held by symbolists as a means to deal with the unknown.

The symbolists have a risk of being too confident in their belief systems. This can lead to a closed mind to new interpretations and responses. The interpretation framework is essentially predetermined for the symbolist, and challenges to that framework are potentially offensive and may inspire rejection of new ideas. If so, this is a thought poison, as was discussed in the preparation chapter. Conversely, this paradigm presets a readiness to deal with or interpret the environment. Through their experience and rules, they are poised to make a response from a considerable background of past success. An intelligence test may reward this ability to apply established relationships and expectations to new situations. A pure symbolist assumes that they have a full grasp of challenges and react accordingly.

Analogizers are from the tribe that uses comparisons to familiar and similar situations in an effort to make an interpretation, decision, or response choice for a new circumstance. Unlike the symbolists, the analogizers do not assume that they have a full grasp of challenges and seek interpretations and responses related to similar challenges. Thus, the assumption that the nature of something somewhat familiar parallels the unfamiliar is in play. When I related tools and their use to intelligence resources, I made an analogy. The touch points of improving performance and expanding ability made the analogy a suitable possibility. An examination of how tools enhance performance provides a familiar experience that has an easy-to-grasp interpretation framework. In this way, the nature of the tool's nuances can be explored, which may guide us to similar ways to interpret intelligence. The analogizer moves through the familiar and makes connections to the unfamiliar as means of discovery. Thus, one can learn about the unfamiliar from the findings of where the analogy holds up or breaks down. It is somewhat like having an old map with a chance of new roads missing and old roads being closed. The guidance may not be perfect, but it tends to enable progress in a reasonable direction (another analogy).

Effectively, this paradigm draws from past successes or failures and extrapolates or applies those actions to a new situation by assumption. For example, the idea that a dish can fall off the edge of a table and be broken can be an analogy for a ship falling off the Earth's edge if it sails too far away. This familiar tabletop experience is projected as applicable to an unknown situation at an edge of a flat Earth. In another example, the habitual action of brushing one's teeth has many elements to it, from dispensing the paste to rinsing the mouth and brush. If one wants to clean something other than teeth with a brush, there may be some common familiar actions that make sense to utilize from that daily practice. The linking of similar situations to new situations is the key to this paradigm. The hope is that the refined response to the most similar and familiar situation serves the new situation well. This style enables leveraging transferable skills and learned lessons as a starting point in a new experience.

The interpretation framework of the analogizer depends on finding similarity. How does this compare to something I already know? Which experience is the most like this new one? A simple example could be recognition of an animal: This looks like my neighbor's dog. It might be the same breed. It was a mean dog. This dog might be mean to me. I will be very careful with this animal. This demonstrates how analogizers project assumptions into new situations and use them. In this case, this learning and connection to a past experience may or may not be appropriate. This may help the person avoid a dog bite, or it may result in an unnecessary avoidance of a friendly animal and its owner. It is easy to imagine how this approach is a place where thought poison thrives. The extrapolation of similar experiences to new ones gives "authority" to the past over the present. The person of this example can carry a fear of dogs that will go unchallenged because of a bad experience in the past. The differences from the past are not being assessed; rather, the similarities are emphasized and assumed to be applicable.

The Bayesians use statistics and probabilistic inference to select the most probable correct responses to a new situation. Gambling is in the domain of the Bayesians. Card games such as blackjack rely on an assessment of success when a hit (additional card) is to be chosen or not (if the total exceeds twenty-one, it results in a loss called a bust). When only a few possible cards could help one get closer to twenty-one, the odds of success are low, and an additional card should be avoided. If almost any card could get closer to twenty-one, a hit is wise. An example of this paradigm at work could be in a traffic situation. Suppose an object is obstructing the path of a vehicle. What is the most probable choice of action to avoid damage? If there is a sudden stop, perhaps there will be a rear-end collision due to an inattentive driver that is following. If the vehicle swerves, it might hit another object or perhaps oncoming traffic. If the object is hit, there will likely be damage, but how much? The decision or choice of action will depend on the situation and the likelihood and magnitude of consequences from each choice. At best, this paradigm makes decisions and actions that are most likely to be successful.

The interpretation framework for this paradigm is full of what-if questions. The responses are alternatives that are evaluated based on risks and rewards typically associated with an objective or goal. Thus, guessing (or statistically testing) the most likely means to reach the goal is the outcome. As with any probable situation, exceptions to the best guess can occur at any point in time. (A person may not expect to draw a playing card less than a three in general, but it does happen.)

The connectionists use backpropagation, which is a means to minimize the error among choices by adjusting the contribution of various factors that influence a result. A simple example for this somewhat complicated concept is a passenger vehicle's navigation system. If a person desires to travel to a destination, the connectionist will examine each combination of road choices and assess the time it takes to cover the distance of the virtual paths that can be selected (that *connect* the current location to a new one). If the wish is to minimize the time of the trip, an optimal suggestion can be found. Similarly, if the desire is to minimize the distance driven, a different path might be suggested. Another choice might be provided in order to minimize the cost of the trip (i.e., avoiding a toll road). Contributing factors of the road selection, speed limits, and distance on each choice are all in play. This paradigm enables virtual experimentation, often called simulation, to test the understanding of the environment to gain the optimal result. The benefit of virtual investigation is that it can be fast and help one avoid experiencing the consequences of a poor choice. Further, it can adapt to changes in an environment in a very practical way. (Suppose there is new construction work on one of the roads that would influence the suggestion.)

The interpretation framework for this paradigm is seeking adjustment of causes and the subsequent effects related to some target result. What are the possible factors that could influence the result?

If this contributing factor changes, what happens to the result? How much should this factor or combination of factors be adjusted to achieve the desired result? An example of this happens when a person takes a hot shower. The blend of hot and cold water follows the position of a control lever. This lever's position is a factor that can make the shower uncomfortably hot, uncomfortably cold, or suitable. In this case, the results are not simulated, and consequences of being uncomfortable are indeed experienced. (This tribe contains "deep learning" that effectively determines the contribution of various independent and interacting factors to emulate the results in a large data set. In essence, it is an extension of simple curve fitting that enables the use of a contributing factor's value to predict a function's outcome: given this "x," you get this "y.")

The evolutionaries use genetic programming to generate logic structures in a learning environment. The idea is that the brain's neurological connections can be mimicked and the structures that connect stimulus to response can be created. Ideally, this paradigm affords the chance to grow knowledge and follow the human mind's development. This process relies on feedback from an action's result to modify the logic structure or management of it, should the result be deficient in some way. This paradigm is well aimed at learning environmental rules or laws, and contending with them as trial-and-error mistakes are made. Conventionally, a computer programmer serves in the capacity of correcting errors in a software program, as old methods that created error are discarded in favor of new approaches that work better. An intelligent device that could self-repair would be ideal in this paradigm. Acceleration of the learning process and the ability to extend the life of these structures may hold tremendous merit in the future. Humans already have this structure and can learn to self-repair when deviations of results are encountered. The challenge to discard thought poisons (bad approaches) rather than continue to serve them is a hazard for an artificially intelligent device that is based in this paradigm, just like us. If one discards failed thinking patterns, what should take their place?

The interpretation framework for this paradigm deals with deviations from a desired result. Is the response unacceptable? What can be changed in an effort to make the response acceptable? When the change is made, did the response become acceptable? Is it necessary to keep trying different things to make the response acceptable? Essentially, the means to correct a deviation is assumed to lie within the resources of the evolutionaries. The learning process comes from largely unguided experimentation: dealing with deviations by trial and error. When no error exists, there is nothing more to learn or actions to be taken. The growth in this tribe depends on firsthand learning from reactions to new experiences.

Exploring the character of the tribes provides additional insight into their nature. A symbolist or analogizer may offer a learned best practice or a similar experience as the only means to an end. It would be somewhat inappropriate to offer inferior alternatives. Bayesians select the most likely single response to yield a desired result and proceed accordingly. Each of these tribes has a chance of failure due to an open-ended assumption that their responses are pertinent (without validation). The connectionists and evolutionaries perceive the symbolist's, analogizer's, or Bayesian's response recommendation as a possible single means of many candidates to an end. The connectionists and evolutionaries seek to manage or identify relationships that link causes (factors) to effects (or results), and a single combination of contributing factors is not likely to be comprehensive in their view. From this, the connectionists and evolutionaries will embark on learning via testing, trying, and failing as effective responses are developed and confirmed. Clearly, innovation is at home in these paradigms as a goal is approached that has never been accomplished before. These paradigms may generate new experiences that expand the boundaries beyond the familiar. For example from the incandescent light research: One cause of filament failure is its burning up, which follows from a chemical change of the filament as it oxidizes. Thus, an unusual environment void of oxygen or air favors longer filament life. This means that the filament and humans cannot share the same "air." Driven by this causal recognition, it was confirmed that a hot, glowing filament in a vacuum (bulb enclosure) did not rapidly burn up. Given how extensive the activities of the connectionists and evolutionaries can be, a Bayesian can serve in a supporting role to make multiple response candidate suggestions that have a good chance of being pertinent. This can narrow the scope of the confirmation investigation with less time spent on frivolous attempts.

The paradigms of the tribes have participated in the evolution of our myths and science. The pure analogizers and symbolists have often projected the validity of their beliefs as undeniable throughout our history and tend to be intolerant of other mindsets. After all, once "truth" is found, there is nothing more to learn, and those that have other experiences or belief systems are unworthy of favorable attention. This stagnation gives rise to the diversity of uncompromising and often conflicting views in political, religious, and even scientific positions and their related organizations since each have arrested at various levels of enlightenment. Imagine if we created an AI device with the "truth" that one can fall off the edge of the Earth in the distance, like reaching the edge of a tabletop. This would make it seem stupid, knowing what we know now. However, the device only has what it has learned as a static resource. As a result, it exactly mimics the pure analogizer and symbolist. Those two tribes need their beliefs and assumptions to be maintained and kept up to date to be healthy. Therefore, analogizers and symbolists should maintain openness to the possibility that the functional truth of their belief is potentially incomplete. For example, the sun rises and sets, but does it really? This is a peculiar and disproven concept that is based on an Earth-centered interpretation framework of circumstantial evidence. In practice, it communicates well and serves as a functional truth. It should not be taken literally. If one asks a symbolist if the sun will rise tomorrow, they will likely say yes and be offended by a suggestion that they are completely wrong, since it never has. Further in our past, it was arbitrarily decided that the Earth was the center of the universe. After all, the universe can be viewed from any place and that place can be called the center of everything, so why not Earth? Some symbolists built a belief system around that perspective to postulate the central importance of human beings in the physical universe as well as in a spiritual one. This belief took a blow when mathematical predictions and observations of nearby celestial motion (transformed to the sun's reference frame) suggested otherwise, with the sun near the center. From a religious perspective, the hypothesis that our central spiritual place in the universe and our physical position are interconnected was disrupted by these findings. With the connection, a need to squelch the physical data (or to punish those that uncovered the faulty assumption about the Earth's physical place) was deemed necessary to preserve the spiritual construct. Yet, without this implicit connection, the symbolist has no threat to the spiritual human-centered belief system, and the physical truth could be accepted.

Let us consider the preparation of a dessert for friends as a way to see these paradigms in operation. As a symbolist, I select one my favorite grandmother's recipes for dessert, with a firm belief that it will be a delight to my guests. I follow the old, soiled instructions and compensate for the unreadable gaps from my previous cooking experiences of a similar dessert (analogizer). When the dessert was sampled by my friendly evolutionaries and analogizers, they find that it is far from perfect and intend to never eat anything like it from me again. (They learned!) My Bayesian friends rudely spit out the dessert and did not hesitate to suggest which ingredients were likely to be the most offensive (i.e., too salty). My good friend, a chef, is a connectionist who suggested adjustments to the ingredients to improve the recipe (actually fixing or improving the old recipe's information). Once the recipe was tuned to deliver a great experience, I am ready to use it in the future without question of its suitability (a symbolist again). My evolutionary and analogizer friends must be encouraged to try the dessert again to learn that it is acceptable now; otherwise, they would reject it based on the past experience. Happily, my Bayesian friends are willing to give me another chance. If some should happen to still dislike it, my belief or hypothesis that this is a great dessert would have failed a test. From this, it is easy to imagine that many of these paradigms could be operational almost concurrently in many experiences to varying degrees.

Upon reflection, it is apparent that the intelligence types and the individual tribes have unique interpretation sensitivities. This means that the awareness of a shared observation or experience may lead to completely different interpretations among them. For example, when a sound is heard, a Bayesian may suggest the most likely guess as to how it was made. An analogizer may say it sounds like a bird. A talented musical-intelligence-type person may explain the pattern and the blending of the sounds. The linguistic-intelligence-type person may explain how the sound makes them feel. The kinesthetic intelligence type might inspire a person to dance in response to the sound. In this way, depending on the challenge, its interpretation will trigger a tribe's paradigm function and similarly the demonstration of an intelligence type, depending on how it matches their respective frameworks. Thus, the interpretation function is part of initiating a demonstration of intelligent ability. For example, an analogizer has to recognize a similarity of an observed circumstance to something familiar. The symbolist may perceive a new challenge as a call to use an established belief system to form a response. The musical intelligence type (ability and ease of sound pattern identification) requires a sound to be interpreted. A person with the linguistic intelligence type interprets internal thoughts and feelings in order to transform them into words. Even if the innate abilities to display an intelligence-type skill or to utilize an AI paradigm (tribe) are exceptional, demonstration will not happen without first having recognition of a challenge or a trigger. This is consistent with the intelligence definitions that require a challenge or opportunity to facilitate a demonstration of these separate abilities.

In addition, two other major intelligence functions can be observed when the tribes and intelligence types are exercised. First, the intelligent action of using what is assumed to be pertinent is present among the AI tribes and is similarly leveraged through the trained responses of the various intelligence types. A reputed intelligent response answers a challenge when the pertinence assumption is valid. Second, the intelligent action of leveraging causes, and their effects that validate resource pertinence to the challenge, is also present among the AI tribes. This action is more demanding, since new knowledge or information is generated that leads to novel responses and potentially novel or, at least, updated interpretation frameworks.

From this, three separate intelligence genres can be postulated that do not require proficiency qualifiers. Each genre categorizes a key unique intelligence function that enables contending with challenges. The intelligence proficiency that relates to the intelligence types, for example, follows from the application and maturity of these intelligence functions.

Throughout this investigation, one can observe that interpretation effectively guides any intelligence demonstration. This is called the interpretive-intelligence genre. Each of the AI tribes has an interpretation bias that leverages information in different ways to form a response to a challenge. One grouping of the tribes embraces conventional or trained responses without pertinence confirmation. This is called the passive-intelligence genre. A second grouping is aimed at generating verified pertinent responses based on causal factors that might be new (perhaps rejecting conventional responses in the process). This is called the active-intelligence genre.

THE INTERPRETIVE-INTELLIGENCE GENRE

Let us define this particular genre. *Interpretive intelligence identifies and comprehends meaningful content; it is the domain of perception.* Thus, the interpretive-intelligence genre filters, judges, and sorts observations with an intent to meet a challenge. The challenge's requirements and unanswered questions are contained in an interpretation framework that enables awareness sensitivity to support pertinence identification. The most basic form of interpretive-intelligence genre function is recognition. Recognition is essentially an almost seamless connection of an observation of a challenge or a resource to a response. There tends to be very little analysis, just a triggered reaction. At higher levels, a more advanced function of the interpretive-intelligence genre is the nomination of candidate responses (opportunities) that are good guesses as to a means to meet needs and challenges. In general, the "environment" is surveyed and interpreted with consideration of some underlying intent. The assembly of a jigsaw puzzle is a very basic example of this genre's behavior. In common practice, a need to place a piece in a given vacant location is a point of focus. The attributes of shape and color combinations can be estimated from the surrounding pieces that can be further refined from an image of the completed puzzle. It is those attributes that establish the requirements in an interpretation framework aimed at this task. During the search of available free pieces, candidate pieces are found that could fill that void, since they are consistent with the requirements of the interpretation framework. In effect, they are identified as pieces with a chance to fit. Other pieces are judged not to be candidates because of incompatible shapes and perhaps a poor color-scheme match. Typically, more than one candidate is nominated, since the interpretation framework does not contain all exact details of a perfect fit. As a result, the candidates are tested by placing them in the void until the correct piece is found. If the interpretation framework used exact measurements of the missing piece during the search, only a single piece would have been nominated.

Suppose a person wishes to ascertain if the emotional state of a friend is favorable toward them. They have knowledge of attributes (mannerisms, tone of voice, posture, facial expressions, gestures, choice of words, etc.) of the friend in a good condition. Similar to finding an appropriate puzzle piece, they translate the current perceptions into a best guess. In effect, based on how they interpret what they see, they form a guess for the emotional condition. If the guess is that the friend is unhappy, an additional test or question is necessary to see if that unhappiness is due to the person or not. This is similar in nature to trying the candidate puzzle pieces in the open space as a final check. It is frequently the case that our interpretation frameworks are incomplete (we don't know everything), and some degree of confirmation is needed to help refine them as a means to account for unrecognized attributes.

THE PASSIVE-INTELLIGENCE GENRE

The passive-intelligence genre features connections of interpretations to learned responses and actions. In this way, previously successful behaviors or responses can be used to contend with new circumstances through a recognition-response dynamic. The learned connections are grown from experience and training. Musical and orchestral performances are excellent demonstrations of the passive-intelligence genre. The triggers of the written music or recognition of the song's progression while playing music lead to a trained response for the next action. One could imagine that a concert without the passive-intelligence training would be chaotic. In an untrained state, it is likely some performer's actions would not be refined or synchronized well with other musicians. Many sports depend on practiced behaviors by individuals as well as rehearsed coordinated actions by team members to produce organized and largely dependable results. A sports team needs all players to be on the same page of the playbook to avoid embarrassing misfires in execution.

This enables a definition of intelligence for this particular genre: *Passive intelligence is the act of recognition followed by an associated response to contend with a challenge.* This defines a situation that has a rapid and seamless connection of observation to reaction. In this way, the passive-intelligence genre does not require anything more than recognition from the interpretive-intelligence genre. If one could apply passive intelligence to the jigsaw puzzle assembly task, each free piece examined would have a recognized location already known for it. The action simply matches the observed piece to a template of all pieces that then orients and moves the piece to an exact final location. It is not necessary to have adjacent pieces to place it. One could imagine that each piece would be handled once and used to populate a tabletop independently until the puzzle is completed. The first pieces would likely be quite far apart from each other.

This genre plays a very significant role as it delivers a vast array of templates from successful connections and coordinated actions. Some hardwired functions fall into this genre that have responses that are triggered. For example, the body's temperature regulation and the production of chemicals to digest food are system responses that are triggered. The transport of energy to the body's multitude of specialized cells follows a very mature structure that is left to its own devices without conscious effort on the part of a person. When we train for specific tasks, we can establish a recognition response for it. In this way, we can build the passive-intelligence resources from actions that at one time took conscious effort to do.

When one wants to play the piano, repetition of coordinated finger actions are associated with triggers that are found in the notes on a music sheet. When these tasks are learned (the result of practice), profound connection improvement is realized, and the mental strain of that ingraining process is no longer part of the performance burden. As this level of proficiency is achieved, the notion that a person is a "natural" at the task seems consistent with how effortlessly they perform at a high level. A famous quote states that doing the same thing over and over and expecting different results is the definition of insanity (from Albert Einstein's frustration with the inflexibility of this genre). However, it is quite the opposite as mastery is gained for many tasks including riding a bicycle, as an example. There are multiple attempts and falls until the balancing mechanisms of the body adapt to the two wheels. This "insane" and recurring failed behavior is essentially like knocking on a door (the same action) repeatedly until it is answered with near permanent success. In the context of the passive-intelligence genre, the refinement derived from repetition yields behavioral strengthening of the response patterns. Such practicing builds and develops a learned automatic behavior, not necessarily providing evidence of one's insanity in the process (although my first real but limited success on a two-wheeler landed me in a neighbor's sticker bush).

In another example, a task to make a special meal for a friend can draw on the experience of past special meals as one duplicates their images and attributes. In effect, a template of lessons learned is applied. The passive-intelligence genre in this way links prior experience to new experiences. It applies an assumption or recognition that the past experience's response is sufficient. The use of reference books and Internet searches are a means to recognize and grow the passive-intelligence genre's resources. In some cultures, it is respectful to use approaches from your predecessors. In fact, anything new is considered risky and dangerous.

The passive-intelligence genre is well suited for artificial intelligence applications in conventional computer programming. The templates of triggers and subsequent behaviors and responses to a variety of circumstances can be coded as rules. The IF-THEN style fits well to sorting through matching observations to preconceptions. Preconceptions can be linked together and associated with learned action templates. At this point, a machine's dependability and its memory stability are better than that of a human. The growth of template connections and associations should only take time as a system is exercised and updated from dealing with reality. Deviations of performance from the intent can be recoded to correctly account for them. Ultimately, a repository of experiences and a multitude of response templates that are well connected will emulate a very talented passively intelligent individual. Voice recognition for navigation systems and music playlists serves as a good example of anticipated triggers being translated into a desired information flow. An extremely simple example could use a computer to respond with "Hello" when it detects an outside voice saying "Hello" or "Good morning" or "Good afternoon." If any of the outside voice triggers (IFS) are detected, THEN it responds with a greeting. By adding a time of day reference to the "IFS," one could refine the response based on the time of day. Should the "IFS" contain voice tonal recognition, it could possibly add the person's name in its response greeting: "Good afternoon, Cynthia." If sophisticated incoming voice-signal processing could detect mood or distress, additions to the response could include, "Is everything okay? Can I help with something?" Perhaps if positive excitement is detected in the voice, a schedule check that reveals an evening dinner party could be referenced in a response. The impression of the machine having awareness and sensitivity to the individual's condition will yield, ostensibly, the beginnings of a relationship.

THE ACTIVE-INTELLIGENCE GENRE

A combination of influences (factors) generally contributes to any condition or state. Relevant factors are considered causal when changes to them will impact the resulting condition. The extent of this correlated change in the result defines the sensitivity of the result to the factor. This means that some factors may slightly change a result while others are dominant contributors. This sensitivity effect enables the resulting condition to be adjusted through altering the factors. The active-intelligence genre leverages these sensitivity assets in the process of meeting a challenge. By contrast, the passive-intelligence genre depends entirely on precedent with a learned response, while the active-intelligence genre could make an entirely novel response. For example, if you were to adjust the flow of hot and cold water to make the temperature suitable for a shower, you used the active-intelligence genre by altering causal factors until the challenge is met. If you simply set the faucets to their middle positions for your shower based on past experience, you used passive intelligence and hope for the best.

With this in mind, let us define active intelligence as follows: *Active intelligence is the act of making a response derived from recognition of causal relationships that pertain to contending with a challenge.* If the interpretive-intelligence genre comprehends causal factors, it will enable the active-intelligence genre to manipulate them to make a response. When a person develops a sense of how to do things or how things work, they are able to interpret the state of the factors and correctly anticipate results. Consider that a golfer may alter the aim of a shot into a detected crosswind to use it as an aid in getting the ball to the hole rather than letting it otherwise push the ball off target. The causal factors of the wind and the aim were blended by active intelligence in forming a response. The extent of that wind correction seems to come from a "feel" of how the causal relationships interact. If the golfer's interpretation framework does not grasp the effect of wind as a factor, the result would likely be a deviation from the intended result. In such a case, this unanticipated deviation presents an opportunity to recognize a missed factor (wind) as part of the learning process. In this case, the interpretation framework of the golfer is incomplete, and factor-sensitivity learning to upgrade it is necessary. This learning is an active-intelligence mechanism and technique that incorporates factor-result sensitivity into an improved and more comprehensive interpretation framework. It is the full recognition provided by a mature interpretation framework that can lead to proficient response selections through factor adjustments that deliver desired results.

A NEW INTELLIGENCE DEFINITION

From this, intelligence can be defined as a function or an action with a few dimensions to it: *Intelligence is an action to interpret a challenge and to apply pertinent resources that are either inherited from past experience, actively manipulated or created through investigation to contend with that challenge.* In this way, intelligence is a set of specialized actions (verb) on information to make a directed response. It is the response's relevance to the challenge that separates intelligent from unintelligent actions. For example, when a person dresses for the weather (i.e., warm coat to react to the "cold" factor), they have demonstrated intelligence. Even if the choice of clothing was not quite perfect for the actual conditions, it was still an intelligent action to contend with the "comfortable" challenge since it was pertinent to altering the result. When the Earth's surface was commonly interpreted to be flat like a tabletop, the familiar experience of objects falling off a table to destruction was considered to be pertinent to distant-travel challenges. The fact that this common knowledge was not pertinent makes the choice to use the related "inherited" resources unintelligent. Rather a choice to use the active-intelligence genre to confirm a response's pertinence to the travel challenge was required to make an intelligent response. Similarly, if one defines a word as it was taught to them (via the inherited definition), this demonstrates passive intelligence regardless of correctness. If they were taught an outdated definition, the response is not pertinent and is therefore not intelligent.

Naturally, we want pertinent reactions to challenges to also be highly proficient. This requires excellence in the interpretive-intelligence genre to recognize pertinence related to the challenge interpretation and response resource selection. In the example of dressing for the weather, a highly proficient clothing selection requires a comprehensive grasp of correctly anticipated weather conditions. In the case of searching for a missing jigsaw puzzle piece, the exact piece's criteria in the interpretation framework will proficiently result in finding the only piece without bothering with similar shape and color candidate pieces. When the demands on the interpretive-intelligence genre are low (recognition only), an expansive resource of credible reference material in the passive-intelligence genre is an asset that supports high proficiency. However, it is not reasonable to think that everything has already been experienced and that our current best practices cannot be improved upon. So a mature active-intelligence genre is required to contend with challenges involving response novelty and to upgrade or update the interpretive-intelligence genre to improve pertinence recognition.

We can merge the passive-intelligence genre and the active-intelligence genre aspects of our definition for the purpose of simplification as follows: *Intelligence is an action to interpret a challenge and apply pertinent resources to contend with that challenge.* This simplification explicitly retains the need to interpret a challenge. Often, the challenge seems like it is a given. Academic testing is an example of that. Given or not, clarity of the challenge is the foundation for knowing what could be pertinent or not to deal with it. For the bulk of this text, we will use the earlier definition since it has a better structure of key functions that have been labeled as the three intelligence genres. The cultivation of proficiency in each genre's function will lead to improved performance of an artificially intelligent device as well as humans. By this, I mean that the likelihood of successfully contending with appropriate challenges should be improved.

VERIFICATION EXERCISE

This new definition of intelligence sets up an interpretation framework that can be used to assess experiences and other points of view. If we exercise this framework, not only do we become deeply familiar with it, but we can challenge its validity and appropriateness. In the process, we might find deficiency in the construct, which can lead to adjustment or refinement. As with any interpretation framework, a healthy skepticism about it is needed for growth opportunities to be entertained.

The intelligence types that H. Gardner discloses were interpreted to be domains or categories in which intelligence can function. Ideally, these domains can be explained in terms of the intelligence genres to varying degrees:

- The linguistic intelligence type is described as a high level of an individual's ability to "express oneself" and to easily grasp the viewpoint of others. This is clearly a high function of the interpretive-intelligence genre. The skill to transform an individual's interpretation framework into another modified framework for the purpose of communication is a result of recognition of a need to do so. Further, accurate recognition of an interpretation framework used by another person would be an essential part of demonstrating proficiency in this intelligence type. The foundational communication elements, such as language, come from passive-intelligence genre. The active-intelligence genre may be important in grasping and using the key factors that lead to strong two-way communication since each person has some uniqueness in their background. When we discussed a doctor explaining a new medication to colleague and also to a child, the suitability of the match of the interpretation frameworks was evidence of this ability. If the opposite frameworks were used (i.e., treat the child like another well-trained doctor), the proficiency in this intelligence type would be very low, even though the contents would be identical but just shared with the wrong person.

- The logic intelligence type is the ability to manage math and logic with ease. The skills for this type are principally in the active-intelligence genre. The relationship of answers or results to various factors is the essence of this genre and is very applicable to this intelligence type. Conventionally, the interpretation or the problem description is provided. This means that the results from the interpretive-intelligence genre are a given. From the given, the manipulation of the information to get answers are made. Naturally, language and other standard practices from the passive-intelligence genre are used to communicate. Further, some logic and calculation processes may also be somewhat habitual and found in the passive-intelligence genre.
- The kinesthetic intelligence type relates to the ease of bodily expression, for example an athletic performance. The interpretive-intelligence genre is important in this intelligence type to trigger physical actions. For example, when a baseball player discerns the spin of a ball, this trigger initiates an athletic response to account for that effect to reach it. A dancer, gymnast, or ice skater may have music or a sequence of actions that serve as triggers for the next action. Typically, the actions that follow the trigger have so little time between them that recognition rather than high interpretation function is essential.

  Thus, embedded habits, training, and methods of the passive-intelligence genre are at the heart of this intelligence type. The embedding may come from training or may seemingly be hardwired in what we call gifted individuals who perform well without much preparation or struggle (i.e., an innate ability).
- The spatial or visual intelligence type is having the ability to create, imagine, and draw images. An artist's techniques translate what is seen to a medium that scales the image

and portrays the image well may be habitual or innate (passive-intelligence genre) and/or part of operating on the factors that lead to the results (active-intelligence genre). The interpretive-intelligence genre can trigger or inspire new images (imagined) and create novel content by using the resources from the other two intelligence genres. Perhaps finding a missing puzzle piece, which is clearly an interpretive-intelligence genre function, could be part of this intelligence type, since it demands the ability to visually grasp candidate pieces and imagine if they can be oriented to fit in the missing location.

- The musical intelligence type is expressed by an ability to listen to sounds and identify patterns with ease. The interpretive-intelligence genre, much like in an intelligence test that identifies the next number in a sequence (2, 4, ___), is employed to determine candidate sound patterns. The active-intelligence genre becomes involved in sorting out the candidate patterns to find the correct recognition. The passive-intelligence genre may be involved, should the pattern be familiar and be matched to the sound.
- The interpersonal intelligence type recognizes skills and qualities in others. This is an interpretive-intelligence genre function that provides recognition. The interpretation frameworks involved in this intelligence type may be quite complex. When a person is observed to be quiet and thoughtful, this may fit an image that the person is kind and careful. When a person is easily upset, intolerance and passion may be qualities of the person. The validity of those interpretations may need to be confirmed, which depends on the active-intelligence genre. High proficiency in this intelligence type can be shown when an effective team is created with talent appropriately assigned.
- Intrapersonal intelligence is expressed in someone that is self-reflecting and able to know personal limitations. This is another interpretive-intelligence genre function that provides recognition. The use of those interpretations could be

used to leverage strength and contend with weakness. The active-intelligence genre can be used to validate or invalidate the interpretation frameworks that suggest personal limitations. That process of refinement can lead to proficiency in this intelligence type.

- The naturalist's intelligence type displays an understanding of living things and has sensitivity to the natural world. The sensitivity comes from an interpretation framework that is tuned in to the natural world. This is from the interpretive-intelligence genre. The understanding of living things may have been learned and reside in the passive-intelligence genre or are rooted in a grasp of the causes and effects in nature (active-intelligence genre). Recognition of how certain types of pollution may or may not negatively affect an ecosystem could be an example of high function in this intelligence type.

From this, the intelligence types that H. Gardner describes can be explained by unique applications of the three intelligence genres. The relative strength of the three genres for each unique intelligence type dictates the proficiency within it. Now let's examine how the AI tribes, from the review of artificial intelligence development, can be interpreted using the definition and the intelligence genres:

- The symbolists use inverse deduction based on philosophy to guide their thinking. The interpretation frameworks are well defined and decided in this tribe. As a result, the interpretive-intelligence genre simply takes new information as a trigger for a passive-intelligence-genre response. The tendency is to avoid challenges to the held interpretation and response paradigms in this tribe. Essentially, this tribe precludes the analysis of the active-intelligence genre.
- The analogizers are from the tribe that uses comparisons of new challenges to familiar and similar situations in an effort to make an interpretation, decision, or response choice. The interpretive-intelligence genre is populated with inter-

pretation frameworks that are looking for similarity. When similarity is found, this tribe operates on the assumption that the nature of something somewhat familiar parallels the unfamiliar. The response will then follow from the passive-intelligence genre to use a "recipe" from a prior experience in the new one. The active-intelligence genre does not contribute unless some investigation is needed to refine an interpretation of similarity.

- The Bayesians use statistics and probabilistic inference to select the most probable correct response to a new situation. The interpretive-intelligence genre is dominant in this tribe, requiring a strong recognition of all possibilities. Further, the likelihood of each possibility is to be estimated. This estimation could come from experience (the passive-intelligence genre) or be tested (the active-intelligence genre). After the estimation of all possible outcomes is made, a recommendation is made to generate a response.
- The connectionists use backpropagation, which is a means to minimize response error from intent by adjustment of the various factors that contribute to or influence a result. This is an active-intelligence-genre function that seeks a given result to address a challenge. This seeking is characterized by systematically testing the result response to various factor changes. Typically in this tribe, the interpretation framework contains the challenge-relevant factors. In some ways, it is like being given a multiple-choice question with a vast number of choices. The answer is in the mix somewhere and this tribe sorts out the best answer. The passive-intelligence genre may need to be consulted to gather known background information behind each choice to aid in the assessment.
- The evolutionaries use genetic programming to generate logic structures in a learning environment. A specific challenge and result expectation must be present to enable pertinent learning in this tribe. In this way, interpretation frameworks (from the interpretive-intelligence genre)

> must be in place to decide what to respond to and if that response is sufficient or not. Based on performance of this logic structure, adjustments or learning may need to be made. The active-intelligence genre resources, which may be derived from trial and error, are translated into logic structures to favor a sufficient response. When the logic structures are mature, they become the resources for the passive-intelligence genre.

Not surprisingly given the contribution of the artificial intelligence tribes to the recognition of the three intelligence genres, they exhibit the functional attributes that fit our definition. The results of this verification check support our verb-like definition of intelligence that identifies the essential key functions that are present in intelligent behavior.

PROCESS REFLECTION

This pursuit started with a goal or intention to facilitate a means to teach or share intelligence. Conventional intelligence definitions (passive-intelligence genre) were essentially vague "you know it when you see it" attribute descriptions for a noun. Similarly, one could consider the characteristics of an animal being used as its definition for recognition only. From psychology, the intelligent attributes are fragmented across specialized intelligence types where the challenges, demonstrated skills, and proficiencies differ. These fragments are evidence that these multiple divisions of intelligence are superficial in nature and lack a fundamental connection to underlying performance drivers or abilities. Since abilities must be demonstrated to be assessed, the definition of intelligence should be verb-like. Thus, a new interpretation framework (interpretive-intelligence genre) for the matter was required. An important question in the growth of our interpretation framework came from the passive-intelligence genre: "What is intelligence similar to that is familiar?" The language of the descriptions of intelligence types suggested intelligence demonstration was similar to skill demonstration. This led to an analogy that tool choice and intelligence resource choice can each be utilized to deliver differing levels of proficiency. The interpretive-intelligence genre then recognized that proficiency was not an attribute of intelligence rather a consequence of it. This is particularly clear when a machine is involved. This framework classified intelligent actions into three separate genre functions, and it is those functions that contribute to intelligent behavior. As a test of this framework, these three functions represented the essential contents that the intelligent activities of the intelligence types and the artificial intelligence tribes required. Thus, this interpretation framework is viable for consideration of intelligence assets.

Suppose we have a large repository of information for the passive-intelligence genre that enables an ability to deal with almost anything that has ever been encountered. In this way, a being with highly developed passive intelligence would be able to excel in an academic environment, by providing answers to familiar questions that have been judged to be correct. For humans, our education process feeds this genre well. We take our teachings, memorize them, and respond with them. We train and build skill proficiency in the passive-intelligence genre (many of Gardner's intelligence types land in this genre). The interpretive-intelligence genre does not have to be exceptional to support the passive-intelligence genre since only recognition of something familiar is required. A more mature interpretive-intelligence genre will identify factor-result relationships and possibly equations that describe them. This insight enables factor manipulation by the active-intelligence genre to comprehend various result conditions and to create new responses to contend with challenges. In each case, the interpretive-intelligence genre is used to extract the responses from these other two genres. Depending on the maturity of the interpretive-intelligence genre, it can lead to effective responses or "stupid" responses. If a challenge is misunderstood (incorrectly interpreted), the response fails to meet objectives. If a goal is inappropriate, and it is not recognized as such, the response that meets that goal may fail to meet the appropriate intended objective. For example, a goal to finish reading a book may miss a more appropriate objective of learning something from it. High functioning (mature) interpretive intelligence will correctly identify the appropriate goal, regardless of how it is initially stated, and prudently leverage the resources of the passive-intelligence genre and/or the active-intelligence genre. Sometimes challenging the conventional wisdom is the best choice, and at other times, it is not (i.e., because of cost and time constraints). Thus, the interpretive-intelligence genre resides at the beginning of intelligence functions and is used to leverage and identify assets for forming a response.

REACTION

The new interpretation framework concerning intelligence contains a set of specialized actions on information to make a directed response. Perhaps it is uncomfortable. Do we have something to lose by changing our view of intelligence? As symbolists, we may have invested ourselves in the idea that we are intelligent based on some test or past accomplishments. We may have socially identified ourselves with others that have also earned a label of being intelligent. The label only sets an expectation for future performance by assumption. An artificially intelligent machine is so named to reflect an expectation of it in a similar way. However, the expectation itself does not deliver performance or play an essential role in intelligent actions. To illustrate, if we call someone a runner, does the person have to be running at the time? Certainly, when the person is running, the label is obvious and clearly valid; otherwise, it is an assumption of ability to call the person a runner. From this, when the ability mechanisms are dormant, the label is irresponsible. This means when there is no demonstration of ability, it is pragmatically equivalent to not having the ability. Consider that the "intelligent" label itself can be a thought poison. If one is projected to have some limits to intelligence, perhaps the person reacts to this defiant poison and works very hard to prove the opposite or perhaps succumbs and behaves in a diminished state. On the other side, one may become complacent and rest on the high marks from a test and do nothing of consequence thereafter. The recognition of these influences can empower a person to treat each challenge separately and not passively follow someone with a reputation of intelligence as the only qualifier. In other words, an unintelligent act can happen amidst many intelligent actions. Conversely, an intelligent act may be a surprise among many unintelligent acts. This means one should avoid the paradigm of believing that a wise person is always intelligent and a foolish person is always unintelligent. Thus, it seems prudent to abandon this unnecessary intelligence label complication. Rather, pursuit of maturity in the three intelligence genres should lead to actions that drive high-quality intelligent responses and high proficiency. Certainly, a machine doesn't require this added burden of self-worth assessment to act intelligently, and perhaps we don't need it either.

CHAPTER 3

PRIMITIVE ARTIFICIAL INTELLIGENCE

Allies is a young artificially intelligent device that is constructed with attributes that can mimic human perceptions and situational behavior. This device is intended to operate intelligently but is untrained, similar to a small child. In other words, there is no structure for these capabilities to be organized or called to function. Once a structure is established however, Allies can begin behaving independently and ideally participate in growing up, so to speak, as learning progresses. Allies is able to gather environmental information through technology that is analogous to our five senses. Allies has sight with cameras, hearing with microphones, touch with pressure and temperature sensors, and smell or taste with gas and chemical analyzers. Also, Allies has the capacity to alter the environment or retreat to a different environment (fight or flight). In essence, Allies has access to the best tools that we have created to extend our influence and grasp of our environment. The control system, or the brain of Allies, contains billions of switches. These switches are able to flip on and off at incredible rates of no less than a billion times per second. Allies has an internal language that defines instruction sets and rules very much like the earliest computer programs. This language associates responses to recognition, and it provides her core passive-intelligence function. The classic IF-THEN decisions can be applied as incoming data cascades through the "IFs" with the responses and conclusions that follow from the "THENs" as various "IFs" are satisfied (i.e., if she hears "Hello," then she responds, "Hello, my friend"). The interpretation framework of questions and comparison references is contained in a static learned network of "IF" criteria.

Allies needs a hierarchy of the thinking paradigms. The most primitive is the paradigm of the analogizers. At this level, the experience base is reviewed and compared to current recognition (IF it matches) to recall previous responses to similar situations in order to apply them. If Allies needs to learn how to identify a cat, she first needs to learn an image of a cat and associate it with a name. When she is presented with a dog, she might at first call it a cat, because of physical similarity and that the cat is the only animal she knows. The feedback that her response is in error leads to learning of a new "template" image and an associated "dog" label. Her searching and comparison methodology, through instruction and detail growth development by her teachers, will eventually enable her to identify all living things properly, even by their biological classification nomenclature. This foundational knowledge base reaches well beyond recognition of animals. It can include almost anything that can be memorized. For example, a complex mathematical problem may have a written solution that is memorized by Allies. When she encounters a similar problem, she can provide the contents of "her" solution image. This is not unlike cheating on a test, where copying someone else's work is used to provide an answer that may in fact be correct, yet is it provided with essentially no grasp of its contents. Despite this lack of awareness, this is a very powerful paradigm that builds links or connections that serve as a resource to find relevant information that can be actively utilized by other paradigms to test and create knowledge. From this training, a very strong passive-intelligence genre emerges for Allies. For example, she can take plain questions, images, and sounds and match them through a search of her memory to make a response. Additionally, she can memorize the multiplication tables rather than adding numbers multiple times. Her quick recall will lend speed and accuracy to responses as long as she has seen the combination before. In this primitive state, she doesn't have to know how the response of the THEN is found. She simply has to connect it to the condition match provided by the IF. If she is asked 3 x 4, then she replies 12. If asked 3.1 x 4.2, then she doesn't know.

When the perceptions that are used by the "IF" part of making a "THEN" response are an exact fit, Allies will be like a brilliant student that is given expected questions that trigger correct responses. However, when the perceptions at best merely resemble some preconceptions in her memory, a failure to respond occurs since there is no certainty in the matching. The foundational information (knowledge database) that the analogizer provides requires some type of similarity selection management. The interpretive-intelligence genre must be more sophisticated than finding an exact match to contend with this problem. The Bayesians (probability paradigm) bring an ability to rank choices through comparison that are most likely to be the answer from what is known. In the case of 3.1 x 4.2, the Bayesians' response is 12, since the "3 x 4" characters are present and 3 x 5 has fewer matching characters, for example. With this, suppose a new animal species is discovered. Naturally, the analogizer's extensive database does not contain it. No one has a name for it. The Bayesians' approach can test the similarity of this new species to known species and make a determination of the highest probability of a relationship. This would support the classification process and aid in descriptions that others can imagine. (The response, for example, could be that the animal is a fish with bull-like horns, probably some type of shark.) In normal activity, the Bayesian paradigm would arrive at a high-probability match to the image and offer the associated name. Memory of experiences held by the analogizer in a similar manner can be retrieved. For example, a previously used shopping list serves in a new shopping experience since it very much relates to similar needs that were met by it in the past. The Bayesians, in this capacity, attempt to interpret information so that it can be connected to the vast resources that the analogizer provides. For example, Allies has a memory of a conversation with you from yesterday. The new encounter will be similar to it in many ways. Allies uses language and voice recognition of you as a trigger to resume the conversation. She then greets you and refers to the connected conversation's contents.

At this level of development, Allies has an extensive burden to transform observations from the environment into an interpretation match through a search of her vast knowledge database that also contains an associated response. This burden can delay responses and yield an impression of a lack of proficiency. Conventionally, highly proficient fast responses are regarded as evidence of intelligence. When high proficiency is demonstrated, the interpretation act is exceptionally brief en route to a response. Further, in many cases of common practice, the interpretation is provided or is somewhat straightforward, which leaves only the proficiency of the response to be judged. This tendency obscured and, in some way, blended the interpretation and response mechanisms, which made it difficult for us to identify the interpretive-intelligence function that is central to our intelligence definition. This could be a good reason why other's intelligence definitions, in one form or another, omitted interpretation and progressed to the "ability and ease" of the response.

The capacity to deliver high-performance responses is the fodder for the identification of intelligent abilities and perhaps spawned the divisions of H. Gardner's intelligence types. For example, the casual observer notes that an athlete is a "natural" because of their amazing and fast coordinated responses. The speed of their reactions is critical to their success. We know that interpretation precedes the response and that can take time, so much so that an athlete may miss split-second opportunities, but does not. It is as if the observations are not processed through the interpretations of "IF" comparisons. The "THEN" happens as a reflex that was simply cued or triggered, and virtually no time for interpretation was required. This ability to recognize and respond quickly is defined as embedding. The embedding of the recognition-response dynamic eliminates decision-making and the delays inherent in the interpretation process. Playing a musical instrument and typing share in this style of triggered action. Through practice for example, an observed letter does not require the keyboard to be surveyed to find the corresponding key and press it. A connection of the visual cue to a finger movement remarkably finds the letter without struggle or delay. In effect, when we form and embed the recognition-response connection, we behave with high proficiency. In this mature condition, we don't require any language or conscious effort to jump from recognition to action. This recognition-response connection is what I will call hardwiring of a specialized interpretation framework to a response. This choice of words implies that there is no logic, search, or decisions made to complete the task. For example, once a light switch is turned on, the wiring feeds power to a lamp. There is no "brain" watching the switch, which then decides to power the lamp or perhaps not. Instead, there is a direct and dependable connection.

My youngest daughter was placed on a padded table moments after being born. The nurse was preparing a small oxygen mask for her. As she brought the mask close, my daughter reached up and grabbed the tubing near the base of the mask and began to wave the mask around. The nurse said, "Hey, look at this. She took it away from me!" Clearly, the baby didn't have language to answer, "How do I grab things?" or even have the concept of what a question is at that point in her life. Her intelligent function happened without the intervention of language or training. This suggests to me that child prodigies, as an example, may function with an innate sense to deliver high function through their special hardwiring of recognition linked to a response. Persons born with a gifting to interpret musical patterns, for example, may have the wiring to do this without the experience of ever articulating or cultivating the finer points that the rest of us would require. It appears that they achieved mastery without any training. This could also be a reason that they tend to have difficulty teaching their skills to the rest of us. Despite their proficiency, they cannot articulate their interpretation framework to us. They spent very little detailed conscious effort with it. They skipped that part because they didn't need to develop or train it. They simply execute with an embedded sense of how to do it. For them, it is like a very sophisticated instinctual response.

These recognition-response dynamics may follow from embedding the entire intelligent action for a challenge. This embedding is evident when a sense of how to respond is in play. Athletic actions perhaps to catch or strike a ball are good examples. In such a case, the active-intelligence genre (noting causes and predictions), in addition to the passive-intelligence genre, can be part of that embedded hardwiring. As a result, some people evaluate and perform with a sense of causes and effects to make natural responses with proficient solutions to problems and challenges as they happen. They seem to be able to grasp the requirements of the solution and address the root cause of a new problem instantly. They functionally answer interpretation questions even if they are not conscious of it. In a college philosophy class, I had a professor that was curious about how far the eye could see. Being an engineering student with a peculiar perspective in that setting, I questioned what he was looking at: Does he consider that our distant sun can be viewed during the day? What about stars? Perhaps my probing questions put me on his "list" so I could be singled out in later discussions. Anyway, he was curious about the possibility that the naked eye could detect the curvature of the Earth as a means to assess the merits of thinking that the Earth is or is not flat. The day of his friendly revenge came when he randomly asked me what angular change in the eye would occur if you were to look one mile into the distance or two miles into the distance. Instantly, I told him, "A very small fraction of a degree." I thought of the tangent function with my height of a couple of yards as one leg and the mileage being the other. I was very familiar with the math (trigonometry) to the point I had a sense of it. I didn't need to make calculations since I knew that my height in that scale is almost negligible. So the angle is negligible to start with; therefore, the change to the angle is even less significant. Apparently, he didn't listen to my response and explained for over half an hour of class time how he spent his weekend researching and discovering "trig functions" and, after several hours in the library, concluded that a very small fraction of a degree was the result. The class broke up in laughter when he used my exact words after he had burned a better part of the weekend it would seem. My interpretation framework was embedded. I recognized the situation and promptly visualized a familiar analysis to make a response. By contrast, the professor's interpretation framework for this task was not initially prepared to deal with it. To the professor's credit, he correctly trained himself. The questions he appropriately asked in his research were already answered in my innate grasp of the issue. I didn't articulate the intermediate questions that he had to; I simply reacted with the answer. My ability to recognize something that I already knew how to interpret gave the appearance of high proficiency. I am sure that at some point in my mathematical training, I was exactly where he was during his uniquely thrilling weekend. My sense and proficiency was learned.

The recognition-response dynamic is a talent that nearly all humans demonstrate in one form or another. H. Gardner basically singled out intelligence types for this talent based on how unusual it is to find a recognition-response dynamic being applied to complex tasks. He did not have an intelligence type for the very complex task of food digestion, since it is commonplace to demonstrate that ability with ease. Another commonplace recognition-response dynamic is for basic language and image identification. When this chore is embedded, the implied questions of the interpretation framework go unstated to the point of being skipped. A person doesn't ask a question when they encounter a familiar word: "What does this word mean?" Rather the passive-intelligence machinery is triggered to automatically find the answer or simply recognize it. In fact, the person might not even use words to interpret it, given that they have a sense of the meaning, and respond quickly. In another case, a fully indoctrinated symbolist who operates with a philosophical approach in dealing with the environment may simply recognize a connection to a standard response. (I happened to be sufficiently indoctrinated into the methods of trigonometry, which led to my response to my philosophy professor.) For a primitive artificially intelligent device, the incorporation of a recognition-response dynamic is capable of yielding great proficiency. This requires a focused connection of observations to the contents of the passive-intelligence genre. This narrow connection avoids the need for vast searches for pertinent information of all that is known and thereby reduces response time.

Highly trained accomplished musicians and highly reputed athletes are said to have short memories of their failures. It isn't that they don't remember. These persons are functioning through their embedded well-trained interpretation frameworks. Consider that a master musician's unlikely error is not pertinent to learning how to play; the person already knows the skill very well. Thus, a random error or current mishap is not pertinent to alter the skills that will deliver proficient future performances, and it is best ignored. In other words, their performance relies on learned responses to triggers, and the failure feedback has no place to be accepted. As a result, their generally reliable recognition-response connections remain available and are not discarded or disrupted. If disrupted, it would compromise the high performance that those trained behaviors are able to deliver in the future. In this refined and mature situation, a closed mind to change is advantageous. This closed-mindedness is the nature of a primitive artificially intelligent device that executes what it is taught without question (passive intelligence).

In a less mature state of recognition-response embedding, the process of securing the connection inevitably has its struggles. The fact is that, the feedback and deviations generated in any learning process have a short life of pertinence as the embedding process becomes complete. I encouraged my daughter, a high-school-aged cellist, in the midst of a practice struggle to reflect on how her errors when she first started learning the instrument are of little meaning now; she has moved on. We agreed that it is silly to dwell on a single screeching note from a performance at the age of ten. The fact was that her skills were largely embedded, but the new challenge was to expand on that skill by making some new actions "natural." She was not relearning how to play, just adding something new that was not yet embedded. She was expanding on her skill's embedding process.

The embedded routines that humans use are typically called habits, which alleviate an analysis burden to form a response. The habits of interest are tried-and-true routines, ideally best practices, which execute when a trigger or cue is encountered. This reflex-like response can be quite complex or very trivial. We can include "habits" to deal with encounters of familiar environmental conditions for Allies. This essentially off loads the task of searching to find a response in favor of quickly making one when a trigger is encountered. Exploring the nature of human habits will help us better grasp them for an adaptation to Allies.

From the book *The Power of Habit* by Charles Duhigg (2013), there are three main parts to a habit: cues, routines, and rewards. The rewards are what come at the end of the routine's execution. The reward may be complicated in that it can have desirable and undesirable contents. The author explains about his workday habit of getting a cookie around 3:30 p.m. The time of day was the cue that triggered the action to purchase a cookie. The reward was consuming the cookie with his colleagues. He tested this reward to find that the social interaction with others was the key element interwoven into his cookie experience that he was really seeking. He modified his routine to include only an interaction with a colleague at that time of day and forego the unnecessary calories. This core positive reward was his actual craving, not the craving for a cookie. The cookie purchase only enabled a circumstance to meet that need. His enhanced clarity of purpose allowed him to use the same cue (3:30 p.m.) to satisfy his need for a break with a coworker and eliminate a negative side effect in his cookie habit. Similarly, he cited how a core craving in alcoholics is very often not for alcohol itself but some other need. This means that the routines we use may not be well directed at our desired reward or, in the intelligence definition context, not well directed at the challenge. Care should be taken to cleanup habitual routines to deliver the reward without undesirable complications.

After a reward is realized, the person waits for another cue for the next trigger of an embedded routine. Most computers use event-based programs that are constructed this way. For example, a computer will be prompted into action with a change in the state of the keyboard's switches (or clicking on an icon). When an event or cue happens, that switch initiates the formation of a corresponding letter while ignoring subsequent key hits until that first one is completed. The routine, basically, is the translation of the switch state to a displayed image of some sort. The result is analogous to the reward for a person's habitual response. If our computers were programmed to behave like us in an unfocussed manner, pressing an "a" would not only deliver the "a" but a few other characters as well. Getting the "a" was the desired reward, which was accomplished. It is possible to clean up the extraneous results after the fact, but that added task lacks efficiency. Correction of our results is best done in the routine that created it. A very visible example of this inefficiency occurs in the manufacture of consumer goods.

A manufacturing process is full of many interacting processes or routines to create a product. Attributes related to product quality are akin to the reward at the end of this habitual undertaking. Upon completion, a defective product can be cleaned up and repaired in order to be made ready for sale. This action requires a new set of cues and routines to correct the problems resulting from the original manufacturing process. Should this supplemental activity yield an incomplete correction or, worse, create new defects; yet another process must come into play, and so on. It is clear that this cascading of errors can be a huge blow to a manufacturing plant's efficiency and cost control. For example, it is found that a fastener (bolt) is loose at the end of the production process. The observation that it is easy to tighten the fastener afterward does not discount the fact that it is ideally an unnecessary complication to the task. The most prudent action is to fix the routines in original manufacturing process so the additional action is not required. The repair costs and subsequent delivery delays could be eliminated by doing so. The process's efficiency and effectiveness will clearly benefit. The same is true with computer or human routines, if they require rework afterward. A new and improved routine needs to be created and connected to the original cues, and the inferior process discarded.

Correction of habits or the embedded recognition-response patterns may require outside intervention. Consider when a person is exposed repetitively to thought poisons, the associated interpretation framework then may become internalized (embedded). This sets up a recognition disposition that cues a response. For example, a person may become surprisingly defensive when triggered by an innocent action and think nothing of it. In essence, the person is like a child prodigy that simply has a sense of things without insight as to why or how they react as they do. This lack of awareness comes from the embedding of the recognition-response dynamic that skips the individual's interpretative-intelligence genre and forgoes any chance to reevaluate candidate response pertinence. If any consideration of adjustment should occur, it comes from a separate interpretation framework, typically from another person. That feedback of a concern might awaken the individual's interpretative-intelligence genre to start testing responses for pertinence in the future. Further, it might initiate some form of intervention to address the issue to support change. Correction of a primitive artificially intelligent device will require external intervention since it cannot self-regulate its recognition-response connections.

A computer's logic readily forgets old "habits" (deleted) when a programmer replaces it with a new routine. The device carries no innate allegiance to failed practices after the updated best practice has been secured. As a good starting point for Allies, the structured belief systems of the symbolists are taught to her as a type of habit. This means that Allies does not have to investigate all of the principles, rules, and interactive relationships that have already been learned by the symbolists; rather, she simply retrieves them. A team is deployed to incorporate this fundamental function of cues and responses into Allies. This includes visual and verbal recognition to communicate and respond to questions with known information. Allies becomes more and more capable as habitual responses and guiding principles are incorporated into her reactions to the multitude of cues that she encounters. It is easy to imagine that Allies becomes very high functioning through this accelerated teaching activity. She is now able to access her vast information resources to contend with expected contingencies. The key point is in the word "expected," since all actions she makes are based on anticipated cues provided by her teachers. It is conceivable that with enough instruction time from an extensive array of clever teachers, it would be an extremely rare case for Allies to be unable to provide proficient intelligent responses to a situation. For some, this capability is enough for an intelligent entity, machine or otherwise.

One can acknowledge that Allies would be regarded as very intelligent in this condition. By virtue of her teachers, she demonstrates "ability" to do so many things with "ease" in the identified domains of intelligence demonstration (H. Gardner's intelligence types). Further, she has an incredible recall of relevant information and an ability to apply it. From these observations, it is clear that Allies has a highly developed passive-intelligence genre and a functional recognition-response connection to draw from it that serves as her interpretive-intelligence genre. Her resources are well suited for familiar challenges, which by nature, does not require an application of active intelligence.

Allies has two major shortcomings as a primitive intelligence device. First, when there is nothing to refer to, she will fail to meet the challenge. Second, Allies is at risk of making an inferior response, when she does an inadequate job of interpreting a request or challenge. This could be due to her inability to properly comprehend the challenge or its context. This means that her interpretive-intelligence genre is not well equipped in this latter case. Her weakness is shown in this sample challenge: Allies is asked to identify the murderer in an unfamiliar murder-mystery novel. First, she has no reference material (passive-intelligence answers) to offer as a standard response. Second, this task requires an evolving interpretation framework. She only has access to established interpretation frameworks that she has learned. By contrast, our action might start the assignment with some basic interpretation framework or hypothesis (i.e., the butler did it). As we read the book, we are finding new information that contributes to the assignment in two ways: First, we test the information for pertinence in our current interpretation framework and choose to use or reject it. Second, the information may reveal that our interpretation framework needs to be revised or updated (i.e., butler or the maid could have done it). This is like seeking the shape of a missing puzzle piece and slowly determining the required characteristics of it. For example, at first, our idea of the missing piece accounts for the color scheme. An adjustment to include shape attributes in our interpretation framework is necessary to seek the correct piece. In effect, learning occurs that refines the interpretation framework. Given this weaknesses, we acknowledge a new challenge to teach Allies how to grow her interpretation frameworks or to activate her otherwise dormant or at least limited interpretive-intelligence genre.

CHAPTER 4

INTERPRETIVE INTELLIGENCE

The essence of the interpretive-intelligence genre comes from a preset disposition to perceive the world in a particular way or (in a simple case) with sensitivity for a particular attribute or combination of attributes. The idiom of wearing rose-colored glasses is a compelling analogy for how interpretive-intelligence functions. The filter of the lens may hide or diminish some things and enhance sensitivity to others. In effect, the interpretive-intelligence genre establishes how we view things. Sometimes these interpretations seem to be embedded in our way of thinking and are generated automatically. In other words, they do not require language in order to function. In practice, it is possible to delve into an automatic interpretation and find that it can be described by a set of criteria or questions that are functionally the essence of the assessment methods used in the interpretation. This collection of requirements, questions, and expected answers is called an interpretation framework. From our preparation chapter, we made a definition as follows: An interpretation framework is a comparison logic structure that is used to classify and organize observations. The probing of an automatic interpretation is not always necessary. In many cases, our interpretation frameworks are very much evident in the form of actual stated questions and expectations. In the familiar controlled education process, the teacher manages the information flow by defining triggers and valid responses.

The teacher asks a specific question; the student responds with a learned lesson. The interpretation of the situation is the teacher's gift to the student by making a request in this process. Since the start of our intelligence definition begins with the act of interpretation, this function is vital to the generation of highly proficient responses.

The underlying intent of the interpretive-intelligence genre is often expressed in simple external requests and goal statements that are provided. The interpretive-intelligence genre has low function in these situations. As with students in a class, the response opportunities are quite limited in scope to meet those requests. As a consequence of this climate, students are not well trained to challenge interpretations or to make requests that go beyond what was taught to them. High function of the interpretive-intelligence genre can be observed when a request or a goal is restated in a more insightful manner. This new interpretation expands the opportunities for an effective response. For example, if a request for a blanket is made, the underlying intent is to raise the temperature of the person. By expanding the interpretation to that of the intent, the blanket becomes only a subset of the possible ways to warm the person. The original request imposed a single solution to the concern and left little room for other opportunities by using a very narrow interpretation framework. This genre is the home of imagination for alternatives. Uncommon and remarkable interpretations are the fodder for ingenuity. Let's examine some specific challenges to assess the nature of the interpretation function.

First, let us try to fulfill a mission of creating a special meal for a friend. The seeking of relevant "ingredients" causes one to ignore tertiary shopping opportunities that are not part of mission. For example, the hardware, lawn, and garden departments will not be a pertinent place to shop for milk, eggs, and cake mix. An enhanced interpretation framework aimed at the "special" part of a special meal might allow one to recognize other opportunities to enhance the meal's experience by visiting the greeting card, florist, and party-favor sections of a store. The maturity of the framework to cover larger and larger dimensions of the attributes of a special meal can result in an exceptional experience. Dare we say a more intelligent or at least a more thoughtful experience? The better suited the contents of an interpretation framework are related to the task at hand, the more proficient the response can be. Questions concerning the best dessert choice and the ingredients are in need of answers. What special theme can be used for the party that the honoree would adore? Should this party be indoor or outdoor, and what obstacles need to be overcome? How many guests should be invited, and who are they? How long should the party be? Are fireworks in order? How about music and other entertainment? Are there schedules and travel concerns that need to be managed? How should everyone dress? Is there a gift that would make the event truly special for the honoree? This may seem complex and difficult, but the consideration of these and perhaps a multitude of other questions could make a special meal very memorable. This requirement structure could be contained in a party plan that has been used in the past. It would provide a shopping list and other answers to questions and serve as an interpretation framework for the event. However, it may not match this situation perfectly. Challenges to that plan to adapt it to this situation will alter the plan's interpretation framework. A great place to start is with a question concerning what has gone wrong with the plan in past. Follow-up questions to contend with those risks should be answered. If the plan could have some unique personalized elements infused into it, what would they be or how can the plan be improved? As a result, the plan is evolved, and the interpretation framework for this party has been built from a largely successful party experience of the past. The new mature plan has answers in place for nearly every imaginable aspect of the party (which establishes resource pertinence). The benefit of using the past experience makes the interpretation task of finding ways to make a special meal much less demanding. By using a memorized plan, the interpretation framework comes from the passive-intelligence genre. When the plan is challenged to be improved, the factors that can make it better are investigated with the active-intelligence genre, since the factors that influence the experience are being adjusted. This is an example of how we leverage known interpretations to get close to a good response without so much effort. The efforts we apply beyond that are specifically aimed at refinement, or we simply don't bother. We may believe that the existing plan is sufficient.

As adults, there is a tendency to turn off our interpretive-intelligence functions and adopt an interpretation framework from the passive-intelligence genre. In this way, adults typically stop interpreting when a conventional interpretation framework is found, like using a party-plan template in the discussion above. With a proven path to a response in hand, the interpretive-intelligence genre adopts a largely inflexible and unchallenged interpretation framework. However, in the case of inquisitive children, they do not have a reserve of conventional frameworks to enable them to stop. Thus, they are quite good at drilling down with almost unending whys as they build their interpretation frameworks. Growth of interpretation frameworks can lead to greater proficiency as the key attributes are better grasped or perhaps expanded. Here is an example:

Suppose a person is looking for a mate with a general sense of ideal attributes or preferences in mind that are projected into the dating experience. When a candidate doesn't measure up to some of those ideal attributes, a person may excuse the deviation (and see only what they want to see, like the tinting of the glasses) and continue to pursue the relationship. Another reaction is to move on from that candidate in hopes of finding a better match. It could happen that the current idea (interpretation framework) of ideal attributes is immature, and a new dating experience leads to refinement of it. In effect, the person learned that some preferred attributes (say hair style or height) aren't really that critical or perhaps this new person has qualities that are unexpected and amazing. Perhaps in some way, the new person sets a new standard. As a result, the interpretation framework used for selecting a mate is developed, refined, and utilized throughout the searching process. This dating interpretation framework can be articulated in the form of questions, when one compares observed attributes to questions that have "correct answers" from the holder's point of view. What does the candidate value? Is the person fun and optimistic? Do they like…? When the unanswered questions stop, the interpretation function naturally stops. This is similar to searching for a piece of a jigsaw puzzle where the participants compare candidate piece attributes to the questions of appropriate colors and shapes to fill a void. If a candidate puzzle piece does not fit, it is rejected, and another piece is considered. Once a puzzle piece is found to fill the void (or all attribute questions are answered favorably), the search sensibly stops.

In social situations, there are often a variety of interpretations of the exact, same circumstance. Some people with a vain mindset arrive at conclusions that any attention received is due to how desirable they are (everyone wants them). Similarly, anyone talking quietly must be talking about them. Conversely, someone may assume that they are not worthy of attention and completely miss genuine interest expressed to them. From our discussion of thought poisons in the preparation chapter, we can see how this can happen. The expectation of what is driving the behavior of others often comes from our own interpretation frameworks. Sometimes people simply get fooled by the expectations that they carry. For example, I went to the Los Angeles airport to greet several international business contacts, some of whom were friends of mine. When my colleagues deplaned, all of them started waving excitedly to me from their gate. This excitement could be interpreted by others as a special situation. As a consequence, many people in the terminal turned to look to see who the fuss was all about, probably a celebrity. I disappointed a lot of people that day.

When interpretation frameworks are not shared among individuals, they will have communication mishaps to some extent. Such an example occurred in an engineering situation in my past. Regrettably, I once made a mathematician's response related to a thermal-performance issue for a vehicle climbing a steep hill while pulling a heavily loaded trailer in the extreme heat of summer. We were concerned that the engine could overheat in those conditions, but it could be mitigated by heat-rejection management. I was asked if the temperature would keep rising after that corrective action, like when a bump in the road is hit and the car rebounds and bounces until it settles. I knew that this system is analogous to filling a leaky bucket with water. The level of water (temperature) doesn't continue to rise, when adding water to it stops (or in this case, heat). Without delay, I said it wouldn't because this system is "governed by a first-order differential equation," which I almost immediately apologized for saying. My response, though correct, sprung from an interpretation framework that essentially only I had. Graciously my VP said, "Don't worry, I know that is genuinely how you think, and I know you are not being pretentious." In a similar manner, any expert is at risk of expressing their thoughts in terms of a very specialized framework that does not communicate well to most others. Expertise is not the only way to invent a specialized framework. When we divide into various groups that have independent or conflicting interpretation frameworks, we are susceptible to having our intentions misunderstood, or at least have difficulties in relating to each other. From a cultural example, I was surprised that the hand gesture by the Japanese to call you closer is the opposite of what most Americans do. Imagine the impression you can make by walking away from someone who is motioning to have you come near. History has shown that differences of interpretation frameworks from political and religious perspectives may distort the interpretation of well-intentioned actions by one group into a heinous act that is found offensive by another.

A shared interpretation framework enables communication with clarity since each of the listeners tends to react in the way that the speaker intends. Great communicators can adapt themselves to another's perspective and relate to them in their interpretation framework. This means that they can readily join a conversation with very little difficulty. When effective adult teachers relate to small children, we can see the adult revert to their childhood interpretation framework to play with the child. This could be expressed in the form of sharing candy or toys and using very plain speech. Typically, any communication from a teacher has an underlying intent to grow the interpretation framework of the student. As a result, there will be challenges to the child that may require rethinking or learning a new way to do something of interest. As a first grader, I innocently reversed this role with my teacher. She held out a few pencils and asked me how many pencils she had, probably to check a box for an evaluation. I told her that I didn't know. She recounted the experience to my parents (every time she saw them for decades): "I knew that he could easily count the pencils in my hand. But he insisted that he didn't know. As I became frustrated, I told him, 'I know that you know, why won't you tell me?' He continued and then said that he had no idea how many pencils I had in my desk or anywhere else." My inability to interpret that her gestures were intended to confine the response to the contents of her hand exposed my tendency to operate less by assumption than by the literal question. This tendency has proven to be advantageous in problem-solving and innovating, since some of the assumptions that impede clear thinking or rethinking are not so strong for me. However, when others hold interpretation frameworks that have a multitude of assumptions and implied meanings, I tend to struggle, given this disposition. (My break from the expected interpretation framework of counting only visible pencils was what surprised my first-grade teacher.)

The use of shared frameworks tends to confine the thinking patterns, and the resulting interpretations become habitual. Such a habit generates a passive-intelligence mindset for the interpretation framework itself, which is characterized by recall of standard answers to questions and challenges. In this way, a sort of allegiance to the framework may form. Individuals may ascend in reputation and authority because of their proficiency in the shared interpretation frameworks. This dynamic entrenches the interpretation framework and spawns a new framework to perceive threats to it. I was struck by the reaction to a modern group of people that sincerely returned to the once-popular view that the Earth is flat. This group found ways to dismiss the evidence to the contrary and suffered consequences in their lives for not holding to the notion that the Earth is more or less spherical. They were subjected to a similar disdain as those that challenged or defied established political and religious norms in the past. From the range of topics that initiate this type of negative reaction, it seems reasonable to conclude that the persecution that one suffers with a given new point of view has very little to do with its correctness or even the topic. Rather, the persecution comes from the defense against the threat to established norms and those that hold them. For this reason, I suspect that those that first broke the flat-Earth paradigm (interpretation framework) in favor of a spherical-Earth interpretation suffered similarly. It is the entrenching of interpretation frameworks that creates incredible inertia against changes in how our surroundings are assessed.

When a symbolist's theory dominates one's thinking, the underlying interpretation framework is already decided. The practical merit of this paradigm is that the symbolists know something that might in reality be correct beyond their immediate experience. They promote ideas that are assumed to be complete, valid, and may hold an allegiance to them. If this framework is challenged by a novel insight that has its origin in a different interpretation framework, there is a mismatch that makes communication very difficult. This clash of perspectives frequently generates a variety of thought pollution as a defense due to unhealthy interpretation-framework allegiances. The intent of this pollution is to infect any challenger and thereby dispense with any evidence (credible or not) that calls for adjustment to their interpretation framework. An analogy might be an octopus that emits a black ink to protect itself when a threat is detected. When norms are challenged, a threat is often perceived. The critics may declare, "This is not how the authorities understand it...," or turn to personal attacks and unflattering labels. Such a response is a characteristic of an entrenched symbolist. The inflexibility of these frameworks and subsequent misbehavior to defend them is terribly unfortunate. The interpretive-intelligence genre is essentially stagnant in these situations.

The entrenching of the framework tends to happen when individuals or organizations gain authority through their mastery of it. As a result, they have the most to lose should the framework be proven to be obsolete. Any disruption may be unsettling to them since their standing and potentially their self-worth is challenged. Generally, any innovation, new information, or novel interpretation can threaten an established interpretation framework, and thereby those that hold it. For example, as scientific methods emerged, the myth-based interpretations of the world, and universe for that matter, were challenged. Similar to a belief in a myth, a scientific theory itself can be used as an interpretation framework in a like manner. A theory may postulate a correlation of observations to possible causes and effects that is untested or unproven. Any challenge to that interpretation framework should be an accepted and encouraged scientific practice to refine the theory. But frequently, the theory serves as a belief that is irresponsibly and inappropriately defended in the name of science to supplant criticism. To illustrate, join me in an assumption that the great pyramids of Egypt evolved rather than being constructed by intelligent beings, which is a competing interpretation framework.

When I have posed this thought experiment, I have experienced remarkable negative reactions. Persons with beliefs that compete with this notion strongly object, even when they use a similar rationale to justify their positions on other topics. Although we share rationale, they are surprisingly reluctant to use it for this theory. This position seems to touch the nerve of the nature of interpretation bias quite well. Like other plausible theories, our interpretation framework is supported by empirical evidence and logical arguments. Observations from mountains to anthills reveal a natural "pointy" tendency at the top of mounds of material. This is one of the key defining characteristics of a pyramid, and this demonstrates the existence of natural causes that deliver the crude shape of interest. In this way, we can empirically suggest that our theory is valid thus far. A popular evolution-style argument to favor our assumption is that with enough time with this fundamental nature in play, our pyramids would form. To support this idea, we dig into the Earth and find that material has been stacked on top of other material for likely millions of years the deeper and deeper we dig—certainly enough time for any and every imaginable shape or collection of shapes to emerge. Further, one could expect that if the conditions were favorable to generate a particular style of material stacking, more than one example would form. From this idea, it is logical to assume that the proximate forces that shaped one pyramid would likely form more than just one. This would be like finding a collection of diamonds in a specific location where heat and pressure were suitable to form them, another natural phenomenon. Well, we have multiple pyramids in Giza. Case closed. Now here come those that wish to challenge our "truth." They say what about the burial chambers? That is easy. They were likely discovered and used for that purpose by the ancient Egyptians. It is not unlike people using water from a river. They didn't make the river, but they benefit from the water. What about entropy effects of erosion (wind or rain) and earthquakes? Well, there has been some deterioration, but these structures by their very existence are evidence of a specialized evolution of materials and refined building blocks that do not suffer largely from those effects. Consider that diamonds are quite robust and stable against deterioration. This is a similar situation that favors our defense. It is easy to imagine that other pyramids existed alongside these robust pyramids in the past that did not have their superior structure. Those with an inferior structure, or not-so-great pyramids, were likely leveled by those deterioration effects, but not these. Further, to date, it is not possible with our technology to create comparable pyramids. The forces of nature through the eons must have done it. This indicates that we cannot test the validity of the theory, and it will remain a theory until that situation changes. This theory is an interpretation that may be correct or may not be. Any challenges to the theory are appropriate and should not be offensive. Further, those that hold this theory should not be held in contempt by those that hold a competing theory or belief. After all, until the far edge of the flat Earth was found to be the completion of a closed path to the origin of the journey, the theory seemed plausible and relatable, but ideally nothing personal. Testing of theories and beliefs with the aim of generating powerful interpretation frameworks should be a pillar of high-functioning interpretive intelligence and, for that matter, real science.

As we have explained about the symbolists, they reveal our tendency to reject alternative theories once one is accepted, especially if it is tested and proven. Suppose our technology improves in the future, enabling us to create similar great pyramids with ease (which comes from a belief in our ingenuity). Our newfound proficiency supports and proves the theory that only intelligent beings built the great pyramids. Actually, that is not true. This hypothetical fact does not discount the validity of other theories that might also be proven capable of forming pyramids. This finding supports the theory that the great pyramids *could have been* created by intelligent beings. This new capability may steer belief away from our theory of natural causes, but in fact, it does not have anything to do with it. Now suppose our geologists successfully find a way to simulate and accelerate the natural causes to generate pyramids (a means to test our theory). That result does not eliminate the possibility that intelligent beings were involved in those particular pyramids. By analogy, suppose a mutual friend of ours receives a birthday cake anonymously every year. If you and I each possess the ability to make a cake, each of us are possible donors. Suppose the truth is revealed that I made this year's cake (it was my turn, and it will be yours next year). Based on this, our friend concludes, via an unsupported reach and a logic error, that you never made them a cake and that I made all previous cakes. Unfortunately, this is a tactic used to erroneously dismiss competing explanations and theories by entrenched symbolists that hold allegiance to their beliefs. Our natural-cause pyramid theory could succumb to this logic flaw when modern human technology can shape the refined building blocks similar to those that comprise the pyramids, and therefore, we conclude that nature could not have formed them. In other words, the origin of the key components of the pyramids is assumed to be only the result from intelligent intervention. When we eventually recreate the building blocks of life, will we similarly conclude that natural causes had nothing to with their (or our) origin and intelligent intervention is the only way it could happen? Such a choice would only support a belief preference that is certainly not based on logic or science. I suspect, like in our thought experiment, theories of intervention and natural causes must remain as possibilities. In a similar circumstance, we seem to have no problem believing that diamonds can be formed in nature as well as by synthetic processes. It would be nonsensical to reject the existence of naturally occurring diamonds based on our ability to make them ourselves.

STRENGTHENING THE INTERPRETIVE-INTELLIGENCE GENRE

Testing and refinement of existing interpretation frameworks can be used to strengthen them. The frameworks account for perceptions and observations to assign meaning. Errors in judgment based on these inputs are typically the fault of an interpretation framework's defect rather than the observation itself. In other words, it is how we misinterpret what we grasp that is at the heart of the fault. To minimize this risk, our education process is used to share well-tested interpretation frameworks to expedite high performance and proficiency. However, in this process, the demands for our own interpretive intelligence to function are quite low since they are not typically part of the structured environments we experience growing up. The student learns expected responses to the provided interpretations and related questions. The student is rewarded when the information is recalled and used. This is the cultivation of passive intelligence. This process, by habit, ingrains a disposition to function primarily in the passive-intelligence genre. However, the information learned can serve as the foundation for defining the attributes that the interpretive-intelligence function depends. When the questions and answers are not given to us, our own interpretive intelligence is required to function. A new interpretation framework will have concepts and expectations that have been previously learned, at least as a starting point, but all of these expectations should be scrutinized and should be challenged. This questioning activates the interpretive-intelligence genre to grow and evolve interpretation frameworks.

One excellent example of growing the interpretation framework comes from merging multiple points of view. In common experience, each situation encountered is subject to an individual's own unique interpretation framework that may be quite distinct. If an individual interprets a circumstance differently than others, depending on the established interpretation framework, the person could be lauded as a genius or rejected as a fool. In either case, such a reaction suggests that the established framework is not comprehensive. When perspectives of many individuals are collected, a multitude of varied candidate-response opportunities to contend with a challenge can be recognized (evidence of a more comprehensive interpretation framework than a single-response nomination). Task teams are a reflection of this concept with a collection of many individual's perspectives to feed the process. Fair and respectful consideration of all perspectives and fitting them into a hierarchy of relevance is essential to manage the situation. Ideally, effective management of the many "voices" can lead to a robust interpretation framework. If the situation is mismanaged, the most popular opinion could be the result, and critical insight held by only a few might be neglected.

The managers of task teams should watch out for a few treasures within their teams. First, thoughtful individuals that may have expansive frameworks on their own (that enable them to have an internal team-like dialogue) may require more time to clarify the elements of their responses and perspectives. These individuals have often weighed much more than one consideration in the formation of their opinion. If they have more insight than the rest of the team, their communication with the team is essentially only for sharing. In effect, the balance of the team is receiving an education rather than contributing. A second treasure in a team is a specialist that carries a deep understanding of at least one dimension of the task or challenge. This individual should be leveraged in related conversations as a means to minimize discussion of low-value superficial perspectives. A third treasure is a good connectionist who has a strong focus on finding the relationships of causes and effects. In fact, a task team manager that is a connectionist can keep the team aimed properly as the path to a solution emerges. If the task team manager is not so inclined, a team member connectionist should be drawn into a functional assistant manager role. This approach (active intelligence) is particularly helpful when an interpretation framework of guiding principles (from the passive-intelligence genre) fail or do not exist. In this case, a new interpretation framework emerges that often requires validation to ensure high proficiency.

It is possible to train interpretive intelligence by maintaining open questions, regardless of the popular answers. In effect, we create our interpretation framework with our own unanswered questions. This function is evident in simple games and puzzles where one keys in on something needed to create success. For example, if two dice are rolled, and a success is a total of seven, a person likely knows that six and one or five and two will be winners and will watch for those combinations. They become an expert in the creation of sevens and instantly know when a seven hits in those ways. They have little concern about the ways to roll a six or a five, for example, and won't watch for that, just that the result is not a seven. This interpretation process sorts or filters information to be considered helpful or not. A problem comes into play when, in this example, if the person has mistakenly decided that rolling four and three is not helpful. It is natural to spend less attention on unhelpful observations and potentially missed opportunities for success. This neglect of attention reveals a suspended interpretive-intelligence function. A pertinence question should be maintained to keep the interpretive-intelligence genre functioning. Why is this asset (or combination on the dice) not helpful? If one finds that it could be helpful (the four and three works), a greater display of interpretive intelligence is enabled by expanding the candidate opportunities and correcting for a misjudgment.

The pursuit of correcting interpretation frameworks is laced with questions that put it to the test. It is unwise to hold an inaccurate or unproven interpretation framework with high regard. In some cases, even issues that seem settled are not. Albert Einstein didn't stop his questions despite the very satisfactory and practical physical law interpretations found by Sir Isaac Newton. Newton's laws of motion, for most of us, are empirically validated through tests and measurements and provide exceptional results. Einstein's special theory of relativity suggested that Newton's laws are faulty, but the fault is well within the measurement error of our typical validation activities. However, in other circumstances the prediction error created by Newton's laws can be measured (i.e., with particles moving close to the speed of light). The magnitude of the error is anticipated in Einstein's work, which serves to validate the theory of special relativity. It is curious that we call Einstein's work a theory and Newton's findings as laws, since it is more likely to be the opposite.

Newton's "theory" of motion has been shown to have limited use and will be inaccurate when rigorously tested. However, Newton's limited domain is immensely practical for us in our daily lives, and the minute error is ignored. Similarly, if we live our lives within a few square miles, flat maps, which have no regard for the Earth's curvature are more than sufficient. In practice, we largely function like we believe the Earth is flat.

When an individual is immersed in a subject, a related interpretation framework is being energized. In research, an investigator is on a constant look out for insight that can be applied to an active project. It has been said the Charles Goodyear discovered vulcanization of rubber by mistake, when a sample of rubber was accidentally dropped onto a hot surface. The fact was, he had an interpretation framework to "see" causes and effects related to rubber stability. If it was by chance that the rubber's heating event happened or not, he could interpret the meaning of the result and use it. He already had a place to put this newfound information into his interpretation framework. Having a "place" to gather new information with purpose is quite powerful. As an engineering student, I was very interested in energy and how to use it efficiently. This interpretation framework gave meaning to many of my studies since I was looking for opportunities to recover wasted energy. When I observed air-conditioning systems that compress a gaseous refrigerant to a high pressure, only to reject heat from it to make it a liquid, I saw wasted energy. Further, when the high-pressure liquid refrigerant is bled through an orifice to a low pressure, to make the refrigeration effect, I saw wasted energy there as well. Those observations coupled with my interpretation framework inspired a successful active intelligence investigation into how to recover energy from that system later in my career. It was an active-intelligence activity since there had been no success in doing so on record. In other words, my interpretive-intelligence genre was required to find pertinent resource candidates to possibly contend with this energy-recovery challenge. Naturally, those resources had to be manipulated and combined in novel ways in order to be successful. (There were no specific best practices from the passive-intelligence genre to help.)

COACHING POINT

One main function of the interpretive-intelligence genre is to nominate candidate resources and recognize opportunities to contend with challenges. The pertinence of the nominations will dictate proficiency when viable opportunities are pursued that can satisfy the challenge. Central to this genre are the interpretation frameworks that provide the structure of how to translate observations into meaning. The frameworks have their roots in questions and criteria that can be articulated as an enabler to manage them. These frameworks can be strengthened in the following key ways: Each interpretation framework should be considered to be a work in progress and not completed. Question interpretations without ceasing, or at the very least, don't defend them as an undeniable truth or as the only answer or perspective. This means keeping the questions active and keep looking for opportunities (like Charles Goodyear). When the questions stop, it has been decided that interpretation is complete, and the interpretive-intelligence function ceases. As a means to remain active, continue to test and verify interpretation frameworks. If errors are discovered, correct them and adjust. When a test cannot verify the validity for some reason, it is prudent to maintain open-mindedness to alternative interpretations that may possibly be correct while the current one may not be. Certainly, one can consider their own point of view to be more likely, but there are usually interesting reasons for other perspectives. History has shown us that the most popular perspective or interpretation framework is often a constraint and in need of correction.

INTERPRETATION FRAMEWORK HIERARCHY AND PRIORITIES

Early in life, our parents tend to set our priorities for us. Our schedule of sleeping and eating are among the earliest decisions made for us. Planned routines are established concerning hygiene and manners. As a child grows, a desire to make decisions contrary to the plan develops without the benefit of complete information.

A parent can support by setting boundaries and rules with rationale for the child to aid them in making better decisions. In the process, the child learns self-control and habitual respect for guidelines or rules (if they like them or not). The grasping of a long-term consequence concept is difficult for a child; after all, their life thus far is, has been, quite short-term. For example, the routine of brushing teeth is annoying. "My teeth are fine, just look at them. What do you mean that they will rot, hurt, and fall out?" The self-discipline to attend to uncomfortable rules cultivates a high-performing person that can value things beyond securing immediate gratification. Strong and often admired people disregard the short-term pain to get a great gain in the future. The most valued accomplishments in life tend to demand sacrifices of time, comfort, and fun. Olympic athletes and soldiers furnish examples of an individual's dedication to a cause despite much personal inconvenience. In addition, some activists may see a rule or general conduct in society that is not consistent with their guiding principles. It is not comfortable to challenge the rule in the short-term, but the evolution of our society into a better condition is driven by persons willing to suffer for it. From this, it is no surprise that how we set priorities as adults depends on how we view the long-term versus short-term benefits and consequences. The parent that facilitates recognition of long-term values does the child and society a huge favor.

Contrary to this parenting approach, parents have been encouraged not to impose artificial consequences for misconduct (rule breaking) as has been done in the past. For example, if a child walks on the furniture with dirty feet, it does not warrant any penalty or an expression of disapproval. Once, our pediatrician in Arizona saw me struggling to get my very young son to wear his shoes after his exam when we were readying to leave her office. She preemptively advised me that any discipline of a child was not the recommended way to raise them. Her position, as I interpreted it, was that the judgment of the inexperienced child should be given the same or a higher place than that of the experienced parents. She said I should just let him have his way; and when he walks on the hot parking lot, he will learn. I couldn't imagine letting him burn his feet and then persuade him to put on shoes. I asked her how her young daughter, of a similar age, was doing in learning how to cross the street to convey my perceived cruelty of her instruction. Perhaps her interpretation framework only saw a competition of wills over a trivial daily life task and my son could indeed learn to deal with that specific task the hard way (a short-term issue). Beyond that, this was an opportunity to cultivate his appreciation for authority that cares for him rather than one that willingly permits harm simply to avoid confrontation (a long-term issue). Anyone, child or not, can benefit from an experienced or a more mature interpretation framework that others have. A parent who yells "Stop" to a child approaching the edge of a busy street may indeed deny them a learning experience of being hit by a car, if the child respects her voice. Often, wisdom (mature interpretation framework) is contained in rules or in the voice of an expert in authority that comprehends and accounts for the consequences of missteps. Naturally, this was the very reason we were leveraging the pediatrician's medical expertise to examine my son in the first place. However, that does not mean that her interpretation frameworks on all topics are above being questioned (or mine either).

An assessment of potential consequences and benefits is central to prioritizing elements of decisions and actions. In news reports, we have seen looting during a riot by individuals that sense there will be no negative consequences for their actions. Perhaps a desire for free electronics is stronger than a consequence risk of being arrested since being caught is unlikely in these circumstances. The thief may realize a benefit, but the consequence to the store owner and the community might be devastating. The shortsighted view of the thief may translate into no future business activity in that area. From that, employment opportunities and taxes that help provide common services will be compromised. Observations about the long-term consequences of various actions have given rise to principles, laws, and rules that protect society. As a thought experiment, if everyone acted against a given law, what would become of the society? Would it destroy key parts or members of the society? Unfortunately, as children, we tend to see our immediate consequences and benefits as all that matters. The merit of functioning within the rules may not be fully understood until the person matures.

When decisions are to be made, interpretation frameworks for separate challenges have to compete. It becomes necessary to weigh each framework's merit and select a compromise or follow one of them as the primary guide. For example, my young daughter fell in love with dolphins and wanted one badly after having a wonderful swimming experience in Florida. Her interpretation framework saw this friendly, amazing animal as a great pet. My "desirable animal" interpretation framework agreed with her. An additional framework of mine considered that keeping a dolphin healthy in Michigan was not tenable for our family. I had some limited awareness of what it takes to keep this animal in good condition, which readily eclipsed our resources. Further, there are likely more demands than the deal breakers that came to my mind. My interpretation framework of resource feasibility for the pet's well-being competed and won against the desire of being able to interact with a fantastic pet every day. These frameworks were prioritized or ranked to help guide our decision to visit dolphins rather than own them.

As in the dolphin example above, frequently there are competing objectives that have their own individual interpretive-intelligence frameworks that enter into making a decision. For example, assume one desires to purchase a vehicle. One framework is for building wealth. The interpretive-intelligence awareness to evaluate the profitability of any expense is functioning in this framework. This could include an assessment that investing in education or a home, if done well, can return a profit in the future and are worthy expenses. The purchase of a vehicle that depreciates is not a good choice in this framework unless it avoids other costs or is used in a business that offsets the expense. Another framework is for projecting an image of success. Anything that is possessed can be viewed as an accomplishment. If a possession is of a high reputation, the accomplishment is interpreted as a greater one. To some, perhaps living in a mansion on a lake with a large boat and several new luxury cars would project a successful image. This framework will narrow the candidate list of automakers and limit the vehicle types that fit the image. In addition, a framework of environmental responsibility may also be in play in the decision to purchase a vehicle. The vehicle's in-use pollution and energy consumption performance should be minimized to support this framework. Consideration of the pollution created to manufacture the vehicle and dispose of it when it is no longer of use are part of this environmentally friendly mindset. A practicality framework also needs to be served. The vehicle must meet certain needs. For example, the required attributes of cargo, passenger, and towing capacity must be met. If an ability to routinely or occasionally carry furniture is a requirement, a compact car may not suffice. Each framework has a different interpretation of the suitability of each candidate vehicle. A frugal vehicle may be old, unimpressive, and have an outdated emission system; but by buying it, the incredible amount of pollution caused to create a new vehicle is avoided. A top-level luxury car may be poor on fuel efficiency, accommodate only two persons, and have excessive associated costs. The interpretation frameworks for this decision must compete for priority to make a suitable choice. On a personal level, my father entered his career with a wife and the beginnings of a family. I entered my career single and with very little outside obligations. When my father saw my new two-door sports car, he later explained to me that he didn't see it as practical and had some internal objection. After he enjoyed a test drive of the vehicle, he thought that for me, in my circumstance, well, why not? My choice wasn't even a consideration in his situation: he had needs to meet that I did not.

In nature, suppose an animal has a decision to make at a watering hole when a predator arrives. The animal has an interpretation framework that avoids predators. To that end, an awareness of noises, smells, other animals and their behaviors can trigger movement to a candidate escape path that has already been identified. Another interpretation framework is to meet physical needs, including acquiring water. The characteristics of good water sources are measured against opportunities observed in the environment. When these two frameworks clash at a shared watering hole, it might typically be best for the animal to hide and wait for a predator to leave prior to drinking. However, should a deep need for water be present (i.e., drought driven), the framework to get water may take precedence, and the animal may drink alongside a natural predator. In such a case, the risk of death from the lack of water is more certain than the predator's appetite. In this case, each framework's relative priority comes from an interpretation of the consequence risks versus the benefits. A clever animal in this circumstance might find a position at the watering hole that enables an effective escape path from a predator (i.e., the predator might have to pass through deep mud to start the chase). In this way, the risk of being eaten is reduced.

The skill to read a circumstance and find alternative choices is a sign of high-functioning interpretive intelligence. In making a decision, interpretive intelligence gathers all of these frameworks related to a decision and interprets them individually and collectively. Ultimately, a hierarchy (priority) emerges that places some objectives above others in preparation to make a decision. The hierarchy is a result of a competition and compromise of what is considered to be important. A selection from the identified opportunities relies on grasping the ramifications of each choice in order make an optimal decision. However, the hierarchy is subject to change when exceptional circumstances are present. For example, the disruption of the priorities of a shopper is the goal of a salesperson. A fantastic deal can inspire a person to purchase an unplanned item.

There are a number of approaches to setting priorities and making decisions that are worthy of examination. Some people claim to have a subjective feeling about a given choice. Others may select the most popular option. Some may experiment with a limited application of their decision before making a full commitment. A person may consider the impact of multiple decision choices and their likely benefits and consequences prior to making a final selection. An enticing support of this style to help make a decision is the prediction of the future. Should a prediction yield unwanted results, one may reject the choice that led to it. The value of using predictions is that the real consequences, particularly from bad choices, do not have to be physically experienced.

Virtual simulation of a candidate decision's performance prior to making a final decision can be exceptionally valuable. Let us consider a vehicle's navigation system. The navigation system embarks on an evaluation of various virtual routes to reach a destination. Based on a few simple criteria, perhaps minimize driving distance or to arrive at the earliest time while avoiding dirt roads, a multitude of paths can be simulated. Typically, the recommended path is comprised of a combination of known public roads. The fundamental minimized path selection is found by drawing a straight line between the destination and the starting point. The closer that recommended path comes to the straight line, the closer it is to providing the shortest practical distance. The physical checking of each candidate route is not necessary, since each path is mimicked well in the virtual environment and rapidly assessed as if were selected. In another example, when some financial advisors recommend an asset mix, they will stress test it with historical data. This is a form of simulation that reveals what would happen if the market conditions of the last ten years were to repeat. In this way, the consequences and benefits of the choices are given some perspective. The fact that the next ten years will not be exactly the same as the previous decade is still a risk, yet it would seem foolish to select an asset mix that would have been a total bust in the past.

Impact ranking is a means to facilitate making a priority of the elements or the functioning frameworks of a decision. From the work of business consultants Kepner and Tregoe (1997), a prioritization method is suggested called SUG. SUG stands for *s*eriousness, *u*rgency, and *g*rowth, which provide a means to rank order tasks or decision choices based on these three attributes. When I was a young driver attempting to enter our very icy driveway one winter, I found myself sliding toward a telephone pole on the edge of our property. It was clear to me that I was not going to make a successful entry into the driveway. If I continued to steer the vehicle in an attempt to make the turn, I would likely hit the pole. I quickly changed my immediate goal from making the turn to avoiding the pole. In this case, all parts of SUG lit up for me. The seriousness (*S* in SUG) of potentially hitting the pole was high because of damage risks and the loss of a vehicle for period of time. If I did nothing, a bad result would grow (*G*). An action to deal with this situation was urgent (*U*). I couldn't wait until the next day to decide what to do. When all three parts of SUG are aligned, it is not difficult to prioritize to the top of the list. However, there are combinations of SUG that are far less clear, when one or two of the three are not present. Consider an information-only report has urgency (*U*) because of an arbitrary deadline. The information is not critical to anyone (i.e., not serious); it simply keeps people in the loop. If the deadline is missed by even a few days, nothing bad will come of it (i.e., no growth). In this case, the report might be one of the last things to complete, particularly if something serious is being handled in its place.

Simple voting is another means to make a decision within a group. This approach is frequently used in the case of a team convened to solve a problem. Participants will individually decide among alternatives. Their choices are combined to find the most popular one. A simple example could be how to revise/improve a form that is used widely within a company. The importance and reason for the form may be held by a few stakeholders in the company. A much greater number of recipients may view the form as only an inconvenience and would vote to delete it. If the goal or aim is to reduce general inconvenience, then perhaps this unbiased vote will be acceptable. If the goal is to efficiently deliver information to a governmental agency about the company, respecting that popular vote may have terminal consequences for the company itself. This suggests that subject-matter experts need to be given more authority than the result of a vote dominated by individuals that represent tertiary perspectives. This style of voting would have a bias to favor those individuals and could be considered unfair. (Note: Pertinence, not fairness, is part of our intelligence definition.) Instead, let us be fair: Imagine if decisions during a medical operation were made by a popular vote from ten musicians and a medical doctor. Perhaps you would be uncomfortable with that situation. Let's add ten amateur baseball player's votes to the mix. Unfortunately, this further dilutes the doctor's voice in making good informed choices. A vote to use the doctor's right hand to make the first incision is made by an overwhelming vote of 20 to

1. The one outlier vote came from the left-handed doctor, who will make the incision. After all, everyone knows (or has been educated to believe) that most people are right-handed, so that is clearly the best choice. If you don't like the conclusion, let's add ten more voters from an elementary-school playground.

The prioritization of competing interpretation frameworks really should be based on the effectiveness to "contend with a challenge" aspect of our intelligence definition. This challenge has to be interpreted and typically takes the form of goal or objective statements. These statements require special attention to avoid constraining the response and compromising proficiency. This is another aspect of the interpretive-intelligence genre. When a goal or objective is clarified and potentially expanded by the interpretive-intelligence genre, it often is necessary to interact with the passive-intelligence genre and the active-intelligence genre in the process. The refinement may be an iterative process, and this leads us to a discussion of goals and objectives.

CHAPTER 5

GOALS, OBJECTIVES, AND THE INTELLIGENCE GENRES

The way a challenge is interpreted can impact the success in dealing with it. As a matter of habit, a familiar challenge interpretation framework might be used, rather than utilizing the power of the interpretive-intelligence genre to assess the challenge. In this way, the passive-intelligence genre asserts similarity of the challenge to other challenges. In the game of checkers, for example, the objective is to eliminate the opponent's pieces. Strategies that enable setting up multiple jumps and trapping an opponent's checkers prove to be effective. The methods and patterns to create the winning scenarios are validated and remembered in a mature checker player. These techniques populate the passive-intelligence response resources that are accessed through association by recognition of patterns that lead to success as proficiency develops. This growth may come from observing other skilled players in action and from personal victories and defeats. Even an ability to anticipate an opponent's actions favor an active-intelligence element to the game that plays out as cause-and-effect understanding grows. Success with this game establishes a tendency to interpret other games similarly and to utilize those strategies. It so happens that many of the strategies and skills prove to be successfully transferable to the game of Chinese checkers. Success in this game reinforces the habitual use of an established interpretation framework for any board-game challenge of a similar nature. Now let's play chess.

Winning in chess results from achieving checkmate, which means the opponent's king cannot escape a threat of capture. Since it is impossible for a completely depleted opponent to win (left only with their king), logic would suggest that the odds of winning improve the closer an opponent gets to that condition. In this way, the challenge to gain a material advantage (having more or stronger pieces remaining on the board than the opponent) connects familiar strategies from the game of checkers to chess. However, in order to win, it is not essential that one has a material advantage of a superior number of pieces on the board. In fact, a clever approach against a checker-minded opponent is to sacrifice powerful pieces to gain strategic positions aimed at the checkmate goal. If one adopts this approach against a checker-minded challenger, the opponent will feel success and superiority as they disproportionately remove pieces from the board. Ultimately, the shock of being suddenly defeated by relatively few remaining pieces exposes the fault of their challenge interpretation. In this case, the opponent's abilities were constrained (or somewhat misdirected) by an underlying idea that successful methods in checkers are requisite in the game of chess. The game's actual objective was replaced by a means to that objective, which is similar to assuming a solution in a goal statement or challenge interpretation. This is a common error in interpreting challenges that may compromise proficiency.

The "Comfortable Cadillac Story" further illustrates this point: One sunny summer day in Florida an automotive engineering group was driving a prototype test vehicle on the freeway. The interior temperature was automatically controlled and was performing well as expected. When the vehicle left the freeway and stopped at the end of an exit ramp, the passengers began to feel warm. In the past, some other models had a low-speed cooling issue in hot conditions that was mitigated by changing the air-conditioning system's inlet air source from the hot/humid outside air to the relatively cool and dry cabin air (actually circulating the interior air). This enables the air conditioner "to work less hard" at providing cold air from the vent outlets in the dash. Given this, direction to adopt this familiar solution that is called recirculation into this new model was made by the engineering group's boss. The challenge statement was framed to find a means to adopt this familiar solution. An alternative interpretation is that the challenge to keep the cabin cool and comfortable in hot conditions at all vehicle speeds was not being met. This goal restatement (interpretive intelligence) does not impose a solution, and its use opens the opportunity to use active intelligence, which demands a fundamental investigation rather than simply copying an assumed solution. It turned out, for this specific model, that the vehicle's motion generated significant airflow through the cabin that was forfeited when the vehicle slowed and stopped on the exit ramp, like turning the fan down. This was due to the unique aerodynamic shape resulting from the model's exterior styling. Further, it was observed that the air temperature in the dash's ventilation outlets when the vehicle stopped was essentially the same as it was while driving at higher speeds. Successful issue resolution was achieved by increasing the airflow (automatically turning up the fan slightly) to sustain cabin comfort when low vehicle speeds in hot conditions were detected. This was a novel solution that was enabled by a revision of the boss's original objective statement. The familiar imposed passive-intelligence solution would have failed in this case: it would have kept the outlet temperatures cool, but they already were cool. This is an example of how a goal or objective statement that assumes a solution not only limited the response options, but it was actually inappropriate.

Initially, the goal statement was not comprehensive enough to inspire an effective intelligent response in the "Comfortable Cadillac Story." The restructuring of the challenge statement enabled a reset in the thinking to the fundamental nature of the concern. This reset suspends the constraints of conventional wisdom and current paradigms, at least for a time. Thus, the characteristics of the broad or higher-level goal were more easily explored. The choice to use passive intelligence or active intelligence, intentional or not, is often a consequence of the construction of the goal or purpose statement. In lieu of a goal statement, a question may be used. The nature of that question, in a similar manner, can impose a solution. For example, "How do we activate cabin air recirculation automatically in these hot conditions?" versus "How do we keep the cabin comfortable in these hot conditions?" In this story, the boss could easily complain that deploying the effective solution rather than his imposed solution was insubordinate, but he was too smart for that.

When we encounter an opportunity, a challenge, or problem to be solved, this makes two primary demands of the interpretive-intelligence genre to fulfill an intelligent action: First, the challenge itself has to be interpreted. Second, the recognition of pertinent resources is essential to contend with it. Effectively, the quality of the challenge interpretation in the first step defines the interpretation framework for assessing the pertinence of the resources in the second step. In this way, the interpretive-intelligence genre can be used to translate goal or objective statements into opportunity enablers that expand awareness of candidate pertinent resources. If a given goal statement is laced with paradigms (assumed solutions), it limits the choices to meet it. As a means to avoid this, the actual deviation of the current state from the desired state should be used in a challenge restatement. The deviation is not that the imposed solution is not yet applied; rather, it is the deviation that the assumed solution is trying to address. Consider that a request is issued to turn the light switch on in a room. The challenge could be to simply flip the switch, or more broadly, to bring more light into the room. With this expanded challenge interpretation, in addition to the light-switch activation, we might open the blinds, light candles, start a fire in the fireplace, use a flashlight, use a lantern, shine car lights through a window, or perhaps activate a different lamp—just to name a few. If the lamp on the switch doesn't happen to work (i.e., power outage or a burned-out bulb), the need to identify other resources to meet the actual goal becomes evident. Thus, the interpretive-intelligence genre can be an enabler of innovation since different resource nominations that have potential to meet the broadened goal are given space to be recognized. These resources for the nominations may come from the passive-intelligence genre (i.e., inherited) and the active-intelligence genre (i.e., resources synthesized through logical manipulation or found through investigation). From the nominations, a response is selected, which follows from our definition of intelligence. To refresh, *Intelligence is the act of interpretation followed by a response derived from pertinent information that is either inherited from past experience or actively manipulated or created through investigation to contend with a challenge.*

From this intelligence definition, contending with a challenge is the reason to act intelligently. Logically then, when the challenge is met, the intelligent action ends. However, there are challenges that are renewed and require ongoing intelligent action to contend with them. Let us define these challenges as open ended, since they can never be completely achieved. This includes maintenance-related goals. In these cases, the circumstances change or degrade with time and require corrective action. For example, these open-ended challenges include replenishing consumables, maintaining health, securing the viability of a business, and keeping a living space in good condition. A challenge of continuous improvement is another open-ended goal. This challenge comes from dissatisfaction with the current state as it is compared to an idea of a better future condition. The result of contending with the existing deviation creates a new current condition that establishes a new baseline that is similarly considered to be insufficient. Thus, a challenge and its defining deficiency remain in place without end. The desired ideal performance or result in these situations is often vague and always unattainable. Unlike how challenges that are met will result in an end to the intelligent activity, these open-ended challenges require sustained intelligent activity. A reinterpretation of the nature of the challenge, goal, or objective could potentially convert an open-ended goal into one that is attainable and vice versa. For example, the following could be interchanged: I want a good score on a test (attainable) vs. I want mastery of the topic of the test (proficiency with no upper limit).

In general, success will be judged by comparison of performance results to what is expressed in the goal or objective statements. There are two classifications of goals or challenges that are common in our human experience, regardless of their renewable condition: First, is a relative goal. This goal type is based on competition and a comparison of performance to others. Second, an absolute goal has its roots in finishing a task or making an accomplishment that has no regard for how others perform. When I was a child, a family of four brothers came to visit us. The youngest of the brothers was a four-year-old named Tony. We had a foot race across our yard. Tony struggled to keep up, and when everyone else had finished, he was just over halfway. He stopped and began to cry. He had failed. He did not beat his older brothers to the finish line; he failed a relative goal. I came back to Tony and knelt down to comfort him. I had him look back at the starting line. I said, "Tony, look how far you came. That is a very long way. I think you did a lot here." He realized that he did go quite far, and we celebrated his accomplishment, and we ran happily together to the finish line. He had not failed in an absolute sense of moving across the yard a very good distance in a short time.

Consider that a sprinter and a marathon specialist are labeled as runners (based on past performance). In some situations, the attribute of speed is more valued than endurance and vice versa. Suppose that a goal to complete a one-hundred-meter race is given to each runner. This goal does not depend on comparison to other race participants; this as an absolute goal. Another challenge is added: to complete the race in the shortest time compared to the other runner, a relative goal. Both types of runners are very capable of completing this short race, which would accomplish the absolute goal. The marathon specialist has trained to use energy resources slowly. This energy management enables running of great distances—and not to use it up quickly like a sprinter does in a short race. Each running specialist employs their essence of being a runner (mechanics and refined movements) during the race. The sprinter dashes out to large lead in the first five seconds. However, the sprinter suffers cramps and hobbles through the last part of the race. His running ability was suddenly hampered. As a result, the marathon specialist wins this short race because of a competitor's misfortune. Without this misfortune, the healthy sprinter would have easily won the race. In this way, a marathon specialist, while applying his same skill set as a runner, can win or lose. The decisive point of this relative performance stems from how well adapted the available resources of each runner is to the task. The sprinter had the best resources to win, but his resources were diminished during the event. Regardless, the absolute goal of race completion was accomplished by each of them.

This leads us to a consideration of relative goal interpretations that arise from competitive situations. Two main stages of relevance occur in competitive circumstances. The first stage rewards proficiency based on real and significant differences. Response choices in this stage depend on causal relationships that influence performance, which means there are pertinent resources that when utilized will give rise to a winner. The sprinter in the previous example lost a pertinent resource when cramps occurred, and the marathon runner won because of a significant difference in running ability at that time. The second stage is much like gambling in which randomness is used to select a winner from statistically equal competitors in an extreme case. From an entertainment perspective, when profound differences exist in the competition's first stage, the results are a foregone conclusion and are not particularly interesting. For this reason, it is convenient to set objective measures of real differences and divide the talent accordingly, such as separating age groups for youth athletics. (A soccer match pitting high-school players against elementary-school players would be painful to watch.) Similarly, a proficiency separation is also the intent of the playoff systems that most sports utilize. Chances are that the predominantly winning teams from the regular season are similar and will make an entertaining playoff competition, while teams with losing records are excluded from postseason play (they may be expected to lose badly). Emerging industries have companies that are competing to gain market share. Real and meaningful differences among companies happen as each is learning how to do things at a different pace. The resulting proficiency is rewarded or punished in the marketplace, which demonstrates the first stage of competition relevance. As the industry matures, the proficiency level among companies tends to normalize and winners or losers at a given point in time are not statistically significant. Evidence of this is found when famous quality surveys become increasingly meaningless as all competitors deliver essentially the same performance. The survey administrators have to reach for new questions that have less and less to do with the primary product or service functions in order to get some sort of ranking to designate a winner in this second stage of competition. In this stage, achievement with these new questions is only important for survey performance and little else.

A friend of mine and I enjoyed playing tennis against each other. We had similar skill levels, and our second-stage competition led to a mix of wins and losses for each of us. It seemed to me that I had a slight, but inconsistent, physical advantage until my friend purchased a new oversized racquet. The power he put to the ball was remarkable, and I was outmatched. In fact, the strings on my small wooden racquet started breaking as he nearly took off my arm with his shots. He was at the next level and I was not and he easily won our matches, which I am sure was fun—for him. Our competition was now in the first stage, which is typified by a real difference.

My friend encouraged me to try his racquet, and the root cause of his newfound power was clear. Since my equipment was now in need of repair, I purchased a similar oversized racquet, which restored our competitiveness. Each of our games was now at a new level, and much more proficient performances followed for each of us. Any friendly bragging rights from our prior win-loss record history with the small wooden racquets (in the second competitive stage) seemed ridiculous and trivial considering this higher absolute performance level that each of us was now enjoying.

If a goal or challenge interpretation is based on the second stage of competition, we tend to overemphasize the importance of minute differences that essentially happen by chance. This means that we have very little control of how to reach the goal other than to keep trying until in success happens to land on us. By definition, there are no pertinent resources that can be applied to contend with the challenge, and therefore, it makes an intelligent response impossible. In essence, no action will be meaningfully connected or helpful. As a result, challenge and goal interpretations to win something in this second stage of competition are of little value. For example, ten world-class runners can be ranked based on one race's result, but what does it really mean to do that? All ten from a practical and statistical point of view are actually equivalent. In this case, the ranking falls to chance, and the results would not necessarily be repeatable if the race were conducted multiple times. This lack of statistical validity undermines the true value of the ranking, but it is popularly tolerated and even celebrated in general. Sporting events and most surveys cultivate this fun and gambling type of atmosphere with awards that find their way to the luckiest among the best contenders. Unfortunately, this encourages a narrow view of competition that implies we have to have a single winner, and that is what matters. This concept that one must lose for another to win is called a zero-sum game. This is a poor challenge interpretation.

Another source of particularly weak challenge or goal interpretation comes from one that is artificially created from independent goals and challenges. Essentially, these challenges are not mutually exclusive but are linked somehow to foster a competition. This means that a nonzero-sum game is needlessly converted into a zero-sum game that has a winner. This conversion rewards counterproductive behavior that incites unnecessary competition in situations where it is otherwise possible to have all winners. Collaboration is generally a casualty of this mistaken style of goal interpretation. I once had a conversation with a young inventor who was, in his mind, competing with me for the most US patents in our company (a relative goal). The *number* of patents was the way he tried to link our independent innovative challenges in order to form a competition. With this mindset, the idea of us collaborating would not help him gain on me should we jointly acquire a patent. However, the meaningful absolute goal of growing our company's intellectual property could ideally be enhanced through our joint efforts. To combat this, I told him that each novel idea stands independently on its own merit. His only patent (thus far) was unique, and it was something that I didn't think of or anyone else for that matter (an absolute accomplishment). The counting and accounting of the number of met challenges is off topic in dealing with the innovative challenges themselves and is best ignored. Similarly, rivalries are typically a form of unnecessary artificial competition that present a risk of encouraging unintelligent and toxic behavior. Suppose one sibling happens to succeed and another sibling has not, as yet, happened to have similar success. Their competition may cause one to resent the other when success occurs and vice versa (an absolute goal of a supportive family relationship is forfeit). In reality, this is not a zero-sum game. Their successes are independent and do not need to be connected by competition; in fact, they could support each other through collaboration and celebrate each other's successes without any negative consequences. This artificial competition in many ways can be a thought poison that impedes proficiency growth as it restricts those willing to offer support—this is a limiting mindset. Challenge interpretations that include this influence should be reworked and replaced with an absolute and ideally unifying goal (i.e., grow intellectual property or develop overall family success).

Goal interpretations that grow proficiency as the primary challenge are useful in helping avoid the pitfalls of an unneeded zero-sum mindset. Consider an example from tennis if an opponent has a poor backhand stroke. To win, it is advantageous to always return shots to that side. This opportunity improves the odds of their failure and ultimately a relative success. At higher levels of competition against opponents that have mastered their backhand stroke, one may find that specialized training to be nearly useless. Basically, becoming a specialist at only beating players that have poor backhand strokes is no longer pertinent. If one wishes to develop proficiency as an absolute goal, it is better to play to the opponent's strengths—and risk losing.

The best use of competition in this circumstance is to grow proficiency, with little concern with who wins or loses. This dynamic plays out in a competition for a starting position on a sports team and in military exercises. While proficiency is first being developed, the relative wins against other similar poor performers have very little meaning. For instance, the fastest elementary-school runner may later be defeated in high school as a result of how the classmates matured. Thus, it is more important to ultimately achieve a high-performance level than to win a series of competitions while rivals are somewhat low performers. The proficiency growth inspired by the competition is where the value is and not the win. This growth builds resources that enable future winning when it is considered to be important. For example, it could be to win a championship or to survive a war.

When winning really matters, an opponent's failure is necessary—a real zero-sum game and a relative goal. Response nominations from the interpretive-intelligence genre need to include a combination of either exploiting an opponent's weakness or by managing the situation to emphasize one's own highest proficiency. In the former case, we want the opponent to act unintelligently when contending with their challenges. This could mean they fail to properly interpret pertinent information (deceive them) related to the challenge or misunderstand the actual challenge (like the checker-chess example). The toxic actions of sabotage and thought-poison propaganda aimed at discouraging a competitor are often used to undermine their intelligent action. In sports, some players will use trash talk in an effort to distract the opponent from a clear focus on their real challenge. Politics thrives on pressing unintelligent positions onto opponents. Should one party meet meaningful challenges in their charge, they might gain approval and retain power. So the opposition party may attempt to impede progress or distort the facts to harm the proficiency of the other party. They might exaggerate nonissues in an effort to occupy the time of the other party as a distraction. This otherwise counterproductive conduct is a means to improve the prospects of gaining power themselves. Manipulation of the situation to play to our strengths is another means to enhance our zero-sum-game winning prospects. For example, a tall tennis player may come to the net rather than remain at the baseline to enable a wider variety of return angles. In some cases, a relative, strength can be created based on an opponent's behavior. Consider that a football team's defense has an objective or intent to impede the progress of the opponent's offense. The challenge can be interpreted from a causal relationship for the defense to have players in the right place at the right time to limit advances by the offense. A defensive football player may recognize an opponent's mannerism change as a pre-indicator of the type of play the team will run. For instance, the opposing running back uses a mouth guard for running plays, for personal protection only as needed. This pertinent resource observation and interpretation fosters an opportunity to trigger more effective actions by the defense. In response, they might abandon the wide receivers knowing when they are only decoys and conversely add pass coverage support that would normally be dedicated to stopping a running play. These actions enhance the ability of the defense to have more players in the right place at the right time.

PERTINENT RESOURCE RECOGNITION

The recognition of pertinent resources is important in contending with challenges regardless of the absolute or relative goal classification. Suppose we wish to fill a glass with water as an absolute goal. The current empty state does not match the desired goal of it being full. Several choices or resources may exist to increase the water level in the glass. They are acknowledged through the interpretive-intelligence genre. These choices could be considered factors that, when adjusted (active intelligence), may enable goal achievement, or at least favor reaching it. If it is raining, the glass could be placed upright outside and filled. A common practice of emptying some water from a full pitcher into the glass is yet another means. If a lake is nearby, dipping the glass into it might suffice. In essence, anything that can change the state toward or away from the goal is a factor. In a negative sense, there can be factors that harm goal achievement. For this example, suppose the glass has leak, which will make it difficult to sustain the state of the "filled" goal as added water escapes. Additionally, if the glass is extremely hot, the water might turn to steam, and therefore, a filled liquid level could not be sustained. So we could patch the leak and use the pitcher to fill a stable glass on a controlled-level surface in equilibrium at room temperature to meet the challenge. Another option is to submerge the leaky glass in a full pitcher of water. Did anyone say the outside of the glass had to be dry? The latter solution might be unacceptable. Why would that be? It meets the goal of having a glass completely full of water. Perhaps the goal should have been restated to include how the glass of water will be used (i.e., for drinking). Some might argue based on their interpretation framework that a drinking glass was implied in original goal statement. Perhaps they are correct, if they share the same interpretation framework as the individual that made the goal statement.

Consider an experiment with a banana hanging from the ceiling, giving a monkey a goal to collect this snack. This experimental configuration is borrowed from Wolfgang Kohler in *The Mentality of Apes* (1925). A short monkey cleverly stacks up nearby boxes to climb up and reach the banana. This problem-solving skill demonstrated active intelligence since the goal was accomplished by manipulating factors in the environment (the boxes were not already arranged for that task). Prior to that adjustment, the monkey had to recognize the challenge to get the banana, an inability to reach the banana by normal means, and identify the boxes as a candidate and pertinent resource to address that deficiency. During the process of achieving the goal, this monkey demonstrated function in the interpretive-intelligence genre in several ways. A tall monkey in the same experiment walks over to the banana and hops up slightly to grab it. The challenge to acquire the banana had to be perceived, and then an automatic action to grab it was triggered. This monkey exhibited passive intelligence after interpreting the challenge, since the goal was met with a conventional approach that has been applied to similar situations in prior experiences. Further, it would be off task to go to the trouble of stacking up the boxes to perform an unnecessary act of climbing.

Given this background, let us consider how to judge the intelligence proficiency of the tall and short monkeys in the experiment. This judgment implies that this is a competition. Since each monkey can collect a banana it is not a zero-sum situation. Therefore, it is an artificial competition. One metric we can use is the time it takes to complete the task. The tall monkey was faster to accomplish the goal, by only hopping a little to grab the banana. The short monkey stacked up boxes and then climbed up to accomplish the same goal. It did, however, take some time to arrange for success. Since this was slower, the race to complete the task was lost. Another judgment factor could be the display of intelligence. The short monkey's innovative success followed from the recognition of the available climbing resources (interpretive intelligence) and the rearrangement of them (active intelligence) to meet this challenge. Since the tall monkey didn't stack boxes, could we fairly conclude that this monkey isn't capable of similar innovation? Of course, the answer is no. By virtue of a height advantage, the resources were not the same as that of the short monkey. The judgment should be that each monkey achieved the absolute goal of securing the snack. They each won. Each interpreted the situation and contended with the challenge successfully with a familiar act, or an innovative act, and therefore, each of them acted with intelligence. The tall monkey had relatively high proficiency since its resources were a better match to the task than that of the short monkey. The poor resource match of the short monkey was overcome through a more complex demonstration of intelligence. The successful "contending with the challenge" part of our definition is the first level of proficiency. The relative speed or elegance of the achievement may be used to rank proficiency, but that is subjective and possibly of questionable meaning beyond entertainment.

QUESTIONING INTERPRETATIONS

Questions, by their nature, can establish or imply paradigms and interpretation sensitivity. Questions tend to set the boundaries of the responses and, therefore, the thought processes from which those responses are derived. Thus, they function very much like interpretation frameworks. Familiar examples from schooling include multiple-choice questions, which have a limited number of response choices. Open-ended questions permit a much wider variety of responses, such as an essay topic. The relevance and quality of the response, or correctness judgment, are measured against norms already shared and anticipated by the instructor. As a student moves through the education process, the typical or preferred responses to expected questions are routinely reinforced and rewarded. This trains or embeds the interpretation and response connection. As a result, thinking paradigms become habitual and dependable, and the interpretive-intelligence genre serves to recognize the familiar. These static interpretation frameworks provide the basis for future interpretation frameworks should the need arise.

The learned interpretation frameworks from our education processes serve us prior to activation of our own interpretive-intelligence genre. Evidence of this genre's "awakening" follows from recognition of the limitations of those teachings that enables refinement or, in some cases, rejection of those frameworks. For example, we were once taught about the four basic food groups in elementary school. We were instructed to eat servings from each group in order to be healthy. This did not seem unreasonable, and many families complied with the guidelines given to us. We accepted this paradigm (interpretation framework) as the way to do things. A meal was not complete if it was missing food from any of these groups. Further, such an omission was upsetting as it implied a disregard for our well-being. In the case of the four basic food groups, we can challenge this guideline with questions: "What evidence do we have for each of the food groups that show they make us healthy? How were the portions decided? Are those amounts linked to health?" If the answers are not compelling, investigation is needed. The questions are aimed at a clear objective of our good health and the factors that influence it. It could be that the four food group paradigm details had economic origins and a loose correlation to a healthy population. As it turns out, it was found that some of these food groups are not healthy for us, even to the point of complete omission from our diets. This means that the old interpretation framework being used to answer the goal/objective question of "What is healthy for us to eat?" has been recognized as obsolete. The revisiting of the objective statement with challenging questions aimed at a clear goal is the key to improvement.

Let us digress to a common childhood western teaching that Santa Claus delivers presents to all good children on Earth in one night. He flies in a sleigh drawn by special flying reindeer fully loaded with everyone's gifts. Further, he manages to deliver the correct gifts through each corresponding home's chimney regardless of the gift's size. For some number of years, children will accept this as truth. After all, it is being sold to them by the people they trust. They will send letters full of requests to Santa and visit his "helpers" at any number of store locations. As the presents keep coming year after year, why challenge a good thing? Yet at some point, questions begin to be raised about the viability of the story. The questions have their roots in common experiences that don't support that such an incredible feat could be accomplished in such a short time. The questions, challenges, and investigation eventually break down the myth. Perhaps peeking out of a slightly open bedroom door to see parents placing gifts rather than Santa was a clue. The first children in their age group to refute the myth are met with some degree of scorn by the people in authority: "You are ruining the experience for your classmates." At some point however, anyone that seriously holds to the myth would be considered foolish. The challenging questions help to break this paradigm. More broadly, questions may lead to a rejection or enable refinement of a perceived truth and even lead to discovery.

A question that calls for a correction of a deviation can generate an innovation-trigger statement interpretation. An innovation trigger can come from a need or desire to create, provide, or improve a function, service, or action. Improvement can take various forms. For example, enhancing completion speed, reducing scrap, using less resources, reducing costs, improving product consistency, elevation of performance, and addressing an unmet want or need (even if it is not yet recognized by others). As before with goal statements, the way we interpret and describe the trigger statement can influence innovative thinking limitations. As an example, a widely published independent survey ranks the interior-cabin heating performance of various automobiles. Some auto manufacturers that rank poorly on the list will use it as a trigger for action. The respondents vote on the ability of their vehicle to provide heat fast enough. The fact is that virtually all manufactures were getting satisfaction levels of over 95 percent on this question, which attains an absolute goal of doing the job well in the industry. The survey publisher ranked the models to artificially create a zero-sum type of competition among the automakers. To form this ranking, a relatively small sample of persons with exposure to largely only one model (that they owned) fed the survey with their opinion. This situation is analogous to observing an individual world-class sprinter running alone and voting that the one seen is the fastest in the world. There is no real comparison or objective measurement to support the subjective impression in the case of the runner or in this particular automotive survey. Although it was statistically foolish to pursue the vehicle heating improvement, it was deemed worthy of effort. It is fun to win, even if it is by chance and to gain the related (somewhat free) favorable media praise. The pursuit of this technical improvement offers an opportunity to examine an example of how the innovation trigger statements can be configured. We will evolve our trigger statement and see how the candidate solutions are affected.

The deficiency of not heating the cabin fast enough is vague. However, one can ask, Are there ways to improve the warming potential of the vehicle? This question activates our interpretive-intelligence genre to answer with candidate opportunities to make heating better and faster in hopes that our odds of getting a better survey score will follow. At the time of this survey, the internal combustion engine was commonplace. The engine's components and liquid coolant gain heat from the burning of the fuel. The hot liquid coolant is used to warm air that is blown into the vehicle's cabin to provide the heating performance in question. The innovation trigger statement could be that the engine's coolant temperature achievement is too slow. The causal design factors are the net heat rejection into the engine's coolant and the heat capacitance of the engine. If more net energy is added to the coolant, the temperature will increase faster. If the heat capacitance of the engine is reduced (i.e., design an engine that uses less coolant and metal), the same added energy, for example, will increase the temperature of the coolant more. This effect is similar to adding a full shot glass of near-boiling water into a depleted cup of tea versus adding the same shot to full cool bathtub. The bathtub might not even register a measurable temperature increase while the tea's temperature would be significantly increased.

The innovation trigger statement could be broader in that the HVAC (heating, ventilation, and air-conditioning) system does not provide heat fast enough to the cabin. The causal design factor is the temperature of the dash's outlet airflow. This system's airflow conventionally comes in contact with a heat exchanger that receives hot coolant from the engine. Thus, solutions that achieve hotter coolant earlier are viable. It should not be surprising that the somewhat narrow trigger regarding engine coolant warming is a subset of the opportunities that a broader trigger interpretation affords. The new trigger suggests that the heat exchanger's efficiency could be improved, somehow, to enhance the airflow's ability to gain more temperature from the coolant.

Additionally, one could use an electrical heater to increase the temperature of the airflow. Further, in heating conditions, the cold outside air is typically warmed up and delivered to the dash outlets, which may require a lot of energy. If one could use heated air from inside of the cabin, for example, the "warming" energy spent would provide elevated dash outlet temperatures faster than using cold outside air as the source. It is clear that this broader problem statement enables consideration of more options than simply finding ways to make the engine's coolant temperature hotter sooner. Unfortunately, this trigger statement is still substantially limiting.

The innovation trigger statement could be revised as follows: The passengers in the vehicle during heating conditions are not comfortable fast enough. Now the fundamental heat-transfer mechanisms applied to a person are available for our resource interpretation: Conductive heat transfer moves energy through physical contact. For example, a seat or steering-wheel heater can be used to warm the person directly. Convective heat transfer depends on fluid movement. In this case, the airflow from HVAC system utilizes this mechanism. Heat transfer by radiation, such as a heat lamp or a nearby hot surface, can also warm a passenger. Opportunities to transfer heat to the passenger with each mechanism can be considered with this trigger statement while the more limiting statements that preceded this, in effect, steer the thinking away from many of these possibilities to address the need. This expanded trigger statement has led to no less than five patents from this author alone.

Ideally, in order to expand the interpretation framework, one is often required to restate the trigger with the clearest and broadest "shortfall" comment. This restatement should avoid the language of existing paradigms that imply a small domain of possible solutions. When the statement is truly broad, the causes of the result will be dominated by fundamental truths (i.e., basic physics) that are pertinent to the trigger's deficiency. As was shown earlier, stopping short of that broad statement will tend to hide possible responses from consideration.

Let us explore a less technical example from an office environment. A survey question asked, Which business forms do you find most annoying and useless? The responses indicated that there is discontent with a particular form. The trigger statement may follow from the question itself, but it is a bit weak. Unfortunately, we lack clarity as to the causes that drive this discontent. We are tempted to make a trigger statement that would say, "Make this form less annoying and more useful." This could be a mistake since the question itself set the parameters of the deviation. To exaggerate, if the question were, Which forms do you find most annoying and useless on yellow paper? This form, on white paper, would not even be identified as a concern. Further, since the question is a relative comparison to other "annoying and useless forms," it could be that this form isn't even a problem, just the weakest among the group of forms that the company uses. It is possible that there is a better description of what is causing the discontent. A general trigger statement could be, "This form is underperforming for those surveyed."

We need to investigate which causes drive this resulting discontent. This spawns many other questions: Is the form difficult to read (font type, letter size, color, etc.)? Is the space provided insufficient to fill in the requested content? Is the request worded poorly or offensively? Is the information updating largely unnecessary? Is the frequency of the request inappropriate? Is it unclear that anyone benefits from this form? Does it take too long to complete? Is it difficult to get the content requested? Does the content change frequently, such that the form is obsolete almost immediately? Is the content reported elsewhere? Does the form lack a request for critical information? Does the form generate hostility among various parts of the company? Does the form require a lot of unnecessary information? And so, it goes. The discovery of the actual causal factor(s) of the discontent is very important to grasp what underperforming means. If the trigger statement focuses on "useless" and assumes that the "annoying" point follows from being useless, the true cause might be missed (i.e., the font selection is "childish" and is simply annoying). If the true deviation's causes are not addressed by the solution candidate, failure to improve will result.

Unchallenged questions create an opportunity to be controlled or tricked. A question, as given, confines the thinking to how a response will be structured. The pertinent reasons behind the triggering question need to be grasped beyond face value in order to make a proficient intelligent response. If the question is so poor, the premise of the question may not even be grounded in reality. In such a case, an intelligent response requires a question revision. For example, leading questions tend to carry assumptions that may be completely erroneous: "When did you stop beating your pet?" One could correctly say, "Never," having never started and therefore could not stop. The "never" may suggest an implication that pet beating is still ongoing since the question set up the premise that beating is ongoing. The revised question can be addressed in a response stating, "My pet has never been beaten." The environment of the question must be cultivated for proficient intelligence to be expressed in response to it. This skill to develop appropriate questions and trigger statements is nearly as important as the level of ability one has to formulate responses. After all, going in the wrong direction will never reach a desired destination. Yet any movement in the right direction, regardless of proficiency, is a sign of progress.

Interpretation frameworks that are questioned and refined without making unnecessary constraints are vital to unleashing proficient intelligent responses and are considered to be healthy. The clarity of purpose and an excellent interpretation framework can enable successful responses. In fact, it is essential to secure that clarity, or the likelihood of a poor response is high. From our daily lives, what things are being done out of routine? To what end are we doing those things? Is there good evidence that what we are doing is effective? Are there other options to consider in doing those things? Is it necessary to do them at all? Where do we see limiting thinking in our lives? Do we impose limiting thinking on others? How can we cultivate open-mindedness in our approaches to challenges? Do we have an overriding biased poison or defiant-poison mindset (selfish, helpful, generous, unfulfilled, satisfied, wounded, entitled, or unworthy)? Why? Does it help or hurt?

SUMMARY

Our goals, challenges, and objectives can be crafted in statements and questions. How this is done will influence our choices or opportunities for effective action. Effort to expand those statements to avoid paradigms and assumed approaches simply broadens the opportunities to contend with challenges. Refinement and clarity of a broad purpose in our statements of goals and objectives can lead to high proficiency. In this way, our interpretive-intelligence genre is enabled to nominate more resources or opportunities that can potentially meet challenges in novel ways.

Proficiency in accomplishment of an absolute goal or relative goal follows from the suitability of available resources. In the case of the monkey-banana experiment, the least proficient participant (short monkey) showed the most innovation. The small monkey used interpretive intelligence to recognize the boxes as a climbing resource. Active intelligence was applied to stack the boxes and climb on them to reach the banana. Meanwhile, the highly proficient tall monkey could conventionally reach the banana without complication. It is quite possible that those with the least suited resources to accomplish a goal apply the most intelligence functions to expand their resources to accomplish it out of necessity.

Challenges and goals can be misinterpreted and be a source of a weakness in making an intelligent response. One risk area comes from relative goals that have origins in a zero-sum game or inappropriately from a nonzero-sum game. An example of valid zero-sum game is winning a war. An invalid relative goal example comes from having to make more money than someone else, to win. This is an artificial competition and is not a zero-sum game. The effort spent tracking and comparing would be better spent earning money, serving an absolute goal of building wealth. Another risk area involves competitive situations. When a competitive situation is in the first stage of relevance, real differences decide the winners and losers. This enables meaningful intelligent actions. The causal relationships can be managed as an act of intelligence to gain an advantage and win. However, the second stage of relevant competition has a level of performance maturity where the contenders are essentially equivalent. Winners and losers are decided by chance. This means that there is no pertinent information to apply to the challenge that can make a difference and change the outcome (no intelligent action is possible). Challenges of this type are essentially only useful for entertainment purposes and can waste resources pretending to be doing something meaningful.

We have explored how the interpretive-intelligence genre and the challenge at the latter part of our intelligence definition interact. The pertinence of the information or response resources that are gleaned from the passive-intelligence genre and the active-intelligence genre depend on proper or clever insight from the interpretive-intelligence genre that connects it to the challenge. The next chapter will focus on the interpretive-intelligence genre in the area of challenge interpretation, given its importance at the beginning of intelligent actions.

CHAPTER 6

INTERPRETING CHALLENGES AND GROWING INTELLIGENCE

Highly proficient intelligent actions come from the high-functioning intelligence genres. The aim of this chapter is to strengthen the interpretive-intelligence genre's contribution in regard to challenge assessment. This is a top priority, since a misunderstood challenge will lead to mistakes that undermine a proficient response. As we have noted, embedded interpretation frameworks create high-recognition proficiency. Because of that embedding, perception sensitivity is enhanced and a response is readily triggered. In a similar manner, baseball players stand ready to react to familiar ball-motion behavior triggers. Those triggers compel them to prepare for the ball as it is headed toward them. They don't put the process into words, but express themselves through movement. They are operating with an embedded recognition-response dynamic. The repetition and familiarity of triggering images (or perhaps questions) can embed an interpretation framework. In addition, responses can be trained to become habitual, which is commonplace for anyone that studies or practices. The functions of intelligence, as we have defined them, offer an opportunity to cultivate and embed their practices and thereby generate new proficiency potential. This supports an ambitious hypothesis that intelligence can be taught to machines and to people.

To that end, we will exercise the interpretive-intelligence genre in this chapter. We will examine many challenges and examples of intelligent actions that can contend with them. The challenges themselves and the ultimate responses are not really of literal concern. These are repetitive examples with the aim of making the process of adjusting the interpretation of challenges familiar and comfortable. It will no longer be the default action to simply accept a challenge interpretation as it is given or presented. This exercise is much like weight lifting not being directly important to being proficient in a sport, but indirectly, it facilitates improved performance. Competency in challenge interpretation is important for us and for any artificially intelligent device we create. Obviously, a person doesn't tend to make an intelligent response, if they answer the wrong question, and neither would a machine. In many respects, this exercise is aimed at increasing the suitability of questions or challenge statements.

Let us revisit our definition of intelligence: *Intelligence is an action to interpret a challenge and to apply pertinent resources that are either inherited from past experience, actively manipulated or created through investigation to contend with that challenge.* It starts with a challenge, and then that challenge is interpreted. When a single-response option is the result of the intelligent action, it is often evidence of impeded interpretation proficiency. For this task, as the interpretive-intelligence genre's proficiency is grown, the diversity of possible effective responses is expanded. To support a more complete intelligent action, information that is commonly known is considered, including available resources. In these data, the challenge may be able to be addressed with a known solution directly. This is much like answering a question on a test. Beyond that, it may be that information and resources can be manipulated or rearranged to make additional useful response candidates. On a fundamental level, investigation of relevant causes and effects can identify a means to contend with the challenge that is largely independent of prior experiences, particularly if the challenge is completely new. Even if the challenge is not completely new, potential improvements and breakthroughs might be uncovered by entertaining the active-intelligence genre processes (even when some might consider it unnecessary).

Frequently, our first interpretation of a challenge is a bit limiting. So at least a second attempt to interpret should be made that dispenses with as much bias or limiting thinking as we can. In reality, some interpretations require even more iterations to open them up. A common error occurs when the challenge statement of a problem mistakenly resembles a hypothesis. It often takes special effort to strip the challenge statement of any supposition of a solution or implied response. One aim of the following exercises is to raise awareness of what that looks like. A pure statement of a challenge opens the field of thought to all conceivable methods of resolution. This enables the interpretive-intelligence genre to "roam free" to nominate a multitude of resource alternatives for the response. In practice, recognition of a single response candidate can be a trigger to revisit the challenge interpretation.

In order to help us visualize the intelligence actions, a table has been created to organize the information and provide a reference between two interpretation iterations. Typically, our first iteration content is a subset of subsequent iterations. For the sake of brevity let's use "[□] +" to refer to using the contents of the first iteration in the second iteration. The final response selection is not important for this exercise and will be left as "To be determined." The table is shown below:

Challenge Observation:		
Intelligence Element	First Iteration:	Second Iteration:
Interpretation:		
Known Information:		[□] +
Resources:		[□] +
Causal Relationships:		[□] +
Resource Manipulation:		[□] +
Investigation to Expand Resources:		[□] +
Candidates/Opportunities:		[□] +
Response:	To be determined	

Consider the following as exercises for the interpretive-intelligence genre:

Challenge Observation:	My hair is a mess.	
Intelligence Element	First Iteration:	Second Iteration:
Interpretation:	My hair needs to be cut.	I want my hair to look good.
Known Information:		[□] +
Resources:		[□] +
Causal Relationships:		[□] +
Resource Manipulation:		[□] +
Investigation to Expand Resources:		[□] +
Candidates/Opportunities:	Cut it.	[□] + Style it, color it, cover it, add features, etc.
Response:	To be determined	

Challenge Observation:	My car is unreliable.	
Intelligence Element	First Iteration:	Second Iteration:
Interpretation:	I need a new car.	I need to improve my transportation situation.
Known Information:		[□] +
Resources:		[□] +
Causal Relationships:		[□] +
Resource Manipulation:		[□] +
Investigation to Expand Resources:		[□] +
Candidates/Opportunities:	Buy a new car.	[□] + Update/repair my car, buy a good used car or motorcycle, ride the bus or train, get rides from friends, move to a more convenient location.
Response:	To be determined	

Challenge Observation:	This sandwich isn't good.	
Intelligence Element	First Iteration:	Second Iteration:
Interpretation:	Return the sandwich.	Have a good meal.
Known Information:		[□] +
Resources:		[□] +
Causal Relationships:		[□] +
Resource Manipulation:		[□] +
Investigation to Expand Resources:		[□] +
Candidates/Opportunities:	Reject the sandwich, money back or replacement.	[□] + Remove unwanted items from the sandwich, add items to the sandwich, select a different menu option.
Response:	To be determined	

Challenge Observation:	It is too dark in here.	
Intelligence Element	First Iteration:	Second Iteration:
Interpretation:	Turn on the light switch.	Bring more light into the room.
Known Information:		[□] +
Resources:		[□] +
Causal Relationships:		[□] +
Resource Manipulation:		[□] +
Investigation to Expand Resources:		[□] +
Candidates/Opportunities:	Flip the switch.	[□] + Activate other lamps, light candles, open the blinds, etc.
Response:	To be determined	

Challenge Observation:	I can't find the hotel.	
Intelligence Element	First Iteration:	Second Iteration:
Interpretation:	Get directions to the hotel.	I need a place to stay.
Known Information:		[□] +
Resources:		[□] +
Causal Relationships:		[□] +
Resource Manipulation:		[□] +
Investigation to Expand Resources:		[□] +
Candidates/Opportunities:	Look up location of the hotel.	[□] + Stay in that or a different hotel, stay with friends, stay in a campsite, skip the trip and go home, etc.
Response:	To be determined	

Challenge Observation:	We lost the game.	
Intelligence Element	First Iteration:	Second Iteration:
Interpretation:	We must fix what we did wrong.	Our proficiency should improve (more good and less bad).
Known Information:		[□] +
Resources:		[□] +
Causal Relationships:		[□] +
Resource Manipulation:		[□] +
Investigation to Expand Resources:		[□] +
Candidates/Opportunities:	Eliminate penalties with disciplined practice.	[□] + Improve play calling, improve reaction time and recognition of opportunities, improve conditioning and endurance, etc.
Response:	To be determined	

Challenge Observation:	My drive to work is too long.	
Intelligence Element	First Iteration:	Second Iteration:
Interpretation:	I need to move closer to work.	I want to spend less time commuting.
Known Information:		[□] +
Resources:		[□] +
Causal Relationships:		[□] +
Resource Manipulation:		[□] +
Investigation to Expand Resources:		[□] +
Candidates/Opportunities:	Find a location to live near work.	[□] + Remote work, move to a location that takes less travel time (traffic direction and speed sensitivity), change working hours to avoid traffic jams, shift working days, change to a job that is closer to home.
Response:	To be determined	

Challenge Observation:	The food prices are too high.	
Intelligence Element	First Iteration:	Second Iteration:
Interpretation:	Avoid paying high prices.	Reduce percentage of income spent on food.
Known Information:		[□] +
Resources:		[□] +
Causal Relationships:		[□] +
Resource Manipulation:		[□] +
Investigation to Expand Resources:		[□] +
Candidates/Opportunities:	Shop at a discount store, use coupons and purchase sale items, reduce restaurant visits.	[□] + Alter the diet to exclude expensive choices, cut out unhealthy items, eat less… gain additional income.
Response:	To be determined	

Challenge Observation:	Our house is filthy.	
Intelligence Element	First Iteration:	Second Iteration:
Interpretation:	Clean the house.	Keep the house clean.
Known Information:		[□] +
Resources:		[□] +
Causal Relationships:		[□] +
Resource Manipulation:		[□] +
Investigation to Expand Resources:		[□] +
Candidates/Opportunities:	Purchase cleaning supplies, tidy up the various rooms, discard unwanted items today.	[□] + Adjust or eliminate habits that clutter and soil the house as an ongoing practice.
Response:	To be determined	

Challenge Observation:	My computer is slow.	
Intelligence Element	First Iteration:	Second Iteration:
Interpretation:	I need a new computer.	Improve the performance of my computing resources.
Known Information:		[□] +
Resources:		[□] +
Causal Relationships:		[□] +
Resource Manipulation:		[□] +
Investigation to Expand Resources:		[□] +
Candidates/Opportunities:	Purchase a new computer.	[□] + Clean wasted memory resources, reduce unneeded software activity, optimize hardware use, add more memory to my computer, etc.
Response:	To be determined	

Challenge Observation:	My job is annoying.	
Intelligence Element	First Iteration:	Second Iteration:
Interpretation:	Change jobs.	Improve working conditions.
Known Information:		[□] +
Resources:		[□] +
Causal Relationships:		[□] +
Resource Manipulation:		[□] +
Investigation to Expand Resources:		[□] +
Candidates/Opportunities:	Find a more fulfilling job.	[□] + Add elements to the job that make it more fulfilling, take on a different assignment, move desk location, wear headphones, socialize during breaks, correct the annoying aspects of the job, etc.
Response:	To be determined	

Challenge Observation:	Teenagers are hard to deal with.	
Intelligence Element	First Iteration:	Second Iteration:
Interpretation:	Things will get better once the child gets older.	Communication gaps and conflicting interests need to be addressed.
Known Information:		[□] +
Resources:		[□] +
Causal Relationships:		[□] +
Resource Manipulation:		[□] +
Investigation to Expand Resources:		[□] +
Candidates/Opportunities:	Wait it out.	[□] + Support the needs of the child, share responsibility, cultivate common interests, etc.
Response:	To be determined	

Challenge Observation:	I want a raise.	
Intelligence Element	First Iteration:	Second Iteration:
Interpretation:	Get more money.	Become more appreciated in my career.
Known Information:		[□] +
Resources:		[□] +
Causal Relationships:		[□] +
Resource Manipulation:		[□] +
Investigation to Expand Resources:		[□] +
Candidates/Opportunities:	Ask for raise, change to a job that pays more, add a second job.	[□] + Highlight contributions, improve visibility, take on challenging tasks, go out of your way to be helpful, self-sacrifice, etc.
Response:	To be determined	

Challenge Observation:	My friend doesn't understand me.	
Intelligence Element	First Iteration:	Second Iteration:
Interpretation:	I want a new friend.	I want to be understood.
Known Information:		[□] +
Resources:		[□] +
Causal Relationships:		[□] +
Resource Manipulation:		[□] +
Investigation to Expand Resources:		[□] +
Candidates/Opportunities:	Expand social circles and attendance at events to build new relationships.	[□] + Share feelings and motivation drivers with your friend, try to understand the friend, improve communication with the friend.
Response:	To be determined	

Challenge Observation:	We are not at the grandparent's house.	
Intelligence Element	First Iteration:	Second Iteration:
Interpretation:	Drive essentially nonstop to the destination to minimize time.	Create a memorable experience en route to the grandparent's house.
Known Information:		[□] +
Resources:		[□] +
Causal Relationships:		[□] +
Resource Manipulation:		[□] +
Investigation to Expand Resources:		[□] +
Candidates/Opportunities:	Leave in our vehicle at 6 a.m. and use the shortest path.	[□] + Plan and visit special areas and restaurants along the way, make it a camping trip, fly to the destination, take a train, ride a bus, bring friends.
Response:	To be determined	

Let's consider our familiar example of the banana-monkey experiment. From the point of view of the monkey, the challenge is to satisfy a triggered desire to get a banana snack. We will populate the table to demonstrate the process of dealing with this challenge. This table is by no means comprehensive, but again, the key point to observe is that the second iteration of the challenge's interpretation created many more candidate opportunities to contend with it.

THE BANANA-MONKEY CHALLENGE

Challenge Observation:	There is a desirable banana hanging from the ceiling by a rope.	
Intelligence Element	First Iteration:	Second Iteration:
Interpretation:	Grab that banana.	Obtain a banana.
Known Information:	A banana is suspended by a rope.	[□] + I am being watched in this experiment.

Resources:	My jumping ability, my reach, my climbing ability, boxes, rocks, sticks, teeth.	[□] + My ability to shake things, my throwing ability, my ability to bat at things, my ability to damage ropes, my ability to look for other bananas. The experiment's observer.
Causal Relationships:	Bring my hand to this banana.	[□] + Bring a banana to my hand.
Resource Manipulation:	Use boxes to elevate my hand.	[□] + Use the boxes to support hitting the banana with sticks or rocks or to help in chewing through or untying the rope.
Investigation to Expand Resources:	Get help from someone to lift me up. Find things to climb on other than just the boxes. Jump from a higher location down to the banana.	[□] + Look for other bananas, see if the rope can be untied or lowered, see if someone can dislodge the banana for me, manipulate the experiment's observer by throwing a tantrum to get it for me.
Candidates/Opportunities:	Simply reach the banana, jump to get the banana, climb the box to grab the banana, jump off a box to get the banana.	[□] + Hitting the banana with available objects, chewing through or untying the rope, get a different banana, stop the "cruel" experiment and be rewarded.
Response:	To be determined	

I would guess that a clever monkey who threw a tantrum would have fooled the observer into scrapping the experiment, when, in fact, the observer would have been outsmarted. Also, if other bananas were easily available, why not just get them instead? The interpretation framework went from a specific banana with a specific way to get it loose to any banana along with multiple means to get possession of that specific banana. Perhaps you can imagine even more candidate actions. If so, your interpretive-intelligence genre is telling you that the exercise stopped interpreting the situation too soon.

Let us continue with a simple deviation from a desired condition that becomes a challenge statement. The correction of that deviation is very tempting to accept as the goal. However, this has limitations and interpreting the challenge more broadly will expand the candidate actions. We will call this example the Laundry Challenge.

THE LAUNDRY CHALLENGE

Challenge Observation:	There is a stain on my shirt.	
Intelligence Element	First Iteration:	Second Iteration:
Interpretation:	Clean the stain from my shirt.	Wear a shirt without visible stains.
Known Information:	The fabric and substance causing the stain, candidate cleaning materials, the location of the stain.	[□] + Location of available shirts owned and for sale.
Resources:	Sink, water, chemicals, washing machine.	[□] + Stores and current wardrobe that contain suitable replacement shirts.
Causal Relationships:	Detergents and stain removers can be successful in cleaning. Rinsing with water often works.	[□] + Discard shirts with stains and replace them. Discard or hide the stained fabric.
Resource Manipulation:	Soaking and treating the stained area with more than normal general cleaning attention.	[□] + Remove the piece of stained fabric, patch the shirt, cover the stain with new fabric, use other garments to conceal the view of the stain.
Investigation to Expand Resources:	Professional cleaner; specialized chemicals for removal for this stain-fabric combination.	[□] + Find a replacement shirt, color the shirt to compensate for the discoloration of the stain.
Candidates/Opportunities:	Give the shirt to a professional cleaner, clean the stain myself.	[□] + Get a different shirt, hide the stain (i.e., tuck in pants) and wear it.
Response:	To be determined	

Another iteration of the challenge interpretation could be "being presentable at a party." The stain on the shirt is not consistent with that objective. This opens up at least one other option to forego the party to avoid the embarrassing stain being seen. In this way, the interpretation of the challenge in the proper context (interpretation framework) is essential. Again, in these exercises, we are not exploring the decision-making process to choose a candidate response; rather, we are emphasizing the increased awareness of other options and requirements beyond the given statement.

Let's take on another challenge. It is put to us as follows: "Our problem is that we need a better cook at our restaurant." In this example, one can attack the challenge statement with a few questions. Why do you require a new cook? Answer: People aren't buying our food. Therefore, they must not like it. Are the customers complaining about the food itself? Answer: Indirectly, they aren't coming in like they used to. We now have a better context of the challenge statement.

Let's insert this issue into the table:

THE RESTAURANT CHALLENGE

Challenge Observation:	Our restaurant is not busy.	
Intelligence Element	First Iteration:	Second Iteration:
Interpretation:	We need to replace our cook with a better one.	We want more customers to buy our food.
Known Information:	The cook doesn't seem motivated. Some of his dishes aren't as good as they used to be.	[□] + Our customer traffic is down. Our fresh-food inventory is suffering since we have stock expiring (not fresh) that must be discarded. There is road construction that impedes access to our restaurant.
Resources:	Talent pool outside of our store and the internal talent pool that could assume the cook's job.	[□] + Management of food quality, how it is prepared and handled. Parking-lot access and seating space. Price and incentive management.

Causal Relationships:	The cook's talent, recipes, and available food.	[□] + When customers have to struggle to get to our parking lot, they may make other choices. Price reductions and specials tend to make for more business. Food freshness impacts the quality of the meals.
Resource Manipulation:	Change the recipes and menu offerings to optimize what the cook makes well. Send the cook to training classes to grow skill.	[□] + Find ways to reduce the struggle to come to the restaurant. Offer specials to see if it changes the traffic. Confirm the impact of food freshness on key dishes.
Investigation to Expand Resources:	Try and compare similar dishes at a competitor's restaurant. Add a new cook to the staff on a trial basis.	[□] + Consider catering and delivery options to bring food to the customers.
Candidates/Opportunities:	Fire the cook and hire a new one.	[□] + Add side-road access to the restaurant, offer specials on the cook's best dish, use fresher food, begin food-delivery service to the customer.
Response:	To be determined	

The alternative expanded interpretation is closer to the true goal and purpose of the restaurant. The first iteration is loosely connected to the goal with essentially one idea to help realize it (via an imposed solution). It could be a misdiagnosis of the circumstance. The second iteration does not discard that possibility as a factor but allows for additional considerations to be made. The challenge evolves into realizing that the restaurant's business isn't sufficiently moving its inventory. With a more appropriate challenge interpretation, the pertinence of the entire scope of what can affect sales is assessed, not just the cook's skill.

Consider a challenge to win a championship. Similar to the example above, the first iteration assumes correcting a given causal factor's shortcoming is the only means to meet the challenge. Should that assumption be incorrect, it can result in actions that are not pertinent to the challenge and therefore not intelligent. In the table, it looks like this:

THE CHAMPIONSHIP CHALLENGE

Challenge Observation:	The team has not won a championship.	
Intelligence Element	First Iteration:	Second Iteration:
Interpretation:	We must have the best collection of active players.	We want to have the best chance to win in all contests.
Known Information:	Some of our players are the best and some are not.	[□] + Our team does not have a competitive edge.
Resources:	Players on other teams that are near the top at their positions can be enticed to join our team.	[□] + Knowledge of which teams are most successful. Our current approach's success-and- failure background.
Causal Relationships:	Good players make good results; great players make great results. Collectively, better talent leads to victories.	[□] + Superior preparation and conditioning can lead to success. Sound coaching decisions can lead to success (plays). Teamwork can outperform individual talent. Weak points hurt a team's chances to win.
Resource Manipulation:	Trade players with other teams to fill gaps in a talent upgrading process. Develop current players into top players.	[□] + Change coaching and play-calling approaches. Assign players to positions that allow them to excel.
Investigation to Expand Resources:	Look for pertinent talent in other sports (i.e., track stars, weight lifters, wrestlers, etc.).	[□] + Scout opponents for weakness, benchmark top competitors, enhance playbook.
Candidates/Opportunities:	Dump weak players and replace them with strong ones.	[□] + Adopt top competitor's best practices, enhance performance from lessons learned, take advantage of opponent weaknesses, develop players and teamwork.
Response:	To be determined	

The championship challenge could be accomplished in a variety of ways. Having the best players could deliver on that result—it is a factor. However, if the talent level is nearly the same compared to the top opponents, the resulting winning sensitivity to that factor might be minimal (or in the second stage of competition relevance). Basically, all teams are very talented, and it is not a clear advantage for any team. In such a case, additional factors that truly improve the chances of winning a championship are worthy of consideration, and if they are optimized, they could lead to multiple championships (first stage of competition relevance). The active-intelligence genre that confirms causes and effects can help decide the most prudent response or combination of responses.

Now let's consider the Babysitter Challenge. The first interpretation is restrictive and somewhat literal with a focus on safety. The babysitter that simply functions as a prison guard could operate under the first iteration. In this case, an expanded interpretation of the challenge serves more fully the objectives of the parents. Recognition of high performance often follows when this occurs. In this way, high performers leverage their interpretive-intelligence genre to exceed expectations by seeing more and delivering more than simply what is asked:

THE BABYSITTER CHALLENGE

Challenge Observation:	Children should not be left unattended for safety reasons.	
Intelligence Element	First Iteration:	Second Iteration:
Interpretation:	Avoid all risk to the children.	Promote children's well-being.
Known Information:	The number and ages of the children being watched. Guidelines from the parents for diet and bed times.	[□] + The unique interests of each of the children. The sensitivities of each to correction and coaching.
Resources:	Their home, television, computer, their toys and games.	[□] + Personal stories and experiences. Supplemental games, special toys and treats.

Causal Relationships:	Activity makes risk of harm—do nothing is safest.	[□] + Reasonable freedom and fun make for healthy children. Learning new things is empowering. Happy children are in a more healthy state vs. unhappy.
Resource Manipulation:	Minimize risk by restricting activities and new experiences. Early bedtimes.	Develop new interests for the children and provide new safe experiences. Discuss school subjects, share experiences. Reward good behavior.
Investigation to Expand Resources:	Restrict activities and force use of time-killing resources like television.	Entertain the children's activity suggestions. Identify new clever challenges together.
Candidates/Opportunities:	Watch TV and go to bed early.	Interactive fun experiences with the children.
Response:	To be determined	

Common sense suggests that the sitter that engages with the children will be more popular with them. This satisfaction could lead to future opportunities and employment recommendations by parents who see the experience as a win for their children. Safe, healthy, and happy is better than simply safe. Expectations are exceeded through the second iteration of the challenge interpretation.

As a student, I was hired as a grill cook for a local lodge. At the end of my first night, the manager came to the kitchen to congratulate me on a job well done, from his customer's feedback. When he entered the kitchen, he paused and looked a bit shocked. Then he exclaimed that he had never seen the kitchen so clean before. His interpretation of a grill cook was someone that prepared the food properly (to the requested level of doneness) in a timely manner. My interpretation went beyond that requirement to having a very sanitary and clean environment to prepare the food to help secure good results. The interpretive-intelligence genre that draws out candidate actions beyond the original goal statement may surprise the person providing the challenge because of their limited interpretation of it. This is a delightful circumstance that is mutually rewarding for the stakeholder of the challenge and the one that contends with it.

Contending with thought poisons is a compounding challenge that can lead to narrow interpretations. The first iteration favors succumbing to the poison or defying that poison, and the second iteration is aimed at dealing with the challenge of improvement. In these cases, the candidate solutions do not tend to intersect because the challenge from the poison is not actually part of the targeted challenge. This is a manner in which thought poisons generate off-topic and inferior responses:

Challenge Observation:	Everyone hates me.	
Intelligence Element	First Iteration:	Second Iteration:
Interpretation:	I am flawed and hopeless.	My behavior needs to improve in the eyes of others.
Known Information:		[□] +
Resources:		[□] +
Causal Relationships:		[□] +
Resource Manipulation:		[□] +
Investigation to Expand Resources:		[□] +
Candidates/Opportunities:	Live in misery.	Become less selfish, become more generous, listen, forgive, be patient with others, etc.
Response:	To be determined	

Challenge Observation:	I am too short.	
Intelligence Element	First Iteration:	Second Iteration:
Interpretation:	I am not appealing because of my size. I need to compensate.	How can I leverage being short to be beneficial in various circumstances?
Known Information:		[□] +
Resources:		[□] +
Causal Relationships:		[□] +
Resource Manipulation:		[□] +
Investigation to Expand Resources:		[□] +

Candidates/Opportunities:	Focus on showing up tall people to compensate for my size in business and socially.	Embrace my uniqueness and my strengths to maximize my contribution to society.
Response:	To be determined	

Challenge Observation:	I am not good at mathematics.	
Intelligence Element	First Iteration:	Second Iteration:
Interpretation:	I cannot excel at mathematics.	Improve my math skills through effort and assistance.
Known Information:		[□] +
Resources:		[□] +
Causal Relationships:		[□] +
Resource Manipulation:		[□] +
Investigation to Expand Resources:		[□] +
Candidates/Opportunities:	Avoid situations (jobs, etc.) that require math skill demonstration.	Study and use tutors to overcome my weakness in this area.
Response:	To be determined	

I will leave the next two templates for personal use:

Challenge Observation:		
Intelligence Element	First Iteration:	Second Iteration:
Interpretation:		
Known Information:		[□] +
Resources:		[□] +
Causal Relationships:		[□] +
Resource Manipulation:		[□] +
Investigation to Expand Resources:		[□] +
Candidates/Opportunities:		[□] +
Response:	To be determined	

Challenge Observation:		
Intelligence Element	First Iteration:	Second Iteration:
Interpretation:		
Known Information:		[□] +
Resources:		[□] +
Causal Relationships:		[□] +
Resource Manipulation:		[□] +
Investigation to Expand Resources:		[□] +
Candidates/Opportunities:		[□] +
Response:	To be determined	

As we have shown in these exercises, the interpretation of the challenge may range from being narrow and limiting to so broad that possible candidate responses seem almost endless.

When an interpretation is provided to a person or a machine, it lies somewhere in this continuum. In effect, the recipient of the interpretation is placed in the middle of interpretive-intelligence genre function and can elect to take that interpretation at face value (like in school) or explore for another interpretation that leads to other possible candidate responses and its related pertinent information. In some cultures and interpersonal relationships that depend on high context, a general meaning or request is understood from a literal and specific comment. In such cases, the comment triggers actions that address an unstated challenge. If your mother says "floor" to you, what does that mean? Do you grasp the context of the situation? Would you demand the use of a complete sentence for clarification? If you are at a loss to know what she means, you lack her context. You do not share her interpretation framework in which the word "floor" is the only evidence that it is in use. On the other hand, if you are aware of her interest in ways (an interpretation framework) to maintain a clean and healthy home (challenge), you might realize that your muddy shoes are pertinent information that endangers the desired condition of the floor. In this situation, the word "floor" may be enough for you to jump back outside and to remove your shoes. In this example, you are literally a walking risk of being pertinent to another person's specific challenge. This is true for variety of challenges that others have and are interpreting you and your actions to assess pertinence. For instance, when a person interviews for a job, the employer has a business challenge and is measuring the candidate with an interpretation framework to see how the person and their skills might be pertinent.

For us and for an artificially intelligent device, an awareness of all goals that are in play in any situation is important to enable proficiency. This means that the goals that we or the device happen to have as an individual are not exhaustive. Rather, they need to be fit into the context of other considerations and objectives. An inability to grasp this wider view is a shortfall of primitive artificial intelligent devices and for selfish humans. An artificially intelligence device that only acts toward achieving its assigned goal may needlessly harm progress on other challenges that are pursued by others. For example, a child that serves himself an entire pie after dinner, leaving none for the guests, accomplished his goal with complete disregard for the needs of others. Similarly, as an example, environmental-protection considerations and meeting immediate human needs are coexisting challenges. It is not a proficient solution to eliminate humans to protect the environment nor is it proficient to destroy the environment and endanger all life.

When coexisting challenges are not intelligently managed, the neglected challenge may ultimately drive the situation to a boundary or a limit as a consequence. Consider a high-school biology experiment that has yeast living in sealed test tubes with varied concentrations of molasses in each. With the lower concentrations, the sugary food source is consumed, and the yeast after some time essentially starves. The higher concentrations favor explosive population growth of the yeast. Ultimately, these samples become untenable for the yeast because of their waste accumulation. As with any living thing, waste is generated and can toxically fill the environment (such as CO_2 in this case, a byproduct of either aerobic or anaerobic respiration depending on the availability of oxygen). The most enduring successful concentrations had enough food to slowly grow the population and, thus, slow the accumulation of waste. Naturally, this slow process without intervention is not a solution for sustainability. Demise is certain, given the confined space and limited food supply. If we wanted to sustain the yeast to avoid the limits of starvation or self-poisoning, we need to regulate the waste accumulation and renew the food source. These are two coexisting challenges that are quite serious, one being keeping a nontoxic environment and the other providing food for the yeast. Cleansing the waste contents of the test tube and keeping oxygen levels sufficient to avoid the very toxic alcohol byproduct of anaerobic respiration are good places to start. Further, replenishing the sugar content is required. If our actions serve only one goal, the consequence of the other's neglect can lead to overall failure.

As humans on the earth, our food supply is being grown and renewed. We don't simply have a silo with grain that once used will lead to certain starvation. Our waste accumulation is our environmental boundary that endangers our goal of sustainability. For example, if our critical waste is the creation of CO_2, we need mechanisms to chemically change it or remove it from our environment. If vegetation can process CO_2 as a portion of their food, it can provide a mechanism of removal. If this is the case, we must avoid plant starvation due to a lack of CO_2 and avoid vegetation destruction that would forfeit this mechanism. In other words, we need to regulate and manage our waste to sustain an acceptable equilibrium. As with the yeast in a test tube, simply slowing the rate of net CO_2 generation does not lead to our sustainability. By analogy, suppose someone brings ten water bottles into their home every day, and they don't remove them. With enough time there is no room for any more water bottles, or them. If it takes a year or a decade to push them out of their house, it does not really matter. The key point is that this situation is not sustainable. There is a limit to how many bottles a house can hold. Thus, the important goal of staying hydrated caused an unintended consequence of not having a comfortable place to live—an undesirable limit of a coexisting neglected goal. In another example, if an organization accomplishes its mission by curing a disease, a personal goal to be the director of that obsolete organization might not happen. Also, if there is a need to correct an employee's behavior, a coexisting challenge for them to remain motivated and respected will need to be part of the response selection. This concept of coexisting challenges adds to the complexity to the next steps in making Allies more than just one that functions as a primitive artificially intelligent device that meets her challenge with disregard for others.

In this way, the sensational threat of primitive artificial intelligence to all of humankind is derived from its neglect coexisting challenges. An interpretation framework of an offending AI device would not completely comprehend the needs of the human race and naturally neglect those needs. Perhaps this is speculation, but it is not unfamiliar. In the past, we have seen dictators endanger all of us via wars and conflicts as a demonstration of serving their self-interests. This is a concern regardless of its origin (human or not). It is the comprehensiveness of interpretation proficiency behind intelligent actions that may in fact control our destiny.

This book identifies the inevitable intrusion of artificial intelligence into to various aspects of our lives as a challenge observation. The welcome intrusions support filling gaps in our understanding and compensating for lapses in our judgment or skill execution. Other intrusions are faulty, and humans must come to the rescue of poor-performing artificial intelligence devices in order to correct them. This fosters a concern that, at times, the conduct of an artificially intelligence device might not actually be intelligent, just like when we do stupid or selfish things. Let's try to put this book's challenge into the table:

THE PURSING INTELLIGENCE BOOK

Challenge Observation:	Artificially intelligent devices are encroaching on human activities.	
Intelligence Element	First Iteration:	Second Iteration:
Interpretation:	People may benefit from knowing more about AI.	Intelligent actions need to be secured for AI and for humans. If intelligence can be taught to an AI device, why not teach humans too?

Known Information:	Published works from psychology, cognitive science, and the artificial intelligence community.	[□] + Knowledge gained from experience in creating software programs and control systems. Knowledge gained from experience in large companies.
Resources:	English skills, library, Internet, computer, software programs, publisher, teaching skills.	[□] + Unique interpretation and logic skills from the perspective of an inventor, computer programmer, manager, and mechanical engineer.
Causal Relationships:	Intelligence is recognized like an object with various attributes.	[□] + Key functions are essential to intelligence demonstration. Proficiency in those functions can be used to develop and secure intelligent behavior.
Resource Manipulation:	The perspectives of others can be combined to facilitate intelligence recognition. Intelligence is a noun.	[□] + Common or relatable experiences can be explored to enable growth of intelligence attributes and applied functions. Intelligence is a verb.
Investigation to Expand Resources:	Consult experts from various disciplines that demand intelligent function to potentially reveal unique attributes.	[□] + Accommodate different interpretation perspectives to facilitate a more comprehensive grasp of intelligence functions.
Candidates/Opportunities:	Write a book that summarizes intelligent behavior and offers examples of varied proficiency for the purpose of recognition.	Write a book that helps cultivate intelligence proficiency by augmenting the health of its attributes, functions, and actions.
Response:	To be determined	

At the next level of intelligent function for Allies, we want her to be able to expand on what she knows or to self-instruct, not only to create new passive-intelligence genre content through investigation but also to create new interpretive-intelligence genre content. This means that she needs to take cues from others to identify their challenges and associated interpretation frameworks and treat them as coexisting challenges along with hers.

CHAPTER 7

INQUISITIVE ARTIFICIAL INTELLIGENCE

A primitive artificially intelligent device can be programmed by teachers to contain questions and answers and to link them together. This "software" intervention by the teachers is the action of learning for this level of artificial intelligence. The device is designed to observe or receive prompts and compare them to what has been stored (preconceived templates) and then follow a connection to a response. This primitive level supports only one part of our definition of intelligence of how challenges can be addressed. Let us now shift our focus within our intelligence definition as follows: *Intelligence is an action to interpret a challenge and to apply pertinent resources that are ~~either inherited from past experience, actively manipulated or~~ created through investigation to contend with that challenge.* This shift of focus does not completely dismiss the background information that is inherited, given the need for resources to help guide and support an investigation. Rather, it is intended to expand on the past experiences instead of simply using them as the sole means to an end. The expansion of what is known comes from the answers to pertinent questions. The questions may serve an investigation or perhaps support decisions that refine a course of action. For example, a medical doctor may ask about a patient's symptoms. From those answers, logic will guide the doctor to other questions and ideally to an effective treatment recommendation. When this style of questioning observations, and probing the environment for new observations, is applied in an artificially intelligent device, it is functioning beyond the primitive intelligence level. Let us call this the Inquisitive Artificial Intelligence level. The pertinent answers to the self-initiated questions fit into an organized interpretation structure. That logic structure serves as an interpretation framework that reaches out for information. Let us call this structure an interpretation logic framework.

Earlier, we took much care to exercise the interpretive-intelligence genre to expand opportunities and candidate ideas related to sample challenges. Typically, a narrow challenge interpretation imposed a single solution that was later found it to be a subset of many candidate solutions. In these cases, the initial interpretation was a fragment of a larger and more comprehensive interpretation framework. Response proficiency improved by adopting this upgraded framework that generated a multitude of choices. In a similar manner, pieces of an interpretation logic framework can be recognized and used to enable use of the entire framework. For example, a device is asked to provide a cup of coffee. It could narrowly decide to get exactly one cup of pure coffee beans. That is not what was intended. If the machine is designed in the context of providing soft drinks, it delivers exactly one cup of liquid coffee, perhaps with ice cubes. The communication will have failed once again, and the results are inferior. However, if an interpretation logic structure that comprehends a suitable cup of coffee is built into the device, the machine would know that an exact cup by volume is not essential. Further, the framework includes the fact that some other content (i.e., milk or sugar) will help fill the cup and what a suitable serving temperature is. The device could use that logic framework to ask questions to refine the response, such as "Do you want decaffeinated or regular?" along with others to make a better response. In this state, the device interprets that the original request is somewhere in a larger interpretation logic framework; and then, rather than literally reacting, it adjusts to a higher level of intent. That adjustment is followed by many questions and requirements that need to be satisfied prior to making a final response. Understandably, any communication with the device functioning this way is vastly improved, since it is now more capable of grasping the intent from a vague request rather than simply failing to respond proficiently. Recall the example when your mother says "floor" to you and you jump back outside with your muddy shoes. This scant information was enough to help you recognize the larger context of keeping the house clean. You internally questioned and answered what the fuss was about and made a response. An inquisitive artificially intelligent device has potential to interact with us quite well, with a similar ability to grasp context. Through context recognition, it is very tolerant of our imprecise and vague communication. However, it could be quite annoying with too many questions to the point that every detail has to be explained—the requestor might as well do the task themselves. This would be evidence of the D2 development level in which high direction is required from the teacher. In order to mature beyond that tedious level, the device should use its own passive-intelligence genre to silently answer as many internal questions as possible (like a glance to your muddy shoes replaces an obvious question to your already agitated mother).

Being somewhat self-centered beings, we tend to project our interpretations and our behaviors into our expectations of others. As a result, our interpretation frameworks are what others have to deal with when they relate to us and vice versa. If I am selfish, I assume that others are also selfish. If I am a thief, I am disproportionally on guard against anything that might take away my things. When others behave in a different manner than we expect, it means that they are using a different interpretation framework than we are. The simple coffee request example above, at least initially, is a great example of incompatible interpretation frameworks.

Incompatibility of those frameworks may lead to frustration, difficulty, low proficiency, and poor relationships. For instance, while dating a friend, I learned that she collected unicorn figurines. In my business travels, I found a small unique glass unicorn in a gift shop. I thought of her and presented it to her as a gift upon my return. To my dismay, she negatively reacted, asking, "What is this for?" I simply wanted to surprise her with something she values as a means to reflect my interest in her. My interpretation of her response (at a clear risk of being incorrect) was that she assumed that I had a motive to generate indebtedness on her part, perhaps a manipulation tool used by her or against her in the past. Nevertheless, I inadvertently trespassed into the appearance of this behavior in her eyes. Our interpretations of the meaning of the gift were clearly not compatible. Stubbornly, I did not adjust my interpretation framework from this incident. (I didn't learn my lesson.) Later, I performed a comparable gesture with a souvenir sweater from a Colorado ski resort for the lady that later became my wife. She was appreciative of the consideration that I displayed. In fact, she has kept it (for decades) and teases me that her boyfriend gave it to her. We happened to share the mindset of being generous without condition of any payback or sense of indebtedness. This example is one of many that supports the notion that compatible interpretation frameworks tend to foster better relationships. This extends from one-on-one to organizational group relationships and affiliations. An artificially intelligent device needs to grasp and accommodate the perspectives and interpretation frameworks of others in order to have proficient seamless communication. Similarly, humans that can relate to another person's perspective can expedite effective sharing and mutual growth. For example, when a person communicates with a small child or an old friend, there is recognition of their interpretation frameworks, and the communication style is altered because of expectations of what is shared and familiar. Despite honest efforts incompatibility risks remain, often we reveal only fragments of our frameworks and do not provide a complete picture. This condition presents a vulnerability to offend. Probing questions from an interpretation logic framework can be helpful to ascertain the perspective of another person. This supports the "getting to know you" part of a relationship.

Cultural and other background differences establish somewhat unique interpretation frameworks in general. In addition, specific experiences and training form the interpretation frameworks of individuals. A trivial example comes from language differences. If an inquisitive artificially intelligent device hears a word in Spanish for example, the entire interpretation framework for communication shifts from English to Spanish. In common practice, we may encounter automated menu choices when calling a large organization with a concern. First, we may establish the language to be used and then the area of inquiry. Later, limited personal information is requested. From that scant identification, an entire history of communication is accessed. Ideally, a connection is made to an expert that grasps the caller's interpretation framework and can begin to address the concern. This logic framework serves as a second layer of the interpretive-intelligence genre. The first layer is use to match perceptions to preconceptions that are typically associated to a pertinent known response. However, in this case, the first layer connects the perception to a pertinent interpretation logic framework. From this example, the phone call itself (first layer) suggested a need for an interpretation logic framework, which is a second layer of interpretation that leads to a response. This second layer is the main attribute that supports the transition from primitive artificial intelligence to inquisitive artificial intelligence. From this somewhat familiar experience, it is clear that interpretation logic frameworks (in this case, a menu structure) can be taught to a machine in a similar manner as any other information in the passive-intelligence genre.

Similarly, some problem-solving methods can be incorporated into the device and recognized as pertinent from somewhat vague concern communication. A device functioning in this capacity will respond with questions rather than answers, particularly at the beginning of the process. These requests for information by the machine means it needs to learn something new, in order to proceed to a final response. Although the trigger to ask the questions came from the familiar passive-intelligence genre, the applied logic structure supports the active-intelligence genre. These logic frameworks are aimed at the recognition of factors that have influence in the situation. *(Recall: Active intelligence is the act of making a response derived from recognition of causal relationships that pertain to contending with a challenge.)* By function, the device will be learning from us via guiding questioning. At this level, a device that meets you for the first time might be given your name, but it asks you for your birth date and your interests. That information is kept for future reference when you are encountered again or to send you a birthday greeting or gift.

The consultants Kepner and Tregoe (1997) researched how the most accomplished problem solvers and decision-makers in their company managed through their issues. Kepner and Tregoe were able to divide their findings into a few key phases. These phases organize an interpretation logic framework in terms of questions, and the answers provide guidance to new questions through a logic structure. The first phase is called a Situation Appraisal, which gathers information without jumping to any conclusions. The concerns are identified and interpreted in this phase. The questions used for this phase of the task include, What deviations are occurring? What decisions need to be made? Clear answers to either of these questions guides the process to one of either of two specialized phases. Those phases are Problem Analysis and Decision Analysis.

When a deviation from an acceptable or desired condition occurs, Problem Analysis is used to find the root cause of the deviation. When a choice is to be made, Decision Analysis is used to clarify requirements and consider the merits of alternative choices. In each case, the method discloses a set of interpretation logic frameworks that is used to probe and manage the concern. Those frameworks were synthesized from key questions that were prevalent in the approaches found from a survey of high performers. The answers to those questions enable a narrowing of the task toward the resolution of each phase, those being solving a problem or making a decision.

If the concern is a problem (deviation), Problem Analysis with its questions is deployed: When did the deviation first occur? What has changed around the time the deviation appeared? How could those changes be responsible for the deviation? How is this situation different from other situations that don't present this deviation (what makes it distinct)? How could this uniqueness contribute to the deviation? How could combining the changes and distinctions create this deviation?

To get a sense of the method, an example was provided in their training material. It was called the Red Sweat Mystery and was explained in the *Wall Street Journal* (March 1980). On a major airline, the flight attendant's necks, chests, and hands are breaking out into a red sweat during the flight. Some believed that they were sweating blood. It was alarming, potentially harmful. The problem needed to be solved to protect the public and the airline. A change that happened around the time of the appearance of the first scary incident was the deployment of a new airplane. Thus far, only these new planes had that concern. But this new plane is widely used internationally and domestically without incident. Through the method, a distinction was found that primarily flight attendants on spring and summer flights between New York and Florida suffered from this malady. In addition, it was noted that these flights fly over water. Upon a closer examination, a safety demonstration for these flights included the flight attendants wearing a life preserver around their necks. This was a distinct behavior from flights that had essentially no chance of a water landing, in which the location of the life preserver was provided to the passengers without a usage demonstration. It turns out that the new airplanes were equipped with red life preservers whose dye leached out and irritated the skin when worn on a sweaty neck. This is a very short summary of the findings of the somewhat laborious task of sorting through where the deviation "IS" and where the deviation "IS-NOT." This framework for problem solving does not require subject-matter expertise of the nature of the "red sweat" or what chemicals could cause the reaction and their origin. Rather, the method depends on a baseline level that is okay and seeks what is unique or what changed that disrupted it. The restoration of the condition to the okay state is the aim. This disciplined interpretation logic framework structure or one very much like it is very appropriate to be adapted to Allies. Allies would only need to "locate" how that situation was altered to enable correction of it. The need and burden to comprehend the complexity of the baseline condition is unnecessary to achieve the desired correction with this approach.

The Decision Analysis interpretation logic framework questions include: What do we need to decide? What are we trying to do? What short-term and long-term benefits do we want? What resources should we use or save? What restrictions or constraints do we have that can influence our decision? What players or organizations are influenced by our decision? What are the must-have elements of the decision? What want elements are there in the decision? What is the relative importance of the want elements of the decision? What are the different choices available? What are the risks for each choice to be considered? From the choices, the must-have elements are essential, and any choice that cannot deliver them should be rejected. The strongest remaining performer in delivering the want elements will create the top choice. If those elements are defined well, the benefits and influences (i.e., resources, risks, and impact on others) will be included in the assessment. Decisions by nature are made at a point in time after which things change. This implies a baseline condition of a decision to do nothing. This is similar to the Problem Analysis in that the background of the baseline situation does not have to be deeply understood. For Allies, this interpretation logic framework and value assessment logic can be adopted to aid in making decisions.

For these phases, her interpretation logic framework provides the function of a guiding-question coach for improving the interpretive intelligence of the requester through collaboration. It is conceivable that Allies could examine the decision data and pick a choice that provides all of the "musts" with the highest delivery of "wants" by using rather simple logic. Similarly, she could point directly to the source of the deviation in a problem based on gathered facts via her questions. This logical process enables factor recognition and a related effective response (the active-intelligence genre) to contend with deviation from a given baseline condition. This means that Allies can be proficient in contending with changes that disrupted a baseline condition. Further, in the case of making a decision, a choice is made to disrupt the baseline condition favorably in the future.

Although her inquisitive artificial intelligence level learns from the environment through investigation, the embedded techniques are predetermined for her by her teachers. For example, if she is asked to estimate the time to complete a trip, the equation of total distance divided by the average speed will be applied. She will then query those two factors of a requestor and be able to compute the answer. The progression of pertinent questions in her interpretation logic framework leads to her response. If that response is somehow inadequate, it is up to the teacher to alter her frameworks to correct for that deviation. As an example of her growth to this new level, consider that she knows to lower a thermostat's temperature if someone complains that the room is too warm (challenge). She also knows that she could lower it too much and create a new problem of being too cold. She carries a statistical knowledge of what a comfortable temperature is (in her larger interpretation framework) and uses that to moderate her response to the complaint. If the request tends to violate those most probable comfortable settings, she will inquire if the person is okay or perhaps is overheated from physical exertion. The response to that inquiry might even lead her to calling a doctor. Further, if her experience does not comprehend a broken air conditioner, she would need to be taught how to deal with those kinds of things as a means to expand her context and ability to contend with the challenge.

Suppose Allies requests feedback or a performance evaluation after making a response as part of her interpretation logic framework (i.e., survey). This feedback could be used to trigger a third layer of interpretation. The purpose of this third layer is to validate the current second-layer interpretation logic framework or, if needed, update and improve it. The approaches to "fix" the second layer, at this point, will be taught to her much like how the second layer was originally formed by teachers. These third-layer structures will allow Allies to alter and upgrade her own second-layer interpretation to benefit from learning based on the feedback that she seeks. Humans, in general, often have great difficulty assessing the relevance of feedback, but proficiency in dealing with it is essential for constructive growth. Let us discuss the nature of the feedback in order to improve our interpretation framework prior to exploring a third layer for Allies.

THE NATURE OF FEEDBACK

The extent that a challenge is addressed (proficiency) comes from a comparison of measured performance with the ideal completed state of the challenge. This actual performance is called feedback, and the deviation of it from an ideal result (target) is called feedback error.

As part of the intelligent action that deals with a deviation challenge, a need to interpret the nature and validity of the performance measurement must be addressed. Consider that an employee receives a performance review with some criticism that identifies an improvement opportunity. In these situations, the interpretive-intelligence genre should be functioning. This means that the reviewer's opinion should not simply be accepted. An important question should be asked: Is the origin of the performance due to a fundamental cause based in the individual, or is it elsewhere? This question is part of an interpretation framework intended to help deal with deviation feedback error proficiently.

Unfortunately, some resources, tools, and processes are not capable of delivering the target performance associated with a challenge. In such a case, an individual may be erroneously "blamed" for a performance deviation. From the world of sports, some athletes that have been cut or rejected by one team are given another chance on a new team and excel. Each team may have essentially the same overall goal and similarly translate it into individual player performance targets. For example, we want to be a winning team. In addition, we want individual players to be among the top-five performers at their positions in our league. However, the team's methods (playbook) and approaches to reach those goals are imposed on the individual players. So the factors of the individual's talent, training and effort, the playbook itself, and situational play selection are intertwined in creating the team's performance. At season end, the team did not attain its goal. A simple evaluation that an individual player didn't become a top-five performer implies that the player is at fault despite the individual's exceptional effort and talent. The player is judged to be a bust, is fired, and replaced. Another team, which shares the same goals, gives this rejected player a chance. This team's clever use of a different playbook enables this player to be a star. This evidence suggests that the former team's system rather than the individual's performance created the feedback error for missing the winning objective. The first team's interpretive intelligence failed to recognize the "elsewhere" source as the fundamental cause of the player's underperformance. As a result, they lost a capable contributor in the process of ignoring their system's deficiency. Had they confirmed that no player at that position has ever been highly successful with their plays, perhaps they would not have blamed and fired that player.

Grasping the fundamental causes of a deviation requires our interpretive-intelligence genre to function. Unfortunately, the correlation of an action to a result does not guarantee causation; otherwise, it would be simple to interpret. Once we had a clothes dryer with an intermittent electrical problem that resulted in an inconsistent startup. In some cases, if one stood on one leg and pressed the power button, it would work fine. Cycling the door could also correspond to a successful power-on event. A litany of random and often silly procedures could be made that at least briefly seemed to correlate to success. However, inconsistency remained as successful actions of the past failed. Our actions were not closely related to the controlling mechanisms of the result we were seeking. Thus, the inappropriate perspective (interpretation framework) led to frivolous correction attempts. A different perspective recognizes that anything related to the power circuit is at the heart of the issue. The power switch and not how we push it is a candidate cause of our issue. Other issues with the circuit may also exist. From this appropriate perspective, only reasonable fundamental cause candidates are cited as opportunities to help us address the challenge to dry our clothes.

When someone receives performance feedback that is not rooted in the fundamental causes of the results, the related corrective actions are statistically irrelevant. It is a waste of effort to try to contend with challenges using information that is not pertinent (not intelligent, based on our definition). In my experience, when I received statistically irrelevant feedback in a performance review, I did nothing special to compensate. At the time of my next review, my vast improvement was lauded, but it was only due to the very low probability of a similar negative perception happening again. Honestly, the reviewer didn't do a good job of verifying the validity of the critical feedback the first time and actually didn't validate my alleged improvement very well either. That aspect of my review was entirely up to chance and not linked to the fundamental causes of my performance. In another case of unconfirmed and off-topic feedback, I was once told that my review's rating should be reduced since I wasn't functioning at a level above my current grade (or, in effect, doing my boss's job). The reviewers cited a specific unmet challenge in our department. I pointed out that my boss, of a good reputation, didn't meet the challenge either. Therefore, it so happened that I was actually functioning at the next level. Basically, I was able to convince my reviewers that the deviation that was cited was not meaningful. The reviewer's feedback was not intelligent since only a candidate interpretation was used without a successful test for pertinence prior to our discussion.

As we just noted, logic (a manipulation of known information) from the active-intelligence genre can be used to examine pertinence of candidate interpretations and aid in discarding inappropriate ones. In addition to logic, statistical methods can be used to screen for shortcomings of interpretive-intelligence genre that fail to connect fundamental causes to results. A statistical approach called the analysis of variance (ANOVA) enables one to determine if candidate factors influence a result for a given set of conditions. In this way, pertinence is established and thereby can be used to improve the interpretation proficiency of the circumstance. Although, this statistical technique has its own specialized complex interpretation framework, the essence of the method is relatable and useful, with a much less rigorous and detailed interpretation framework.

The concept of ANOVA can be demonstrated using a customer-opinion research experience. A survey of passenger vehicle performance was conducted. Satisfaction with various aspects such as fuel economy, audio system, and cabin capacity were queried among others. The aim was to improve the overall opinion of our products. To aid in understanding, imagine that hundreds of persons that filled out the survey could vote by entering a "happy" room or move to stand in the "unhappy" room. Minivan owners were asked about their opinion of fuel economy to divide into these two rooms. About 25 percent of them went into the "unhappy" room. This seems terrible and might inspire management to make corrective action that assumes that any dissatisfaction is unacceptable. But the goal was to favorably influence the *overall* opinion of the vehicle. The participants in each separate room were then asked to provide an overall rating of their vehicle. When the two room's results were compared, they were the same, as if their room choice didn't matter. This means that improved fuel economy (to move some individuals from the unhappy to the happy room) would not help with our overall opinion-improvement objective. For another question, the participants divided into the two rooms based on their satisfaction with the cabin capacity (ability to carry what they need). Only 10 percent went to the unhappy room. When the overall vehicle opinion from each room was gathered, the unhappy room people were very unhappy with their minivan compared to those with no concern for cabin capacity. If one could remove (or convert) these unhappy persons from the survey, the van's overall opinion would become the happy room's substantially better overall opinion. To do so, the answer to this pertinent question is required: What is it that they wanted to carry that didn't quite fit (plywood)? As a result of this analysis, it is recommended that the company should *not* dedicate effort to reduce fuel-economy dissatisfaction given the overall satisfaction improvement goal. Rather, it should examine how to alter the van's design to accommodate items/persons more comprehensively. This does not mean that fuel-economy dissatisfaction will not be at risk to become a factor in the future, but for now it is not. As it was at the time of the minivan customer survey, no competitor was delivering significantly better fuel economy (and had similar unhappy room percentages close to 25 percent). Now, if the fuel efficiency technology advances in the future, the current performance might become a reason to hate a vehicle. Not surprisingly, when small compact car owners were surveyed, those who disliked their fuel economy did not have a high overall opinion of their vehicle. Further, being cramped in the cabin wasn't terribly satisfactory, but they didn't really care, since their overall opinion didn't change with this factor (similar overall opinion in each happiness room). This survey example appears to support the reasons that people selected these two very different types of vehicles in the first place. It is interesting to note that the fuel economy of the small compact vehicles as a whole was much better than that of the minivan, but it was a sensitive weak point for that group of owners. This shows that the use of ANOVA tests the result-factor sensitivity for a particular (local) situation at a given point in time. It does not generate an equation or a rule that necessarily describes all experiences. It does enable us to find a meaningful step in the right direction from our current "location" or circumstance.

Think of the methods of ANOVA as standing on the ground and reaching out with a stick in all directions that can "test" the result of the choice should one take a step accordingly. For example, the stick could reach into a hole or perhaps touch a wall, and that information can help guide the direction choice for movement. Let's suppose one is hiking in the mountains and wishes to get to a high point to view the sunset that will happen in thirty minutes. The choice of direction with the first step will likely change the elevation. If a stick is used that is able to reach out the length of a single step, it could touch the ground all around to find the best direction to take to climb up a bit. With this short stick, the action might find the top of a foothill by accident, since a single step in any direction from it would be downward. This process stalls and does not meet the objective. However, if a "very long stick" that relates to the total number of steps that could be taken in thirty minutes is used, one could find a high point that is within range in a similar manner as the short stick. It is easy to imagine that the mountainous terrain is not well organized, and perhaps going down in the short term along the path enables reaching a summit in the thirty-minute time frame. This surveying process with the short and long sticks build a topological map around a starting point. This methodology is useful for interpretive-intelligence genre candidate screening for pertinence since it can identify potential relationships (or sensitivity) of a result to a fundamental factor or choice of action. In some cases, it may be enough just to know what does and does not influence a result—and avoid wasting effort and resources on candidate solutions that are irrelevant (make no difference). From an appropriate or pertinent feedback interpretation, effective corrective actions can then be made.

In common practice, a final result of an action is used to judge success or to find performance-feedback error. We will call this conclusion feedback for this end-result type of assessment. Cooking is full of conclusion-feedback behavior. For example, the relative quantity of various ingredients and the cooking time and temperature are captured in an instruction set. The ingredients in a cake are decided by the recipe. The suitability of the balance of them is judged after baking when the cake can be sampled. If it is in some way inadequate, the recipe is modified, but the current cake is essentially a loss. Similarly, a washing machine has various settings that have correlated time and other factors to a cleanliness result for a variety of laundry load types. We trust they will deliver as expected. The user of the washing machine may see a poor final result (the clothes were not clean) and change the settings for the next time. In this case, the user takes the conclusion feedback and modifies instructions of how to operate the machine. The user may select a longer wash cycle. Perhaps, after completion, the result showed some improvement but not enough. The user may elevate the water temperature for the next attempt. Suppose that attempt cleans well, but the laundry's colors bled out to some extent. Eventually, through much trial and error, warm (not hot) water for a slightly longer wash time is found to give the desired result. Once those final settings are found, an open-loop instruction set (held by a passive-intelligence genre template) can be created. Open loop means that a result is delivered from a given process that does not have regard for feedback; one simply gets what the process delivers. Another open-loop scenario example comes from a task to fill a bucket with water. An instruction set suggests that if the water faucet is wide open for thirty seconds, an empty bucket will be filled appropriately. One simply operates the faucet for thirty seconds, and the task is accomplished. In essence, the learned instructions are followed and subsequently generate the result in an open-loop system. Confirmation is suspended. In a similar way, Allies's second-layer interpretation logic frameworks are well-defined (open-loop) actions that are assumed to be effective based on past experience.

Consider clothes dryers with a variety of open-loop settings to deal with clothing types (i.e., towels vs. delicates) to help the user accomplish the aim of dry clothes. If the user follows the clothes' sorting constraints, it tends to do fairly well. However, there can be several reasons that cause varied drying performance results. The initial condition of the clothes from the washing machine (i.e., knotted or spun almost dry) and the clothes themselves (i.e., fabric type, thickness, and how many) will influence the drying time. Active-intelligence research that correctly accounts for these varied initial clothing-condition combinations (causes) will likely generate a complex template with a multitude of tedious details to be captured. A manufacturer might create hundreds of settings for the user to navigate so that benefit from this extensive study can be realized. In theory, it is possible to do this, but at some point, the burden to account for the complexity of causes exceeds the practical benefit in the result and is abandoned. This means that slightly damp and slightly over-dried clothes are tolerated as a result, but it is not clear what will happen with a given laundry load. When we surrender to this complexity burden, we elect to call these influences random effects. These random influences will generate variation in our results that we have deliberately chosen not to manage. As a result, we should prudently accept the variation caused by them. In my opinion, this "too burdensome" stance seeded the formation of Edward Lorenz's Chaos Theory. The theory alleges that downstream result variation is caused by small differences in initial conditions. Given a cause is cited, is it really chaos? Philosophically, are we just lazy by not accounting for all of the detailed initial conditions, like the condition of the wet laundry?

A more sophisticated means to fill the thirty-second bucket described above is to confirm the bucket's water level and manage the faucet accordingly during the process of filling to a target level. If the faucet's water flow is unusual because of a water-pressure issue (high or low) or partial clogging, the open-loop fill time of thirty seconds from the passive-intelligence directive could fail to some degree. The open-loop method does not account for these unexpected influences. To contend with this variation risk, the management of the faucet can be linked to the level of the water in the bucket. This means that the faucet will be wide open for a while and the level of water in the bucket rises. The faucet closes gradually as the target level is approached until it is shut off at the desired water level. This is an example of a closed-loop system. In this case, the water level in the bucket is continuously monitored, and the factor of water flow is modified based on that condition. The current condition is compared to a target result to calculate a deviation as a feedback-error signal. This means that when the feedback error is zero, then the measured result is at the target. We will call this feedback style continuous feedback. A distinction between continuous-feedback and conclusion-feedback corrective actions is that continuous-feedback action happens during the task and conclusion-feedback corrective actions happen after the task's completion. Closed-loop systems are not uncommon, and we frequently find ourselves making the adjustments or "closing the loop" ourselves. For example, if a person prepares popcorn by powering a microwave oven based on the frequency of kernels popping, they have also used a closed-loop approach. When the frequency of popping is decreasing and has become low, the power should be shut off. If not, perhaps another continuous-feedback error indicator of smelling smoke will inspire the power down. In some cases, we have assistance with our closed-loop activity. In a building, a thermostat is used to maintain a preset room temperature target. This target temperature is subjectively decided somewhere between too hot and too cold. A control system that operates the furnace or air conditioner compares the target temperature to a measured temperature to generate a feedback error. If the measured temperature is above the target (warm), a positive error is found, and the air-conditioner runs. If the measured temperature is below the target (cool), the furnace is called to operate. A closed-loop system is characterized by real-time condition monitoring and corrective responses during the approach to a desired result (target).

In some cases, it is possible to convert part or all of a conclusion-feedback task into one that utilizes continuous feedback. In doing so, corrective actions en route to task completion can be made with a closed-loop process. In the case of clothes dryers, a humidity sensor may be used to monitor the moisture of its internal air and, thus, the clothing it is processing—this is continuous feedback. Even though a guideline open-loop time and heat setting may be selected by the user, the humidity sensor can detect when the drying task is completed and terminate early or extend time as needed. This closed-loop action may save energy in some cases as it consistently delivers dry clothing. Suppose that we monitor the condition of a cake as it is baking (continuous feedback). This means that we can detect when it is done and avoid burning it or removing it too soon, regardless of the recommendations from the recipe. In this way, continuous feedback and an application of closed-loop corrections can be used to at least partially compensate for an underperforming open-loop task instruction set. Ideally, a closed-loop control supplements the open-loop action to refine and converge on the intended target performance.

In addition to pertinence of feedback measurement, the challenge, target, or goal needs to be interpreted as part of an intelligent action to assess a deviation. This consideration initially assumes the existence of a deviation. However, that point needs to be verified. For example, a reviewer cites a deviation of not performing job in a conventional and expected way and marks it as a demerit. Yet the offending unconventional approach is more efficient and accomplishes the desired overall results. This makes a "correction" to the reviewer's image of the target unwise, except to get a good mark on the review. Such case follows:

Early in my engineering career, my task was to determine the calibration values for a passenger vehicle's computerized automatic air-conditioning controller. Calibration is basically a set of reference numbers used by the onboard computer's logic (algorithm) to manage a system or function. Good calibration is perhaps like dressing appropriately for a party. The person is the same regardless of the attire, but the suitability of the person for the circumstance can be influence by wardrobe selection. In essence, my job was the selection of appropriate "clothing" for each environmental condition. This conventionally meant that the calibration values (reference numbers) were derived from several weeks of iterative trial-and-error experimentation with a somewhat rare prototype vehicle in an expensive climatic wind tunnel (the cost of just two days in this facility could buy a nice new car). This activity was typified by testing the performance, correcting it, and verifying—unless further correction was needed. The starting point was usually based on another model's calibration (wardrobe). Since that approach was rarely adequate, I chose to theoretically calculate my model's calibration as a starting point of my testing. I proceeded to find that my testing was largely verifying rather than developing and iterating. At best, one try in each condition proved to be enough. This dramatically reduced my consumption of wind-tunnel test time and related costs. After an early job completion, my reviewer complained that I did not have a battery of baseline test data to prove that I had made improvement en route to my new results, I only had on-target results. I pointed out that I had more than enough reserve time to test an inferior calibration, if he felt it was important to have these data. However, I explained that I didn't see the reason to spend resources, time, and money on proving something that we already knew was not adequate was, in fact, inadequate. The expectation to perform an expensive job conventionally was not met by my activity, but the meaningful objective of getting the calibration developed was met. This is an example of how an approach-based objective or target interpretation can create an irrelevant deviation.

When dealing with feedback, we need to avoid tampering with a generally good approach when a largely random unusual deviation happens. Suppose a chef is baking a cake and there is a brief power failure interruption that causes the temperature in the oven to drop for a period of time. This causes the cake to not be completely baked. Naturally, the recipe should not change to extend the cooking time or raise the temperature for future use based on this rare experience. Similarly, an individual does not require feedback, coaching, and explanations of how to do a well-known task when an unusual deviation occurs. To illustrate, I was a trip leader for a vehicle development program, and I had two very high-performing technicians that supported me. Once in roughly ten years of working with them, they failed to turn on a vehicle's data-acquisition equipment at the start of a field test. This meant that we conducted a test on one of our seven vehicles that cold (-30°C or -22°F) early morning (4:00 a.m.) in the mountains with no performance-data record. A guest evaluator asked me if was going to scold them in front of the test team and essentially throw a fit like his bosses usually did when an error was made. I told him. "Of course not, they feel terrible about the error because they care so much, as they have shown so many times before." I am confident that it will never happen again, which is the best result I could possibly want. My talented staff certainly didn't need an explanation or a refresher lesson of how to turn on the data-acquisition system. They probably had done it successfully over a thousand times in addition to the twenty of twenty-one times that day. I don't need them to alter their approach because of fear or be distracted by a degrading tantrum from me. It would be an error to concede a very good behavior that delivers excellent results. Their mistake was a random and rare occurrence.

In another instance, corrective action was necessary for a process that depended on inexperienced evaluators to press a button to indicate their vehicle's location near specific milestones along a test course. We needed the observations and opinions of these nonengineering evaluators to become more certain that our performance and designs were not only tuned to experts but for the needs of our typical customers. In nearly every flight of daily tests (multiple vehicles tested multiple times), someone in the team made a mistake and failed to press the button properly. This required time-consuming offline rework of the data to estimate what should have happened. There is no tantrum I could throw aimed at the well-intentioned evaluators that could completely compensate for our process weakness. Further, making this voluntary activity less pleasant was not an option. Instead, we found a way to detect the course's milestones with the data-acquisition system and remove our dependence on the evaluator's concentration and action. In many cases, if we don't like the feedback error, we likely need a more capable system or process. Otherwise, we should be tolerant of the feedback error since it is caused by the system that we created, which includes the sources of result variation that we didn't bother to address.

An excellent demonstration of this dynamic was shared in an experiment by Dr. Deming in *Out of the Crisis* (1991) in which the sources of variation are not prudently tolerated. In the experiment, a funnel is placed above a target, and marbles are dropped through the funnel, with the hope that they will land in the center of a stationary target below. Since the narrow opening of the funnel must be slightly larger than the marble so it can pass through, the marble's exit position will have some variation that will be reflected in the resulting landing point on the target surface below. The marble's imperfections, its spin and speed as it approaches the funnel's exit will contribute to the scatter of the landing points. These factors are not controlled or easily predictable and can be thought of as random; they are substantially the initial conditions of each individual marble in the experiment (burdensome details). Suppose the center of the funnel is precisely aimed at the center of the target with a laser. Then we conduct multiple experiments of dropping marbles, which reveals some scatter evenly around the center of the target below.

This experiment has conclusion feedback, which means we don't know our error at the target until the marble lands. Further, the path of a marble cannot be altered after it has left the funnel exit, which means that there are no closed-loop control actions to correct the path to hit the target. If open-loop funnel aiming is corrected based on its conclusion-feedback error, let's see what happens. If the marble misses to the left slightly with the first attempt, the aim is slightly adjusted to the right to compensate. The implied assumption is that the first result is representative of the process and it will repeat. The intervention will compensate for that error and subsequent attempts should hit the target every time, so further adjustment is not required. Now let's drop several marbles through the funnel. The experiment's scatter is not distributed evenly around the target's center. Its average location is to the right. Well, clearly this system is not being managed very well, as some bosses might conclude. One adjustment of the aim is clearly not enough. It is lazy to think only one adjustment would be sufficient. A performance review could cite this laziness, and now management needs to be involved. So diligently an adjustment based on the error from each and every marble drop is made in response to the laziness criticism. Sadly, the scatter around the target doesn't get better. In fact, the scatter becomes much greater (worse), but those involved were hard workers and had involved management (congratulations). Unfortunately, what happens in this case is that the ongoing adjustments amplified the random causes, and this resulted in a much smaller percentage of marble drops close to the target. Therefore, it is best to hold the theoretically correct aim and not to tamper with the system in response to the uncontrolled variation sources that created the feedback error. The key point is to know when the error is generated by random (uncontrolled) factors and avoid reacting to them; otherwise, the action may make matters worse.

Performance feedback is important in the development of active-intelligence genre responses. The discovery via tests and trials to figure out how things work and eventually work well is part of the learning process. The AI tribe called evolutionaries holds a paradigm that is based on learning. The learning depends on the information that results from the device's responses to a variety of situations. This means that credible feedback and prudent management of it is absolutely vital. For example, if a device is learning how to pick up a ball with a single handlike gripping mechanism, attempts that bump the ball away would quickly be altered to avoid that type of contact. By experiment, the device could learn that high success can come from approaching the ball from directly above with the gripping mechanism. When a high degree of mastery is secure, that learning process can stop (it is "enough"). This means that new performance assessments should be ignored. Despite this mastery, when a failure happens, perhaps because of a wind gust or an unsettled ball placement, the device should not attempt to relearn how to pick up a ball. Instead it should simply try again, which will very likely result in success. If there is no threshold of performance that is considered "enough," the device would continue to try to learn how to deal with randomness in the task and become less stable in its performance. The degradation of performance from tampering with the funnel-marble experiment emphasizes this point. The adjustments that follow randomness (having undetected and unpredicted causes) will be counterproductive and waste the device's processing resources. This acceptable tolerance logic is important to manage any learning methodology since it sets a boundary of "enough" that prevents new lessons from being counterproductive.

Let us assign a task to Allies to keep the fuel level in a vehicle at full. She takes the vehicle to a nearby station and fills it to capacity. She returns and finds that some fuel has been consumed. She promptly returns to the station and adds a bit of fuel to satisfy the objective. Then she returns and again discovers that some fuel has been consumed. This perpetual task is created by the management of the feedback and the target. In this condition, Allies compulsively travels to the station to the exclusion of other tasks. Perfectionists and addicts in the human experience often behave this way and compromise their productivity. There is an ongoing deviation that requires attention that leaves little time for much else other than tending to it. These conditions need a healthy feedback management system. It must have an "enough" criterion that is short of perfect target achievement to stop the compulsion and break the obsessive cycle. For Allies, when "enough" is achieved, she is free to accomplish things far beyond filling a fuel tank. "Enough" could take the form of a limit to the number of trips allowed in a day. It could be that the action to fill the fuel is triggered by being near empty rather than not being full (called hysteresis). There are a variety of ways to prevent this compulsion; but there will be a period of time, perhaps most of the time, when the objective of the fuel level being full will not be precisely met. We tolerate the feedback error since it has its origin in our process and clearly not in Allies's lack of diligence. (This is a good lesson for bosses who give performance reviews to diligent workers.)

When somewhat incapable processes are used to execute a task, they need to have an "enough" criterion to shut down wasteful actions. Otherwise, the task quickly becomes compulsive in dealing with random variation with very little progress. A popular business approach called management by objective may set performance level targets that overlap with a healthy "enough" criterion. In such a case, I observed one executive dealing with this corporate style with great frustration because of a lack of real progress. It seemed that when one issue was resolved, another emerged to take its place. He astutely drew a comparison to the carnival game called whack-a-mole. The issues that popup, like a mole in a hole, get hit and then another pops up. In this analogy, the causes for each mole showing itself were not related. Further, if a given mole were neglected and not whacked, it would retreat into its hole seemingly without reason. In fact, this analogy held quite well for our seemingly random vanishing and appearing of various concerns in our management priority lists. Without sufficiently improving our process capability, we were destined to vainly "whack" away and to disappoint.

When an "enough" criterion is necessary, it is indicative that the method used lacks capability. From Allies's fuel-fill example, a fundamental cause of the fuel-level deviation lies in the vehicle delivery process. To contend with this factor, we can eliminate it. Suppose Allies could bring fuel to the vehicle or store the vehicle at the station after filling it. These new processes are capable of delivering the objective of a full fuel level without compulsive behavior or conceding to less-than-ideal performance, while the old process cannot. This is like getting a better playbook for the "failed" athlete that led to success in the new situation.

THIRD-LAYER INTERPRETATION LOGIC FRAMEWORKS

The third-layer interpretation logic frameworks are designed to take feedback from the second layer's performance, in order to refine its open-loop responses. From our review of the nature of feedback error, we have seen that there are several risks to being proficient in adjusting the second layer. For example, the first part of the deviation is the target itself, which may be based on an inferior (or perhaps irrelevant) goal or objective. Just like in our goal statement review, targets need to be challenged to ensure a high-level focus that is truly meaningful. The feedback measurement is the second part of the feedback error, which is comprised of fundamental causes (causal relationships) and random effects. If the causal relationships can be adjusted, real improvement can be realized to reduce feedback error. In this way, pertinent corrective action is an act of intelligence.

However, when a given process is not capable of delivering the target performance, persistent feedback error is guaranteed. Thus, efforts to correct this feedback error are not pertinent and often cause compulsive and fruitless behaviors that lead to ineffective and potentially harmful future results. In this circumstance, an artificially intelligent device or a human might destroy or disrupt statistically successful approaches in favor of one that only momentarily compensates for an error and then underperforms thereafter. Some inferior processes do not comprehend at least some of the causal relationships because of the analysis burden or simple neglect. Therefore, this omission creates a pseudo random influence threshold for the process. Regardless of how the process dictates the random influence threshold, to struggle against it consumes resources and yields very little value.

To avoid overuse of feedback when dominant random effects remain in a process, an "enough" criterion should be used. This requires recognition that the performance of the current approach is at its capability limit. This criterion sets a feedback error level at which corrective actions can and should stop. Making the requirements for "enough" stricter or closer to the target is a temptation that only leads to fruitless efforts to fix random effects with actions that are not pertinent since it reaches into the random influence domain. The third-layer interpretation logic frameworks will need to determine when to use an "enough" criterion. In addition, the third layer will need to consider that when "enough" is applied to a second-layer process, it is evidence of an opportunity for a new more capable process.

The revisions to the second-layer's logic will ideally improve the final result or response. Typically, we are using conclusion feedback to motivate changes from the third layer. The third layer will apply an "enough" criterion to stop tampering with the second layer. In essence, the second layer's methods are to be optimized to their capability limits. It will use the presence of "enough" as a trigger to seek other pertinent causal relationships to include in the process. Even when the dominant causal relationships are accounted for, the open-loop nature of the second layer will likely have some final result variation. A closed-loop process that monitors progress of the task prior to completion may be able to safeguard the proficiency of the final result by making en route adjustments. Any second-layer open-loop process is similar to the throwing action of a quarterback in the game of American football. This player executes arm motion to deliver the ball to the ten-yard line in the vicinity of a running wide receiver, for example. Once the ball is in flight, there is nothing more that the quarterback can do to alter the outcome.

Naturally, there are sources of uncontrolled variation that will influence the location of the ball. The ball-position variation at the point of the catch could be due to the wind, an opponent tipping the ball, the quarterback's misjudgment or inability to execute as intended. A coach can act in the third layer to offer refinement suggestions (arm angle, foot position, etc.) to the quarterback, but that can only benefit future performance. However, in real time, the wide receiver tracks the progress of the ball's flight and alters running speed, path, hand position, and body angle to make the catch. The receiver accounts for an incredible amount of position variation by using a closed-loop approach. The receiver's continuous feedback corrections that occur during the task can compensate for a reasonably proficient open-loop action by the quarterback. This means that a third-layer action could be to apply this concept of closed-loop continuous feedback rather than attempt to perfect an open-loop action that has a capability limitation. This approach provides a safety net for the second layer's inadequacy in dealing with burdensome details.

Let us return to the coffee request. The open-loop second-layer actions are assumed to deliver as expected. However, condition monitoring for liquid level, smell, and temperature could be used to ensure the suitability of the response should there be some unexpected problems with filling, brewing, and heating of the coffee. This closed-loop pertinence confirmation during the task supports high proficiency.

CHAPTER 8

RELEVANT RESPONSES

Artificially intelligent devices that are primitive or inquisitive can contend with known challenges or anticipated variations within challenges. If the challenge is simply to recognize an object and respond with its name, a primitive function is demonstrated to meet it. This function is supported by a first-layer interpretation framework that has a trigger-response style to connect the challenge to learned responses. If a challenge is more complex, the first-layer interpretation framework recognizes the pertinence of an interpretation logic framework. These logic frameworks provide the anticipated context of the challenge in that it organizes known information and holds a place for unknown information that is pertinent to the challenge. Pursuant to the unknown information within this context, the logic structure gathers additional challenge details to support full use of this second-layer interpretation framework. This creates the inquisitive function that enables an artificially intelligence device to grasp our vague requests and to enter into a relevant discussion via questioning. The pertinence or relevance of the responses is implicit in the trained connections of the triggering challenge to the response. The device essentially inherited the result of an analysis that decided or assumed the pertinence of information in the response. Similarly, humans that follow belief-based interpretation frameworks operate with the assumption that what they have been taught is pertinent and will use it to navigate to a learned response. The sophistication and comprehensiveness of these passive-intelligence resources enable highly proficient familiar or anticipated responses to challenges.

With a large experience base, the artificially intelligent devices with these two interpretation framework layers offer capabilities that can address a majority of challenges. Thus, the development and preservation of the passive-intelligence genre's resources are very important to enable meeting challenges. To that end, let us reflect on our human experience that grew our capability. As a student, a triggering question is answered and practiced until an embedded proficiency of the response is realized. Most approaches to this learning process typically have some amount of repetition. Flash cards, peg words, photographic visualization, and substitute visualization are among the devices that, through practice, can expedite the memorization process. The proficiency resulting from this process is typically tested and scored to reinforce the permanence of it. Some have claimed that if you don't use learned information, you lose it. This suggests that periodic reinforcement of the learned information is necessary and valuable. An example of memory reinforcement comes from dealing with an early application of a microcomputer. This computer contained a memory section called RAM, which stands for *r*andom *a*ccess *m*emory. This section's hardware was capable of withstanding frequent modifications without wearing out. Further, and perhaps more importantly, the superior speed at which this memory could be modified enabled fast calculations to be executed by the computer, which enhanced its performance and capability. Now a little technical background: Each memory address, called a byte, groups eight separate associated locations that can hold a voltage or not. These individual locations (called bits) will hold a "one" when a voltage is present. When no voltage is present (or grounded), a bit contains a "zero." One can picture this with eight adjacent slots in a box that can hold a single AA battery or be empty. The computer's processor can check each slot to see if it presents a voltage or not as a means to "read" the information. Of course, the microcomputer didn't mechanically arrange batteries into the slots (bits); rather, it energized the locations with special miniature electronics in the act of "writing" the information. Conventionally, it can be assumed that a "one" is made by a voltage close to five volts. If one address (byte) contains 01101101, it has five of the eight locations that hold a voltage. It turns out that the hardware at that time had difficulty retaining the voltage in the RAM's bits. This meant that, with time, the electrical charge leaked out of the "ones" and, if left alone, all addresses would eventually contain zeros; and all data will be lost. This situation is very much like the familiar leaking bucket that loses electrical charge rather than water. With that in mind, suppose we could check each bucket before it is empty to see if it is supposed to be full, and if it is, we top it off. However, if we wait too long, all of the buckets will be empty, and we would lose our chance to recognize the intended condition. In order to preserve the memory's condition, a software routine for the microcomputer was used to frequently read each address in RAM and rewrite the same value to the location from which it just read. Without grasping this "leakage" background, this lengthy task seems silly and wasteful of computer processing time. It is like I repeatedly ask you your name and then I tell you what your name is. However, if your recollection of your name is fading, this "silly" routine reinforces the integrity of your memory. This practice of revisiting each address does not have a purpose other than to exercise and refresh the memory. In other words, there is no directed use of the memory resources. Our subconscious mind, perhaps in our dream state, appears to exercise our memory resources for us with a similar lack of intent.

Empirically, when humans consciously direct the use of their memory resources through practice, it appears to keep them refreshed (the "use it" action with our memory). From this, I hypothesize that we utilize our dream state to internally exercise, reinforce, and maintain the biological hardware of our memories. Thus, ongoing repetitive activity with our memories, subconsciously or otherwise, should make our passive-intelligence resources more stable and enduring.

When the passive-intelligence resources are not sufficient to deal with a challenge, an expansion of pertinent resources is necessary. For example, if a person or a device mistakenly identifies an object, the passive-intelligence resources are inadequate. The recognition of the mistake comes from the feedback error, which triggers the second-layer inquisitive interpretation framework to seek and nominate names with associated images from books and other records as possible corrections. Once a relevant response is found, a specific corrective action of adding a new object's image and name to the learned resources is made. It is the second layer's (interpretation logic framework) protocol that manipulates or collects pertinent information en route to the correction. If there is an issue with the logic of this protocol, a further corrective action is required. This follows from the third layer's interpretation logic framework that recognizes an inadequate response (for example, adding access to new databases that contain the desired information). In this way, the passive-intelligence genre is assembled with connected pertinent information. Clearly, adding missing content is one way to expand the passive-intelligence genre's resources.

Another way to create new passive-intelligence resources is to combine or manipulate known resources. Consider the banana-monkey experiment, in which the short monkey manipulated the box resources to enable climbing to reach the suspended banana. The boxes alone in their original location were not relevant to the challenge, but when stacked, they enabled a viable candidate response. This type of expansion of pertinent resources is preceded by response nominations from the interpretive-intelligence genre. These candidate responses are derived from recognition of factors that can influence a result. The active-intelligence genre adjusts, combines, or manipulates factors through some form of feedback and determines each candidate's proficiency. When a successful result is achieved, the passive-intelligence genre can collect the factor-based responses for the purpose of trigger-response resource growth and future reference. Thus, a recollection of a past experience is used rather than repeating the investigation or learning-factor adjustment sensitivity for future related circumstances.

The learning that occurs in the passive-intelligence genre is gathering memories or information (responses) and connecting them to similarly trained interpretation triggers. The passive-intelligence genre's established triggers are not essential to the other two intelligence genres. In fact, they might actually get in the way. The exclusive dedication of the response resources to an associated trigger can be a type of thought poison. This is similar to thinking that boxes can only be used for storage. Thus, the main reason to reject boxes as a climbing resource is that "no one has done it before," as far as we know. In this way, the established interpretation triggers set up the paradigms that tend to confine the response resources only to their connected purpose. However, the passive-intelligence genre's resources may be able to be utilized in new ways, in order to contend with a challenge. In these cases, the interpretive-intelligence genre may very well violate those paradigms as it entertains novel uses of the response resources and disregard the connected trigger. This is the nature of a high-functioning interpretive-intelligence genre that does more than simple trigger-response recognition.

It is important to note that a high-functioning interpretive-intelligence genre nominates factor or resource adjustment opportunities that can be used to form responses to a challenge that may or may not be successful. The relevance of each candidate response is not clear until some confirmation is conducted, which means it requires testing by the active-intelligence genre. Suppose a challenge is to open a lock that has a simple three-dial zero-to-nine combination. The passive-intelligence genre does not know the combination, and inquiring of others does not lead to the answer. If we had the combination, we would have all of the necessary pertinent information that we need to contend with the challenge. Without it, we require new information to answer this challenge. The interpretive-intelligence genre nominates dial adjustment as the factor that will lead to successfully opening the lock. The active-intelligence genre proceeds to adjust the dials to all possible permutations of three digits as candidate dial-setting responses, of which only one will be relevant and meet the challenge. Confirmation of each setting is made by attempting to open the lock for each one. With incredibly bad luck, each of the one thousand settings is checked until finding the desired outcome on the final attempt. The number settings for each dial were exhaustively manipulated and combined with each other. The relevant response was among them.

Let us shift our focus within our intelligence definition as follows: *Intelligence is an action to interpret a challenge and to apply pertinent resources that are ~~either inherited from past experience~~, actively manipulated ~~or created through investigation~~ to contend with that challenge.* As before, this shift of focus does not completely dismiss the background information that is inherited, given the need of known resources to manipulate. Rather, it is intended to expand on the past experiences instead of simply using them as the sole means to an end. This part of the definition permits a response that finds a pertinent arrangement of information, like seeking the lock's combination. Among the resources that may require manipulation to contend with challenges include equations, altering the state of various factors that influence a response, and the manner of combining resources. Resource manipulation in and of itself does not ensure an intelligent action since a multitude of resources that are not relevant can be adjusted and combined. Pertinence is a key part of this definition to make the action intelligent. Discipline in the information manipulation can come from grasping the causal relationships involved in the challenge. This permits a narrowing of response-candidate nominations to those that at least have a reasonable probability of being pertinent.

As human beings, we have little tolerance for irrelevant responses. In fact, entertaining irrelevant response nominations may cause us to feel stupid and embarrassed, when we discover that they are. Because of this, we tend to manage our interpretive-intelligence genre to keep our dumb ideas to ourselves. Functionally, there is an internal simulation of the expected outcome of our candidate-response ideas that may be based on experience, education, or a gut feeling to screen and decide on our public response. This screening action is from the active-intelligence genre that operates to test for relevance. When the internal simulation utilizes the disciplined benefits of causal relationships, it will mimic reality and thereby demonstrate high proficiency. In many cases, a strong and credible sense of these causal relationships may enable us to arrive at obviously relevant responses. For a meal, a chef may have a sense of how much salt to add to a dish to avoid being too much or too little. The resulting taste suitability depends on the factor of how much salt was added. With this sense, the chef successfully adjusts the factor without precise measurement or calculation. Similarly, an artist's drawing may need to consistently abide by a sense of realistic lighting and shading principles in forming images or their efforts will be considered a failure. The spin that a bowler puts on the ball at release influences the ball's resulting position at the pins. This factor is manipulated without the benefit of mathematical analysis from the laws of physics. Likewise, a golfer or a place kicker compensates for the influence of the wind. Through use and experience, many of us refine our sense of the challenge's factors to strengthen our internal simulation that builds our active-intelligence genre's capability. The better our grasp of the realities of the challenge (how well our internal simulation matches reality), the better we can screen out our irrelevant or inferior responses.

Innovation and invention place a high demand on the interpretive-intelligence genre and the active-intelligence genre. From our intelligence definition, the challenge or goal statement has to be interpreted and pertinent resources have to be recognized to enable contending with the challenge. Since innovation, by its nature, does not have a corresponding trigger in the passive-intelligence genre to lead to a response, an expansion of that resource is required. The causal relationships associated with the challenge help establish a pertinent interpretation framework for the task. Reflecting on the background of the challenge often provides insight into the causal relationships. For example, in the case of electric vehicles, the individual cells that comprise the battery pack will function most efficiently when they are all at a uniform (isothermal) optimal temperature. This desired state is not met when the cells discharge energy and give off sufficient heat to cause the cells to exceed the optimal operating temperature. Conventionally, a cooling fluid is moved through the battery pack to protect the cells from overheating. As the fluid cools one cell, heat is gained, causing a temperature increase for the fluid. The fluid continues to the next cell and gains more heat and so on. The result is that the cooling fluid enters the battery pack at a relative low temperature and exits at an elevated temperature. The consequence is that the temperature uniformity of the battery pack's cells follows or, in some way mirrors, the fluid's temperature-rise profile. In effect, the method used to cool the battery's cells dictates the nonuniform temperature distribution among them. In this way, the conventional approach creates a deviation from our ideal balanced temperature state. A strong grasp of these relationships can enable us to seek factors that can influence our desired result. We can structure these relationships to form an interpretation framework that is uniquely adapted to this challenge. The quality of this interpretation framework will be reflected in the relevance of the candidate responses it nominates.

If we wish to find a candidate solution to address this battery cooling concern, let's construct an interpretation framework in the form of questions. How do we secure an isothermal battery pack and reject heat from it to maintain every cell near the optimum operating temperature? Supporting questions are as follows: How do we transport heat away from the cells? How can we prevent a significant temperature rise during heat transfer from the cells? So now let's measure our experiences against these questions as a means to find resources that present factors and behaviors that can be used to form candidate solutions. At mealtime, we observe a boiling pot of water during the food-preparation process. From our schooling, we know that when the water is warming up prior to boiling, the temperature of the liquid water rises steadily as heat is added.

When the water boils, the temperature of the water persists at 100°C (the boiling point of water at a pressure of 1 atmosphere). The creation of water vapor, or steam, from the liquid is where the added energy is spent instead of increasing the liquid's temperature. This fits with our interpretation framework that picks up heat and remains at the same temperature—a candidate resource for our battery-cooling concern. If we let the water boil away, the pot's temperature will go up. So we must keep liquid water in the pot. In order to do so, we either recycle the water vapor or add new liquid water to the pot. If we add new water, it needs to be at a very similar temperature to the existing liquid, or we may mess up our isothermal goal. Thus, it seems convenient to recycle the water vapor. How can that be done?

This is a new challenge that has grown from a candidate solution. If we meet this challenge, the original challenge could be met.

A long, hot shower follows dinner, and the question is still in the back of our minds. Upon completion of the shower, the bathroom's mirrors are dripping wet with condensed water from the humid air that was made in the process. This situation is recognized as one that converted water vapor back to liquid water. Now we can combine these two resources to address our challenge. First, the battery cells add heat to a liquid so that vapor is formed, which takes the heat away while leaving the liquid and immersed cells at a stable temperature. The vapor can be remotely cooled to reform the liquid, and that liquid can replenish the original reserve to create a cycle. From our familiar gravitation-field resource, we know that the vapor will naturally escape the liquid and will migrate to an elevated location. Energy can be removed from the vapor to reform the liquid, and it can fall back to the pool via gravity. This means that the natural dynamics of making and condensing vapor is a substitute for the need to pump the cooling fluid. These observations and resources have been matched to the causal relationship and requirements of the heat-transfer process found in our interpretation framework. Thus, we can combine these resources to nominate our candidate response. This response is fundamentally viable to address our electric vehicle battery-temperature-uniformity issue. However, it may or may not be relevant to our challenge.

Now with a viable concept of pertinent resource properties and factors, the active-intelligence genre is needed to combine or manipulate the available resources to make a successful response. This is similar to the short monkey recognizing that boxes could be used for climbing to get a dangling banana, but the boxes aren't yet in position and may collapse under the monkey's weight or have other concerns. This cooling solution candidate cannot use water for a couple of reasons: One is that, the battery's target operating temperature range is not 100°C. Another is that water will freeze and expand to potentially damage the battery structure when not in use at low temperatures.

Among our passive-intelligence genre response resources is knowledge of saturated fluids, specifically refrigerants. The connected triggers for such fluids come from its use in an air conditioner, heat pump, or refrigerator. The exclusive connection that such a fluid can only be used for those devices needs to be disregarded. With this freedom, we learn that the nature of a contained saturated fluid has a temperature-and-pressure relationship that is maintained by phase changes between liquid and vapor. This means that management of the pressure of such a fluid can uniformly control its temperature. These observations and interpretations were contributors to related patented solutions that can be summarized as follows: A saturated cooling fluid is managed to keep the liquid temperature surrounding the immersed battery-cell enclosures uniform in the target operating temperature range. The vapor forms in bubbles as the liquid is heated by the cells that escape the liquid en route to a condensing heat exchanger. The condensed liquid cooling fluid is returned to the battery cells.

This example reflects how the interpretation framework's questions carried the requirements that dictated the pertinence of the response. The normal-life cooking and showering observations were essentially tested in that framework to see if they might be helpful. The interpretation of the experiences nominated a candidate solution's factors in concept only. Nothing was proven yet. The candidate solution formed a hypothesis that posed new challenges. In the process, we shifted from the initial challenge of making the battery cells isothermal to "how do we sustain a saturated fluid's condition in applicable environments?" This progression of challenge refinement and migration often happens in the creative process. The initial challenge could be met if the next challenge could be met and so on. In this case, there is a commitment to the belief that a saturated fluid will be able to meet the original challenge. The new challenges come from working with saturated fluids. If a suitable fluid did not happen to already exist, the challenge could be to create one that would have the appropriate properties. The challenges related to the chemistry, safety, and costs could then be the next focus. At some point, the task of interest may seem far away from the original challenge. This migration in research is sometimes referred to as a rabbit hole, which is essentially a paradigm founded on connected cascading beliefs. The interpretive-intelligence genre may furnish multiple conceptual candidate factors to deal with a challenge. Each of them may have their own unique and possibly unrelated rabbit-hole pursuits for the exact same initial challenge.

When the candidate response is so well conceived, it essentially answers the challenge and the active-intelligence genre can readily recognize the nomination's pertinence. From an engineering example, corrosion and failure of a part was occurring when a feature collected salts and other debris during use. Conventionally, some might respond to improve the protective coatings of the part to avoid this unwanted failure. However, if one fills in the feature so that no debris can accumulate on the part, the issue will certainly be resolved. From aerodynamics, it is noted that airflow can have two main reactions as it encounters surfaces. First, the air can adhere (attach) to the surface and follow its contour. Second, the air can deflect away (separate) from that surface, perhaps like a foul tip of a baseball. Depending on the conditions, one or the other might be the interaction that governs the airflow's behavior. If a candidate design solution depends on the airflow staying attached to the surface, for example, it will fail should the conditions arise that the airflow deflects and separates from that surface. From this grasp of the causal relationships, a design structure that favorably harnesses both possible reactions rather than counting on only one of them will be successful. Thus, with all bases covered, the relevance of the design solution is obvious and assured (and no equations and calculations were necessary).

Candidate responses are not relevant if they do not contain or adjust factors that are present in the challenge's causal relationships. When a factor is found to influence a result, it is a candidate cause of it, or at least a contributor. The causal equations from physics and other sciences are examples of a definitive means to connect causal factors to responses. For example, one can control their speed while driving on a long trip. That choice will largely determine the time it will take to complete the trip. When the causal factors can be controlled, they enable us to alter the results with our management of them, and that is a key characteristic of a relevant response. There are three classifications of relevant factors or causes of a result according to the book *The Elements of Reasoning* (Munson and Conway 1996).

First, triggering factors tend to be the factors that change closest in time to a change in a result. When we turn on a light switch, we could call this the cause of a lamp being lit. However, there are standing conditions that enable that final act to be successful. The lamp requires electricity to be lit. The availability of the electricity to the circuit in question depends on its connection to the power lines. The power lines are fed by converting another energy source to make it useful for the lamp. The energy source itself may have a great deal of complexity involved in making it available to the electric company. In this case, the proximate cause is the light-switch activation. The standing conditions dictate if the proximate cause is relevant to the result or not. If there is no power in the electrical grid, the switch can be toggled endlessly without influencing the result. I have heard people say that they are independent and don't need anyone. This springs from a lack of recognition of our deep dependence on the standing conditions that are pertinent to our life experiences. Sure, we can buy our own food, if the local store can dependably keep enough in stock for us.

The second type of factor is called an unusual factor. Sometimes we say the cause of a result or event is due to an unusual factor within a set of sufficient conditions. Sufficient conditions are similar to standing conditions in that they are essential for the event to happen. Suppose a friend falls down the stairs when one of the steps comes apart. If they had not been walking on the steps in a gravitational field, the event would not have happened. However, we don't tend to blame the person for the fall. Their action was not unusual and is not considered to be the cause. We check for the number of nails used to secure the broken step and find them to be typical of all steps in the structure that do not have any concerns. Thus, the installation is conventional and is not considered to be the cause, despite the fact that if the stairs were never installed, the fall they experienced could not have happened. When we examine the nails that were used to secure the broken step, we find that some have fractured in an unexpected way. We see this as unusual and designate the faulty nails as the cause of their fall. It is not uncommon for humans to question their part in creating the sufficient conditions that had negative consequences and feel that they are at fault. If I asked the friend to get something for me that caused them to climb the stairs that broke and lead to their fall, I had a part in setting up the sufficient condition. By extension, the person that placed the object such that it required the steps to be used contributed another part of the sufficient condition set up. The creator of the object is also responsible for the reason for them to use the stairs. If that object did not exist, there would be no reason to use the stairs. When we adapted the inquisitive intelligence function to Allies to solve problems, a deviation from a baseline "healthy" condition was noted. The logic incorporated a methodology designed to disregard the factors that are simply sufficient conditions. For this example, the fact that the friend traversed most of the steps in the staircase successfully, the logic directs the attention to the failed single step. It was the unusual factor that is recognized as the reason for the failure. Corrective action for the unusual factor allows the sufficient conditions to exist without incident.

The third type of cause is identified as a controllable factor. If a roof of a building collapses because of the weight of a massive winter snow, the collapse is due to gravity, which is a factor that we do not control. Thus, we don't typically suggest gravity as the cause, although it certainly is. If there were no gravity, any amount of snow on the roof would not cause damage. Instead, we focus on the fact that the snow accumulated in a manner that exceeded the capacity of the building to support it. We can control how the snow accumulates on the building's roof by the shape that we make for it. For example, we can make the roof very steep so that the snow will fall off at minimal levels of accumulation. If we make the roof's shape too flat, a large amount of snow accumulation is possible, and that design (or neglect to remove snow from it) is regarded as the cause. Likewise, many illnesses arise from microbes in our bodies. Our immune system that resists those microbes can be strengthened or weakened by controllable factors of rest, hydration, staying warm, nutrition, and vaccination state to name a few. We might say that we get sick because of a weakened immune system. Evidence of not getting enough sleep and having a chill by not dressing appropriately may be cited as causes because we could control those factors. The microbes are the actual cause of the illness. In these examples, the controllable factors provide a means to deal with the actual causes that can help us minimize their harmful impact. The actual causes still remain uncontrolled and unaddressed.

Suppose an inquisitive artificially intelligent device knows the relationship from physics that the distance travelled comes from the following causal equation: distance = time x average speed. If asked how far we travelled in the last hour, the device asks us what our average speed during that time interval is. After receiving our response, the logic structure multiplies that speed by an hour and reports the distance. Let's ask the device to answer the following question: We wish to average 60 mph on a two-mile trip, and we have already driven an average of 30 mph during the first mile. On average, how fast do we have to drive the remaining mile? The device hears "average" and from the passive-intelligence genre responds "90 mph," since the average of 30 mph and 90 mph is 60 mph. This device has no mechanism to assess the pertinence or correctness of this answer. It is an open-loop response with an assumed pertinence that is a characteristic of the passive-intelligence genre. The active-intelligence genre is needed to see if this answer is appropriate or not. The causal equation combines the factors of speed, distance, and time; but the equation it is not configured to react to this particular question. This requires a manipulation of the causal equation to fit the problem. Given that the distance is provided to us and speed is in the answer, let us interpret this problem in terms of time, which is an unspecified underlying causal factor. If we rearrange (manipulate) our equation (and define average speed as speed for simplicity) in terms of time, it looks like this: time = distance/speed. First, we will interpret the final objective in terms of this parameter: How much time does it take to average 60 mph on a two-mile trip? We divide two miles by the speed and get 2/60 hour or two minutes. This means that our two-mile trip must take exactly two minutes. This also means that in the last mile, we must go fast enough to finish the entire trip in two minutes. So how much time remains for us to complete our second mile? From the first mile, the time that has been spent is time = 1/30 hour or two minutes. Thus, we have no time left to complete the trip to average 60 mph. It cannot be done. If we had a goal to average 15 mph for the same two-mile trip, we have 8 minutes (2 miles/15 mph = 8/60 hour) to complete the trip. We used up two minutes to finish one mile at 30 mph, so we have 6 minutes (1/10 hour) left to finish the second mile. Therefore, we require an averaging speed of 10 mph. If the same average-speed interpretation error is made as before (half of 30 plus 0 is 15), the device would conclude that zero mph would be the speed for the second mile to average 15 mph, which erroneously suggests that one can complete a one-mile trip without moving.

Currently, this capability to arrange, combine, and manipulate known information to adapt it to challenges is beyond the artificial-intelligence structure that Allies has. The insight to rearrange the causal equation for pertinence in the problem above is lacking. However, Allies is capable of guessing answers, such as the 90-mph guess. If she were able to test that guess for pertinence, she could refine her guess through successive guesses (called iteration) until she finds the answer. In this case, she would see that 90 mph in the second mile creates an average speed for the trip of 45 mph. So she would increase the speed in her next guess. Eventually, her guess of 10,000 mph for the second mile yields an average speed for the trip of just over 59.8 mph. If she had a grasp of what a reasonable speed is, she could correctly conclude that it is not possible. The results from this type of trial-and-feedback error-correction approaches are often called numerical solutions. It is this very function that is behind the training practices of "deep learning" at the foundation of some AI approaches, which adjusts the relative impact of factors through guided guessing to find the best fit. One limitation of this approach is that it is data-set specific. This means that results or responses fit the context of the problem or data that was used to train it. If the challenge moves outside of that context, the training process would have to be repeated to account for any changes that could potentially generate a different result. If our travel challenge required a 40 mph average speed instead of 60 mph, the results of the 60 mph context are no longer useful. The essential enabler for Allies to function in this manner is the capability of simulating or testing a response to assess feedback error en route to a relevant response.

From our combination-lock challenge, let's imagine that there is an audible clicking noise when each dial is set to its correct number due to the mechanism of the lock. This sound is a causal relationship for the final lock combination. The interpretive-intelligence genre notes that each dial can independently be turned to its correct position and then the lock will open. This means that with no more than thirty adjustments, the successful lock combination can be found. The relevance confirmation changed from repeatedly testing the ability to open the lock (up to one thousand times) to the confirmation of each individual dial's clicking sound. Either this approach or checking everything can find the answer (meet the challenge) and are intelligent actions in the end. They differ only in proficiency. The "clicking" approach was guided by a causal relationship that significantly reduced the effort involved in checking combinations that are not correct. From this, it is apparent that the "manipulation" aspect of the intelligence definition can be accomplished through an exhaustive arrangement of all known information of the passive-intelligence genre and observed external resources without regard for causal relationships. It is the testing of relevance that connects the causal relationships to the trials at the point of confirmation. Such a mechanism for combining information can be created for an artificially intelligent device and is incorporated into Allies. Unlike when we trained her passive-intelligence genre to have only pertinent combinations of information, this process attempts to use anything and everything without a constraint of pertinence. This means that she will merge even somewhat unrelated concepts, ideas, and information for the purpose of making a variety of candidate responses. However, her response candidates that are based on irrelevant information are not intelligent. Thus, Allies has a considerable burden of doing unintelligent things when she is attempting all possible responses. Clearly, this approach is not terribly proficient. Yet our intelligence definition does not require proficiency. Contending with the challenge successfully is what is important, and ideally, a subset of her vast search contains pertinent resources that can be applied proficiently.

Perhaps the human mind has a similar information manipulation mechanism. If this is the case, it subjectively supports the advice to “sleep on it” to find inspiration, renewed perspective, and new combinations of ideas when dealing with an issue the next day. In effect, our subconscious mind interprets new arrangements and connections of resources for the challenges, which may or may not be pertinent. From experience, when I have been immersed in a subject, even my dream recollections tend to be relevant to my study. To reinforce this point, scary movies watched before bedtime empirically seem to correlate to nightmares for some people, as if the sleeping mind combines internal memories to scare them. If this is the case, challenge-related thoughts prior to entering sleep would be a better choice than a scary movie to favorably leverage this asset. Given our disposition to react better after some delay, perhaps an artificially intelligent device also needs to “ponder” what it knows in an effort to make a response. Conceivably, Allies could be designed to laboriously combine all known information in her own sleeplike state or a parallel “subconscious” activity to support candidate response nominations.

This robust check-everything approach for Allies means that she will have a huge task of rejecting low-quality response nominations. This burden can be reduced through relevant attribute sorting. By analogy, consider a large collection of apples that are of a variety of colors, sizes, and ripeness as a representation of her information resources. The challenge is to collect fist-size red apples that are not overripe as is indicated by a lack of firmness or a rotten smell. Logically, all of these requirements have to be met to be acceptable for our apple collection. It is not necessary to inspect every apple for all of the requirements once any single requirement is not met for a given apple. This suggests that we can pass a single criterion through the entire apple collection and gather all the candidate apples that meet it. The choice of the first criterion should deliver as few as possible successful nominations. The reason for this is that the next task of applying a different criterion to the candidate batch of apples will be as small as possible. For example, suppose 99 percent of the apples are not rotten, 30 percent are red, and 80 percent are fist size. If we sorted for rotten apples first, we would have just about as big a sorting task (99 percent of the collection) for the next applied criterion. If we sort by color followed by size, then we will likely have around 24 percent of the original collection to inspect for the unlikely chance of rottenness (if there is no bias of size related to being red). If the apples were organized by color for example, our search task would have been largely completed. If the resource information that Allies learns is classified or has assigned asset attributes as she learns it, her sorting for pertinent resources will be much more proficient. This means that her passive intelligence resources will be required to additionally carry asset-attribute details. Those attributes create another path to those learned resources beyond the passive-intelligence genre's trigger-response connections. In this way, we can facilitate recognition of the pertinent learned information for a given challenge. For example, when Allies learns about cardboard boxes, she assigns asset attributes for cardboard boxes that might include Container, Organizer, Building Blocks, Hiding Place, Combustible, Shield/Protection, Paper Material Resource, and Insulator among others. The attribute of "building blocks" would help her identify this resource for a short monkey to enable reaching a suspended banana. Her known information that has asset attributes that do not contain climbing, building, or reaching would be ignored. Similarly, we ignored all apples that were not red in our analogy. The interpretation of the challenge will dictate the asset attributes that are pertinent and help guide the search. As an upgrade, Allies will search her information's asset attributes that have likely pertinence to a challenge for candidate response nominations.

General boundaries or constraints can be used by the interpretive-intelligence genre to filter (or sort) through the response candidates. This screening will prudently reduce the analysis burden of the active-intelligence genre that is charged to establish relevance or prove otherwise. These logic structures that arise from screening approaches can be held in the passive-intelligence genre that will be called upon when a need triggers it (second-layer interpretation framework). These structures will be subject specific and will provide rejection criteria for candidate response nominations. For example, the laws of physics should not be violated. Legal limitations and laws should be observed as a requirement. Poisonous materials should be avoided. Damaging side effects should be circumvented. Extreme condition requirements must be met. The timeliness of the response must be adequate. Even if this filtering logic is not perfect, it should be able to reduce some of the burden of the final pertinence confirmation.

The challenge statement itself can provide the interpretive-intelligence genre with candidate solution-rejection criteria. This supports the main purpose of interpretation frameworks to generate or manage candidate responses. From the isothermal battery cell challenge, if the cooling medium cannot be isothermal when the heat is added to it, we should reject that candidate solution. This screening could leave us with phase-changing materials that might move from solid to liquid or liquid to vapor that meet that criterion. Substances that transform chemically and react similarly would also offer an acceptable nomination. If our passive-intelligence resources contained other means to meet that criterion, they would remain viable candidates. The fact is that, even after applying this criterion, we may have several options that offer their own challenges to be proven to be relevant by the active-intelligence genre. While the passive-intelligence genre tends to offer a single response, the active-intelligence genre typically contends with a variety of response options. An expectation of a single response to a challenge is familiar, given our conditioning to expect only one correct answer for a test question for example. However, this is typically not the case and often supplemental requirements are used to decide which viable response will be selected (i.e., the cheapest or quickest might be among those criteria).

Another tactic for Allies to find pertinent information and reduce the burden of a comprehensive search of all passive-intelligence resources involves analogies. In the case of an analogy, even an imperfect analogy may identify mostly useful information that can be tested for pertinence with a lesser content of irrelevant information. When we use analogies, we substitute our new interpretation framework with an old and familiar one. The old framework has pertinent information already assigned to it that, at least initially, is assumed to be relevant to the new one. Where the analogy holds, the grasp of pertinent information is expedited like striking a vein of gold while mining that connects successful findings to more successful findings (another analogy). We used a "tool" analogy when we were considering the proficiency aspects of common intelligence definitions. The analogy helped us reject proficiency as part of our definition. The relative proficiency level of a hammer or a nail gun may be circumstance specific, yet each could meet a challenge to drive a nail. The basic proficiency to meet the challenge is what is relevant. One cannot say that the hammer is not relevant to the challenge simply because the nail gun is faster. The familiar interpretation framework of addressing challenges by the use of tools helped us treat the concept of intelligence in a more tangible manner (called reification).

SUMMARY

Responses from the passive-intelligence genre have a built-in relevance. The primitive and inquisitive artificially intelligent devices function under an assumed response pertinence instilled by their teachers. When the passive-intelligence genre fails because of the absence of a trigger or an associated response resource, a proficient response might be formed through combining and manipulating the existing information resources. The attributes of those resources can help the interpretive-intelligence genre to find relevant factors and response candidates. An example of this was from the challenge of opening a three-dial lock without knowing the combination. Initially, the factor of adjusting the dials was all that the interpretive-intelligence genre offered to contend with the challenge. The active-intelligence genre tried to open the lock for all permutations of dial settings until the challenge was met. This serves as an example of how an artificially intelligent device can be designed to generate and nominate all possibilities from what it has been taught. In this way, the passive-intelligence resources are assumed to contain factors that can be manipulated to answer a challenge. In such cases, confirmation feedback, like checking to see if the lock opens, is essential to see if the response is relevant or not. When this function is added to Allies, for example, she can act in all dimensions of our intelligence definition. She is able to use pertinent inherited information, manipulated information, and results of investigation to contend with a challenge.

Allies approach of checking all combinations of everything that she knows is tedious and time consuming. If we asked Allies to assemble a jigsaw puzzle from a starting point of a corner piece, she would begin checking all available solitary pieces in all orientations to see they fit into that piece. As pieces are connected, the process moves to new locations, and exhaustive checking again continues until the challenge of completion is met. As humans, our tolerance for this approach is quite low. The discouraging action of many failed attempts is something we wish to avoid. We would use attributes of puzzle-piece color and basic shape requirements to reduce our confirmation task for filling a given void. These attributes are associated with adjacent pieces and serve as causal relationships for the task. Although not essential to Allies completing the task, if she were able to utilize this insight into the causal relationships, her number of "foolish" nominations will be significantly reduced. Thus, the active-intelligence genre function of relevance confirmation (trying to fit the piece to another piece) will be much more efficient. In this way, insightful interpretations (from the interpretive-intelligence genre) ease the burden on the active-intelligence genre that seeks to confirm the details surrounding the pertinence of the candidate responses. From this, it is clear that the three intelligence genres will interact when new and pertinent resources need to be found.

CHAPTER 9

GOING BEYOND THE PASSIVE-INTELLIGENCE GENRE

When Albert Einstein stated that insanity is doing the same thing over and over and expecting a different result, I believe it was out of his frustration with the dominance of the passive-intelligence genre that tends to shut down the other two genres. Short of the varied execution of an intended response, the mechanism to initiate a different result comes from a change in interpretation, which requires a functioning interpretive-intelligence genre. With the passive-intelligence mindset, new interpretations are forfeit in favor of simple recognition, and there seems to be no desire for the alternative responses that would compete with the connected response. Clearly, Einstein became regarded as genius by not abiding in this stagnate recognition-response behavior. It was his high-functioning interpretive-intelligence genre and his active-intelligence genre that matured his interpretation frameworks and made his contribution exceptional. He deployed attributes of the scientific method by testing and refining hypotheses and theories en route to his key accomplishments. In order to act scientifically, one must interpret observations, form or modify hypotheses, test and challenge the hypotheses, analyze and interpret the observed results, and repeat as necessary. The interpretive-intelligence genre organizes observations to set up a candidate hypothesis that reflects an understanding of the causal relationships. The active-intelligence genre acts on the hypothesis content to test to see if it is valid or is in need of revision. Once the hypothesis is refined, the causal relationships are confirmed. Then those relationships may be leveraged to contend with related challenges. In this state of higher understanding, past approaches and historical responses may become irrelevant, especially if the old approaches deploy an inferior connection to the causal relationships. This progress potentially leads to rejection of the familiar past conventions. Those who function primarily in their passive-intelligence genre value and protect those conventions. In these cases, sharing of a new interpretation framework may take considerable skill or it may simply not progress for these closed-minded persons, which can be very frustrating.

As an inventor, frustration with the overused passive-intelligence genre was found with decision-makers that would cling to the conventional. They might say, "If it isn't broken, don't fix it." This gave rise to a personal philosophical statement: "If it isn't broken, raise your standards." Meaning that if one can elevate the requirements (i.e., seek greater efficiency and value), the idea that something is perfect and not broken often gives way to noticeable flaws and improvement opportunities. Initially, I was not aware of how this perspective enabled my interpretive-intelligence genre to function, but it did. I questioned designs, processes, methods, and approaches that worked as a means to make them work very well. Early on, challenging my theoretical education's interpretation frameworks to explain and anticipate physical observations forced close examination of them. Often, my interpretation framework confirmation testing (active intelligence) exposed a lack of refinement in my understanding or perhaps how some simplifying assumptions limited the pertinence of the frameworks. This practice nurtured an awareness of significant causal relationships that propelled my academic and professional ability to contend with challenges. In this way, I trained not to rely solely on my passive-intelligence genre. A personally intense experience exposed value from this behavior when I was given a thermodynamics examination that covered the first twelve chapters of our text. To the dismay and distress of our class, we had lectures on only the first three chapters. I didn't know this at the time, but my ability to answer around 25 percent of the problems fit the image. I felt panic with the realization that I would fail this exam and how that could negatively impact my future. I had no passive-intelligence resources for 75 percent of the exam! I settled down a bit, after accepting my plight, and toyed with the remaining problems based on the foundational causal relationships contained in the first three chapters. It turned out that I was able to develop responses for the rest of the exam that made some sense, at least to me. When the professor cited the error in scope he doubled our exam scores to get a class average of 50 percent, my 78 percent was converted to 156 percent.

During my efforts to better grasp my theoretical education, I found that some of the theories were developed to a level of nearly debilitating complexity. When this happens, there are consequences. If theory communication is desired, the details may require a very mature interpretation framework on the part of the recipient. This may necessitate considerable education (to develop a shared interpretation framework), or there will simply be only a few likeminded persons that can understand it. If the complexity comes from details that contribute to only a small part of the estimated results, from a practical sense, that complexity could be neglected; and a larger audience can grasp essence of the theory. When one neglects those low-impact details, simple descriptions of the theory may emerge that allow for conceptual explanation of main effects. Thus, effective communication is fostered with a relatively simple focus on dominant causal relationships while the minutiae are pragmatically regarded as such.

For example, while serving as an aerodynamics technical committee member at General Motors, a communication gap between our research arm and our development engineering staff was apparent. One of our research scientists developed a polynomial equation to aid in the selection of front-end heat exchangers (i.e., radiator) for new models. Most of the vehicle development staff did not have any interest in making the complicated calculation and preferred to conduct physical testing of available parts to make their heat exchanger selection. After checking the mathematical expression, a simple one-term "squared" relation approximated the polynomial quite well. This simple equation was easy for the development engineers to grasp and use as they selected more appropriate heat exchangers for experiments and reduced their physical testing demands. In practice, the physical test measurement error was greater than the difference between the single term and the well-studied lengthy polynomial equation. In effect, with this simplification, the development engineer could now function at a practical level as well as the scientist. Our research scientist acknowledged the value of this practical approach. I admired and appreciated the open-mindedness to abandon his work in the interest of being effective rather than being correct (literally to the nth degree). The pursuit of perfection in theories may fall into the "enough criteria" management that was discussed in chapter 7. Without it, one may obsess on nearly insignificant details that add little value. On the other hand, the theory's small true and statistically valid errors may help us unlock important causal connections that are relevant in other circumstances. Einstein's special theory of relativity is such a case where most of us do not require the theory's nuances, but it makes a significant step toward grasping the genuine attributes of nature, and it enables a more appropriate reach beyond our normal experiences should a challenge reside there (near the speed of light).

The theories that are developed using the scientific method start with observations, and variation in those observations are the subject of interpretation for the purpose of explanation and prediction. The scientist fundamentally believes in cause and effect that give rise to variation in observations. Thus, the theory's interpretations are typically tested through active-intelligence confirmation of cause adjustment to secure its validity. However, in some cases it is nearly impossible to secure the validity of the theory in this way. This means that the theory's pertinence is a belief, or an assumption, and not actual science (kind of like believing in myths in our past). In this state, the theory resides in the passive-intelligence genre with assumed pertinence. Let us cite some examples of the scientific theories that attempt to explain variation without rigorous confirmation (unverified by managed replication). First, the big bang theory for the universe suggests a very "compressed" beginning of all that we know. The theory, at least in part, is based on the apparent increasing separation of various visible stars. Thus, given our knowledge of object motion, we postulate that these stars were once concurrent at a single location in the distant past. In this way, if correct, we apply our understanding of the laws of motion from that beginning and explain where the stars are observed today. Further, we may predict future positions based on these laws. Thus, position variation and proliferation of the stars in the heavens is not subject to randomness; rather, they support our concept of the laws of motion. Another example is the theory of evolution. Some have interpreted the theory to mean that all life came from a simple single cell. We postulate that mechanisms affecting life generate diversity through mutation of the cell or the cell's "offspring" and an ability to combine with other cells in symbiotic relationships. Further, the most suitable mutations, as defined by environmental conditions, have an advantage for survival while those disadvantaged mutations tend to become extinct. Thus, this theory shares a similarity to the big bang theory in which a simple beginning is acted on by mechanisms that lead to variation and diversity in the future. A question such as, "Where did the material come from for the origin of the big bang or the beginning of life?" is not a question about variation and is therefore outside of the scope of science. Theories often start with a "given" ideally simple condition with minimum variation and work from there to vast variation. It is curious to consider why we think things have to have a beginning. Is it that we have a beginning and an end and impose that interpretation framework on other things? Is this analogy flawed, or have we yet to discover its flaw?

Passive-intelligence theoretical training (verified or not) is a dominant part of our education process with assumed recognition and response pertinence. Naturally, when students take a class, it is somewhat typical that they leave the class knowing a bit less of the topic than the teacher does, even with excellent grades. In the preparation chapter, we discussed the Situational Leadership Models of Ken Blanchard and Paul Hersey. Their models identify development levels or stages of task proficiency and link them to leadership behaviors that help facilitate growing task competency in others. Critics of this model claim there is poor correlation to enhanced business results by using their methods. One reason could be that the business organization's approaches are not enhanced through the training and, at best, are simply sustained. I interpret this critique as more of an indictment of the neglect of the interpretive-intelligence and active-intelligence genres during the passive-intelligence training to mastery of a specific task. The leader provides instruction and is the mentor throughout the process. Similar to the teacher-student scenario, it should not be surprising that a duplication of the leader's capability is an expected ceiling of performance. A means to excel beyond the training involves expanding on the ingrained passive-intelligence resources by using the other two intelligence genres. Using the multiple genres may build on the learning points and drive out-of-the-box thinking, which may or may not meet with approval. The leader, teacher, or mentor at the D4 level tends to hold to trusted paradigms that have led to their personal success and may come to embrace their reputation as an expert in them. Should new interpretations and causal relationship information be expressed, it may be perceived as a threat to the leader's standing. As a result, the leader may wish to disregard the new information in order to protect an "authority" status and the means that led to it. In this way, the leader lacks openness to the possibility that there are better ways to perform. This effect tends to suppress the growth beyond that of the leader's proficiency and it protects the status quo. Should this happen, this is a form of mental paralysis. Thus, when a new experience happens and "a proven method" fails, the paradigms are defended, and blame is often placed elsewhere in an effort to keep those paradigms intact.

I experienced an example of this mental paralysis early in my first "real job" as an engineer. My new boss and assigned mentor often declared, "If it isn't broken, don't fix it." His experience of many years gave him awareness that disrupting a good condition through change can create problems and that should be avoided. From this background, he considered change to be a risk rather than an improvement opportunity. With this mindset and using standard methods, my boss refined the performance of a prototype vehicle (a vehicle that closely resembles the vehicles that will later be mass produced) just prior to my joining his team. As part of my training, he assigned his model's responsibility to me for confirmation testing that would be conducted when the first few vehicles from the assembly line were available. This delegation of responsibility would enable him to manage our department's entire production-vehicle confirmation activity for several different new models without the task of attending to the one model that he personally developed. In this opportunity, I could prepare and test the new vehicle as a means to gain experience. This was a very good plan to grow my familiarity with the development processes and expected outcomes. Unfortunately, during confirmation testing, my production vehicle underperformed relative to other models to a level that I feared was unacceptable. This meant that I was the one that had to report the disappointing performance shortfall to our management. Given that this result came from my boss's work, he chose to deny the concern and followed up with attempts to discredit me (the new guy) for bringing it up. He was able to persuade his bosses that this condition was not a concern. Personally, I believed that my boss's work with the prototype vehicle must have been superior to what I experienced. So I began an investigation of how this could happen. From the performance data, I could estimate that the geometry of a key component was out of specification (not made correctly) in his prototype vehicle. This caused my boss to make unique specific adjustments for that design flaw that later caused problems with the updated correct design in my testing. Further, given this geometry and knowledge of the correct geometry of production parts, I was able to calculate how to undo those adjustments to restore my boss's intended performance for the production vehicles. My hope was that this root cause would help my boss recognize a part supplier's error and soften his stance against me for detecting the problem. However, my boss was not receptive to these findings either. "This is not an issue!"

At that time, it was customary for the company's top executives to evaluate the first few production vehicles in personal use prior to ramping up production-line speeds. This was kind of a high-level trial run that helps the executives confidently endorse our products. Should an issue occur, this early timing enabled corrections to the production line and to repair only a few vehicles if necessary. Once everyone was happy, we could accelerate the mass-production process and begin delivering products to the public. One day, news came down to our department that a chief executive issued a strong complaint consistent with my observations from our confirmation test trip. Our department's executives were accountable to the chief and needed to make a rapid response with corrective action. My boss announced that he would handle this highly visible concern himself (undoing his transfer of responsibility to me). He proceeded to an out-of-state wind tunnel to restart the lengthy vehicle development process that he used when working with the prototype vehicle. He declared that I was going off the deep end with my geometry study and that I would not be allowed to support the testing "because of my stubbornness." Given the high level of concern, our department's top executive was receiving real-time status reports from this remote testing so he would be ready to update the chief executive as needed. He was aware of my study from the "stubbornness" announcement and asked me to join him in his office for the updates and to provide my estimated corrections. During the first update, the preliminary findings from my boss's iterative testing were converging on my recovery-solution estimates. The executive recognized this, called attention to the validity of my work, and told my boss exactly what to do to fix untested concerns based on my document to expedite progress and skip most, if not all, of the time-consuming trial-and-error development activity. There were two operative challenges in this experience: First, resolve the performance issue. Second, minimize the response time. One response came from the passive-intelligence genre to conduct the full development process. The recognition of an underdeveloped vehicle was the interpretation framework connected to the conventional response. A second response from the active-intelligence genre was to correct the factor that caused the performance issue. The interpretation framework for this response was based on recognition of a causal relationship deficiency. Thus, separate interpretation frameworks competed to address the first challenge, and the most appropriate one was selected based on completion timing.

In another example of competing interpretation frameworks, there is an account of King Solomon settling a dispute between two women who claimed to be the mother of the same child. The actual mother was functioning with an interpretation framework that recognized the causal factors of good things and threats related to the well-being of her child. Through great care and commitment, she had successfully navigated through the pregnancy. The other woman was likely operating with an interpretation framework of jealousy. This framework recognizes a personal asset deficiency that triggers a response to compensate for it. From this, the child's status is interpreted in different ways by the two women. The king's challenge was to recognize which woman carried the mother's interpretation framework. If one can present a suitable challenge, each woman's framework would lead to a telling response. If the child were to be destroyed, the selfish-jealous framework would have a partial win, denying the mother her child and achieving an asset match. The mother, when faced with this unthinkable choice, continues with responses that demonstrate a selfless commitment to the well-being of the child. When King Solomon suggested that the baby be divided into two equal parts with each woman getting half, the mother quickly conceded the child to the other woman. With this confirmation, Solomon awarded the child to the woman willing to surrender it. The king tested (active intelligence) each woman's interpretation framework through its response to a challenge to enable his ability to interpret and respond wisely.

Our tendency to follow an expert's opinion is a passive-intelligence genre response that makes us vulnerable to exploitation. One such case was attempted when an automotive-part supplier had accidentally manufactured defective parts that they wished to furnish to our vehicles to avoid the cost of scrapping them. The external appearance and structural integrity of the parts were consistent with good parts. The defect was in the internal routing of the fluid that flows through the part. The mistaken internal structure actually trapped some of the fluid within the part instead of letting it pass through as intended. I was concerned that this "trapping" created a degradation of performance, and I would not allow the parts to be used. The supplier sent two "technical experts" to remove my concern about the vehicle's performance degradation. They wanted me to accept their technical interpretation framework by simply recognizing their expertise and trusting them (passive intelligence), which would lead to their favorable financial judgment. The conversation started with credential sharing by their experts. I asked why they came, since their expertise should clearly identify that these parts are not acceptable. This set them up to try to prove their expertise that, they believed, was critical to persuading me. They made several failed attempts to get me to accept their judgment that the defective part cannot be responsible for any degradation of the system's performance that we had experienced. Then I asked them if they had ever seen similar performance degradation in their prior experiences. One of the experts enthusiastically responded that they had seen this before, seizing the chance to build credibility with me. "It happens when there is not enough fluid in the system."

With that, I pointed out that trapping fluid in their defective part means that the rest of the system does not have enough fluid. This is the same problem. In this example, if my interpretation framework was not rooted in causal factors, the appeal to passively accept the pertinence assessment of alleged experts would have likely been successful and compromised our product.

A secondary challenge to "raise the standard" renders the existing response "broken." In this way, the original challenge's interpretation framework is typically inadequate to contend with the new standard. From an engineering example, the development process of a vehicle's interior automatic temperature-control system required expensive and time-consuming iterative trial-and-error testing. This observation can be interpreted to have two challenges within it. First, the challenge is to provide the proper temperature for the passengers in all conditions. This statement bears an interpretation framework based on temperature performance. It turns out that this paradigm of *temperature* control found its way into the system's control logic that depended solely on temperature relationships. For example, the logic sensibly delivers warmer air to the cabin the colder it gets outside. The missed causal factor of airflow functionally assumes that the fan speed has nothing to do with results (i.e., low, high, or off doesn't matter). Let us revise the first challenge by means of a different interpretation framework: The first challenge is to provide the proper heat flow (temperature delivery through airflow) for the passengers in all conditions. The second challenge is to make the development process more efficient. This second challenge is how the standard is raised and a proficiency deviation is recognized. Unless you recognize the inefficiency in the development process (multiple test iterations are required), the situation is not broken. We can revise this vague open-ended efficiency-challenge as follows: the second challenge is to eliminate repeat work in the development process.

In order to better grasp the influence of the causal factors, a computer simulation of the physics, heat transfer, and thermodynamics that included the related temperatures and the airflow exchange with the vehicle's cabin was refined. After using the simulation to successfully predict bad physical test results and good physical results from the factor settings and operating conditions, the causal relationships were confirmed. As a result, this virtual simulation was used to replace the vast majority of the physical trial-and-error testing. This simulation tool accomplished the primary temperature performance goals and was part of a more efficient development process. This is where the revision to the second challenge is important. Two separate computers are being used to accomplish the task—repeat work remains. Let us "raise the standard" again in the form of a question: Can the computing demands be integrated into the vehicle's onboard computer and eliminate the simulation requirements?

The response to this new challenge came in the form of a revision of the vehicle's control equation and logic to better account for the physics (causal factors of airflow and temperature). With this, the vehicle's logic internally adjusts and iterates the settings for varied airflow conditions to converge on solutions for each unique circumstance in a fraction of second. By this means, an engineer would be able to measure and incorporate a new model's basic heat-transfer characteristics into the vehicle computer's settings once and deliver refined results without using an external simulation program (or extensive iterative physical testing). In retrospect, it could easily be acknowledged that the earlier condition was "broken" compared to the new proficiency of meeting the elevated standard.

When "If it isn't broken, don't fix it" is the mindset, it tends to quiet the interpretive-intelligence genre, and responses are conventional with the intent of not disrupting the unbroken state. With this "not broken" mindset, there is a tendency to accept only one established response nomination, which is the character of the passive-intelligence genre. When this tendency is rewarded with successful responses to challenges, one may conclude that the interpretive-intelligence genre's multiple response resource nominations are not necessary.

However, if the condition becomes broken, a new response is necessary to meet the challenge of returning it to an unbroken state. In some cases, a person may have previously seen how to repair this condition and simply apply what they remembered as their successful response (passive intelligence). Another person that is familiar with how things work may readily recognize which contributing factor adjustment is needed to correct the situation (active intelligence). These two types of simple intelligent responses are likely quite sufficient when contending with isolated challenges.

If the corrective response influences other coexisting challenges, those challenges are used to "raise the standard" that may demand more than a passive-intelligence response or a single causal-factor adjustment. When "If it isn't broken, raise your standards" is the mindset, it tends to activate the interpretive-intelligence genre that enables recognition of improvement opportunities. Essentially, the state of being broken is assumed to be the result of raising the standards, and this requires a new response. Often, a new response is very difficult for the "unbroken" mindset to accept because of their lack of recognition of a shortfall. This presents another challenge of breaking through the barriers that the passive-intelligence genre presents.

When dealing with others, it is advantageous to recognize their interpretation disposition to facilitate effective interactions. This means that a grasp of how they interpret and respond to challenges enables us to treat their behavior as a causal factor related to updating a response for the better. For example, if you are sharing a new idea, a person that is passive-intelligence driven needs emphasis on the familiar aspects of the idea. The aim is to make as little as possible novel to the person so that only a very small venture into the unknown is required to receive the idea. Conversely, an active-intelligence-driven person responds best to an appeal that relates causal factors to the new idea. In this way, the new idea is simply a logical consequence of arranging understood causal factors perhaps in a novel way. I once had a boss that had a passive-intelligence expectation of a result that my test activity should yield. When my results did not match his expectation, I offered an analysis based on familiar causal factors that indicated that my results were reasonable. As he read my analysis, he said, "I believe this and this, so logically I have to believe this result, although it doesn't feel like I should..." This caused a shift in his interpretation framework to better include pertinent causal factors from the bias of his passive-intelligence genre.

Given that the predominant human mindset lies in the passive-intelligence genre, we are very much biased by our unquestioned training. Similarly, the artificially intelligent devices that rely on the passive-intelligence genre will carry a bias. This was not always the case for us. When children are building their interpretation frameworks, they can assume very little from past experience out of necessity (they have almost no past to reference). A child is full of unending questions, it seems. They are examining each circumstance and struggling to grasp how to deal with it through a cascade of whys. As we mature, we are placed in an education process that tends to suppress our questioning skill by giving us the answers to the questions that are prejudged to be important for our passive-intelligence genre's resources. As a result, we use the passive-intelligence resources to conduct our lives for the most part. In this way, most of us have become desensitized to our surroundings after learning to ignore "unimportant" things.

Thus, there is a strong tendency to react to our environment in repeatable and predictable ways. For example, we may sit in the same seat in a classroom every day. We may travel to work the same way every day at the same time. These activities become automatic and almost thoughtless. Do these types of reactions to our situations have value? Of course, they do. Are they creative? They are absolutely not. Do they need to be creative? The key word here is "need." If one does not perceive a need to change a response to the environment, there is no motivation to react differently. Personally, I have a favorite dish at one of my preferred restaurants. As a result, my ordering process is very simple and familiar. In fact, the wait staff has come to expect my selection. Does this mean that there is only one meal option of merit at the restaurant? I seriously doubt it. Yet I act as if there is only one. If I considered the culinary attributes of my typical choice that are most appealing to me, I am grasping for the causal relationships that make a good meal for me. Perhaps the texture of the vegetables and crispness of the breading on the meat and tenderness of meat along with the spiciness level of the sauces are factors. Once I figure out what I like, I can use that as an interpretation framework for other dishes on the menu. The sampling of new meal choices is an active-intelligence function that looks to confirm my "factors" of a good dish. If I find a new favorite after this investigation, guess what? Yes, I will probably order that choice every time hereafter. This example shows how we may be willing to investigate for a while, and at some point, we decide that we have done enough and simply copy previous experiences in the future. One of my favorite jokes identifies this tendency. It involves a mother and daughter cutting off the ends of a ham prior to cooking for a thanksgiving dinner. The young daughter dared to question why. Her mother said she was not certain, but it is how grandmother has always done it. So they asked grandma about it. She said the ham wouldn't fit in her small pan if she didn't trim it.

This quieting tendency of our interpretive-intelligence genre gets occasional shocks when discomfort stirs our awareness. This can happen when an unexpected event or surprising information does not find a comfortable connection in our passive-intelligence genre. An extreme example can be found when a family member aggressively pursues a cure for a disease afflicting a loved one. The distress triggered the awaking. In order for us to deal with it, we need to interpret what we observe. In this state, we begin acting like an inquisitive child as we gather all information that we can to grasp and handle the challenge that the new situation presents. It is not childish in a derogatory sense; rather, it is the awakening of the interpretive-intelligence and active-intelligence genres that children often possess. For example, if a person perceives a strong need to get home faster, they may find alternate routes and departure times, or even alternative ride choices to accomplish the task. These situations effectively "raise the standard" for the response. This subsequent awakening dynamic may be possible for all challenges. Is there a need to do things better, faster, cheaper, or entirely eliminate the need to do the thing itself? These questions trigger the interpretive-intelligence genre to nominate candidate choices to respond to a need. This awakening can be deliberately sustained by keeping various questions in the forefront of our thinking: What would make the commute easier? How can this situation be less frustrating? Why is the carpet always dirty here? Why do we always have quality problems in this process? Why am I nearly always late for meetings? Why do I always sit in the same place in a classroom? How can I make my relationships better? How can I best use my talents? Is there a better answer? Why do we have these traditions? For many of the questions above, we might be simply doing what we have commonly done and never reconsider them. If so, we are functioning out of a habit and the embedded solutions from our passive-intelligence genre.

Another source of "raise the standards" or "don't fix it" triggers may come from supplemental interpretation frameworks used by others. The external assessments from those frameworks tend to fall into three basic classifications: encouragement, discouragement, and disregard. The classification for encouragement and acceptance supports intelligent behavior to contend with challenges. This reinforcing interpretation framework is founded on a shared belief that a challenge can be met (raising the standard). This alignment bolsters the intelligent function and fosters a high-achieving mindset in the recipient. A hallmark of this can be observed in wishing someone well and offering support. That expression can inspire confidence and strengthen the desire to succeed in the person receiving it. The other two classifications can be taken as thought poisons by choice.

If taken in this way, the poisons may lead to an end to intelligent activity regarding challenge achievement (leave things as they are).

The next classification covers discouragement and rejection. In the simplest form, an assessor's interpretation framework's criteria are not met and a rejection can follow. That rejection is typically discouraging to the one being assessed. The one being assessed can elect to believe the assessor and end the pursuit of the challenge or to take the feedback in order to "raise the standards" for future performance assessments. Consider a person that tries out for a sport and fails to make the team. This rejection can be the end, or it can be a call to improve their performance. Unfortunately, many times the discouragement is expressed from flawed interpretation frameworks. When an inventor receives discouraging feedback, flawed and incompetent interpretation frameworks may be exposed. Frequently, the obvious and weak-minded judgment that "no one else has done this before" is the only reason given to reject a novel idea. Had a good reason for rejection been offered, it would enable clarification of the actual challenge and an opportunity for a more appropriate response. In another example of interpretation incompetence, a university's guidance counselor discouraged my wife from embarking on a second career as a nurse. He likely projected an assumption (passive intelligence) based the history of unsuccessful people that tried to become a nurse into her situation. Undaunted, and to her credit, she disregarded the counselor's discouragement, excelled academically, and supported the medical community's response to COVID-19 as a nurse. His inability to interpret my wife's skills, motivation, and past accomplishments was at the root of his flawed assessment. In another case, an uncle might want to be the most successful person in the family and belittles the attempts and accomplishments of other family members. This flawed interpretation framework comes from jealousy and is deliberately incompetent, discouraging, and should be ignored; otherwise, thought poisoning may occur.

The disregard classification is for a neutral response, which essentially is a suspension of judgment. Unfortunately, the recipient of this interaction typically believes that there are reservations on the part of the one assessing or that they don't care. This suspension of judgment does not necessarily mean indifference to the situation or discouragement, but such an interpretation presents a risk to harming intelligent action by the recipient. Individuals that tend to have a binary view (some call it black and white) recognize a lack of an enthusiastic endorsement and are discouraged. The fact is that this classification makes neither an encouraging nor discouraging assessment. In this classification, the assessor is giving their interpretation framework an opportunity to form and develop prior to making a judgment. This follows from recognition that the maturity of their ability to judge with their framework is currently inadequate. In my opinion, this thoughtful pause is underused in many human interactions, perhaps because of this risk. As a result, we often pretend to know things based on our passive-intelligence resources and jump to rapid conclusions without interpreting very well and potentially make uninformed assessments.

A job interview provides an example of how a personal interpretation framework on the part of the interviewer may influence the hiring process. Perhaps a candidate with exceptional job-pertinent credentials is seen as a threat to the hiring manager that has lesser credentials. In this case, the manager may discourage the candidate from joining the team or perhaps simply reject them to protect their standing within the company. In addition, personal style, appearance, or other compatibility markers may play the role of providing a personal-preference interpretation framework that competes with the hiring challenge's appropriate interpretation framework (i.e., he rudely chewed gum during the entire interview). Nepotism is another example of a personal-preference interpretation framework disrupting an appropriate interpretation framework for the task. Rather than selecting a candidate based on merit, acceptance is essentially guaranteed because of a relationship between the candidate and interviewer. When we interpret the use of personal-preference interpretation frameworks to be unfair, we are rejecting the behavior with our own "fairness" interpretation framework since it does not meet our requirement to serve the true purpose of the interview of finding the most capable person for the job. (The fact that a prospective employee has a mouth full of gum should not prevent them from being the best candidate, unless it is a speaking job.)

Upgrading the passive-intelligence resources is prudent, given our propensity to rely on them. As a means to detect best practices, a company may conduct a competitive benchmark investigation to find how others deliver similar products or services. This passive-intelligence-genre research style connects new response resources to familiar triggers. This means that the research findings reveal alternative responses that deal with a shared challenge among competitors. At one time, I was asked to consult on a research project that involved a new approach to a problem that was based on a benchmark discovery. When I examined the content of the competitor's technology, it was clearly at a disadvantage for cost and performance responsiveness (the main factors related to the challenge). I pointed this out to the project leader, who justified this activity by telling me that a competitor was doing it, so we should do it too. It wasn't too much later that news came out that the competitor abandoned that technology, which was used as the main reason to similarly terminate. In effect, the interpretation was left to the competitor. In such a case, this "following" mindset ensures that the competitor is the leader, even into failure.

In another example, consider a challenge to make a given soft drink more appealing to more people. One option is to copy a successful competitor's drink and hope to get their favorable results (benchmark). This action will make the updated drink an alternative in the marketplace. Management might be comfortable with this update since the success in the market for that flavor has already been demonstrated. However, because of the similarity, it is not reasonable to expect to be more successful than the competitor. Rather than simply taking a benchmark competitor's approach, what if we could make an excellent new drink that would become the top performer? It would be preferred to employ the active-intelligence approach that depends on a grasp the causal relationships or factors that lead to a successful soft drink. If one truly knew the physiological mechanisms that could create an optimal pleasurable sense of taste for a soft drink, the research could aim at confirming the blending of ingredients to achieve high performance through those mechanisms. If these mechanisms are not well understood, one can test those mechanisms to determine how they behave. With that knowledge, sensitivities can be found and optimized. This can be done by means of using the plateau-cliff principle to test responses. For example, a drink can be formulated to be too sweet or not sweet enough. Other sensitivity related to carbonation level and other key ingredients may also have their own acceptable content limits. To that end, a confirmation taste test experiment with various formulations is conducted with a significant number of persons. In this case, the response sensitivity to the selected ingredients is tested to help refine the recipe. Further, the competitor's benchmark drink can be tested as a market-viability reference. If the new formulation performs better than this benchmark drink in the taste testing, that fact may persuade management that it can outperform the competitor in the market. If this task were delegated to our artificially intelligent device, Allies, she would try all combinations of all possible nontoxic ingredients in a taste test as a means to judge pertinence to find the best recipe. It is this feedback from confirmation testing and the interpretation of how to adjust the recipe that enables this novel response's pertinence recognition and proficiency.

Different challenge interpretations are not always competing; rather, they reflect separate and valid points of view. In some cases, the interpretation frameworks may be merged to enable high proficiency. The consolidated interpretation framework enables identification of pertinent resources so that all concerns may be appropriately addressed. When we form effective task teams, we blend multiple perspectives into a single interpretation framework that ideally gleans the most important content from all members with the intent of addressing diverse and unique needs related to the shared challenge. In a simple example, two people are attempting to make a decision about a shared meal selection with two different ways to interpret food choices. One may have food allergies and will, out of necessity, seek to avoid certain otherwise appealing foods. This person is challenged to be comfortable after the meal where others might not be. The second person does not have this restriction and has a set of favored food choices that the first person might need to reject. These coexisting interpretation frameworks are related to the same challenge, and the response choice must be pertinent to both frameworks to meet the challenge. To that end, there are some "overlap" food choices that can be agreed to be pertinent to each of them.

When one can account for multiple interpretation frameworks, there is an optimization of the response that ideally generates "wins" for all concerned. For instance, a person working on a project may not want to be interrupted by expert support. They want to be able to own the result. This was the case when one of my engineers had a somewhat difficult technical challenge occur in our area of responsibility. Personally, I enjoyed solving this type of problem and had distinguished myself in doing so in the past. I conveyed that I would happily support issue resolution, but doing it alone would likely be very satisfying and enjoyable. Thus, I left the support decision to the engineer. This is a management example of accommodating the interpretation framework of a subordinate with the aim of career enrichment. We shared the goal of fixing the issue, but how we conducted ourselves in the process served additional needs. This approach to meeting the main challenge accounted for another coexisting challenge and perspective in the process. This characteristic of responding in a manner that satisfies multiple challenges and their related interpretation frameworks is a sign of a mature and intelligent function that enables a wide range of successes through improved response selection that serves each of them.

The dominance and convenience of the passive-intelligence genre has certainly made our lives easier, and it is readily adapted to artificially intelligent devices. It is simply based on experience. However, the passive-intelligence genre presents an obstacle to progress by holding to the familiar as a distinction. The most proficient individuals do not rely entirely on the passive-intelligence genre, and they do so by probing and asking questions of what many may consider to be decided (keeping their interpretive-intelligence genre awake). When those questions do not have previously known answers, the active-intelligence genre can be used to seek and adjust resources or factors that contribute to contending with the challenge.

The scientific method is a good example of this probing and testing of contributing factors through the formation of hypotheses. These hypotheses are equivalent to interpretation frameworks that recognize causal factors and, through testing, get refined. The dissimilarity of the interpretation frameworks that support the passive-intelligence genre or active-intelligence genre can be a source of great conflict since the trusted ways may need to be discarded. This is true among individuals as well as at an organizational level.

CHAPTER 10

COLLECTIVE INTELLIGENCE

The advantage of the (collective) intelligence of teams versus that of an individual was the topic of a training seminar. In the seminar, a test created by social psychologist Jay Hall (~1962) called NASA Exercise: Survival on the Moon was given. The challenge was to rank a list of fifteen assets by value for a task of making it back to the mother ship after missing (and crashing en route to) a landing point on the moon. If a respondent ranked the assets exactly as NASA did, it generated a deviation score of zero. If, for example, only the top two were out of order, each position would score a demerit of one each for a total of two. If one asset ranked ten places from the NASA rank, that item was awarded ten demerit points. In order to do well, the somewhat familiar interpretation framework for survival on the Earth needed to be adapted to the environment of the moon. In such a case, the absence of oxygen and the lack of a polarized magnetic field on the moon made a box of matches and a magnetic compass virtually useless. After individuals in the seminar completed their tests without knowledge of the results, they were assembled into several separate small groups to negotiate the rankings among themselves to complete a single test for each group. The results of this exercise were intended to demonstrate that a group is more proficient than an individual through comparison of the test scores. This premise generally held up with the team scores being better than the individual's scores within that team, except for an individual in one group. In addition, that group's score was much better than all of the other groups. The administrator of the seminar disregarded this as an anomaly, and the message that teams are better than individuals remained the paradigm of choice for this training session. It is reasonable to believe that the blending of various interpretation frameworks has potential to be more insightful than that of a single individual. However, if through negotiation the blending does not improve the interpretation framework, it is easy to imagine how this "anomaly" was created. In this case, the insightful perspective was in the minority of the subgroup, and the consensus voting to complete the test compromised the top performer's overall proficiency in the group's score. In addition, the top-performing individual's interpretation framework elevated the subgroup's relative proficiency because of a better overall grasp of the differences between the Earth and the moon during the negotiation process. This seminar's experience demonstrated the interpretive-intelligence genre's resource-selection proficiency through the ranking of the assets (by pertinence). It did not demonstrate that a group's interpretation is always better than an individual's interpretation as was assumed.

From the seminar's result observations, collective intelligence appears to "normalize" the interpretation framework as it tends to resist influence from outlier perspectives. The improvement of group scores versus individual scores for all of the individuals except for one essentially discarded some of the poor thinking that was not collectively shared. Similarly, a portion of the top individual's perspective was not completely accepted by the subgroup, which discarded some exceptional thinking. In other words, the same group-think dynamic that at least partially discards poor thinking also functions to disregard narrowly held exceptional thinking en route to a somewhat competent interpretation. This phenomenon is familiar to those that bring unique, expert, or specialized perspectives into a group setting when contending with creative and innovative challenges. Typically, members of the group have a large constituency of passive-intelligence agents including those in authority. This means that any consensus or leader-based decisions will likely be from familiar passive-intelligence resources. Thus, the enlightened individuals, who are using the other two intelligence genres, are impeded by the group's established interpretation frameworks and their inflexibility or inability to grasp alternative perspectives. A similar inertia is experienced when new ideas are being "sold" to those that have their thinking based in passive-intelligence paradigms.

Based on the premise of the moon-challenge seminar, it may be somewhat disconcerting to acknowledge that an individual can surpass the performance of an entire organization. However, it should not be so surprising when one notes that the majority of scientific and technical breakthroughs historically have a single individual (or at most a few persons) that are given credit for them. Further, the most appreciated artistic and literary accomplishments tend to have their origin in an individual's unique perspective (interpretation framework). The many accomplishments of Galileo Galilei are among the most impressive examples of this in the sciences. In a very literal way, his telescopes enabled an interpretation framework that others without them could not grasp. He was able to track celestial object motion and mathematically anticipate their positions. With these data, he could draw conclusions about the nature of their behavior. Later, Newton and Einstein launched their notable contributions with the benefit of the interpretation framework that Galileo cultivated (they cited his foundational contribution). These enlightened individuals readily surpassed the existing conventional wisdom through the use of their superior specialized interpretation frameworks.

When specialized interpretation frameworks are needed, blending of their insights with lesser interpretation frameworks is foolish. For example, if you enlist a medical surgeon's help, you don't want them to compromise their training based on the most popular opinions of nonmedical experts.

When we form organizations with the intent of addressing a complex challenge, we typically reach out to others for their expertise (and interpretation frameworks) and skills to help us. For example, this could mean calling an ambulance, a doctor, and an insurance company to address a health issue. When this is done, several distinct roles are defined that carry unique specialized interpretation frameworks without significant intermingling. This respect for expertise boundaries enables high proficiency without normalizing and subsequent degradation of each expert's interpretation framework. These organizations tend to have a hierarchy of specialized functions that may have a multitude of specific tasks associated with each one. Some functions depend on direction or are interconnected to the responses of other functions. This gives rise to authority structures that may mature into an organizational culture through time. This is familiar to us from the beginning of our education process, in which we experience being trained by persons that are in a position of authority that enforce rules related to our behavior. As children, we are not in a position to challenge their authority and tend to simply follow their lead. As a means to secure our compliance when we abide by their rules, we may be rewarded, or at the least, avoid punishment. During our development in this setting, we may form bonds and expectations with our teachers as our performance aligns with their beliefs, approaches, and lessons. In other words, we are rewarded with their approval when we reflect their interpretation frameworks and responses to them through high scores on tests, etc. Given our years of exposure in this environment, we become accustomed to being led by authority figures that carry a perception of expertise and high capability. For many of us, this pattern is reinforced during early employment. The leaders in a company are granted authority over the employees much like the teachers that readied us to begin working. Successful employees tend to achieve mastery of the organization's specialized cultural approaches and conventional ideas that have led to meeting the company's objectives in the eyes of their superiors. Additionally, we may choose to participate in a variety of organizations that carry unique cultures with belief paradigms to help address other personal and collective needs.

Many organizations carry a primary or a coexisting challenge to instill an interpretation framework in their membership, and that leads to a cultural bias. When successful, the organization becomes populated with persons that share beliefs, approaches, and ideals. Evidence of this is clear when we recognize the existence of a variety of distinct academic disciplines, societies, religious, and political institutions that carry differing interpretation perspectives. This mission or challenge to persuade members to a more enlightened perspective can be a great service to their well-being. Aside from the sharing of paradigms, a sense of belonging can be comforting to the lonely or marginalized when they are embraced for having a shared interpretation framework with others. For example, persons in some degree of crisis (over the cliff) may reach a healthy plateau by adopting an interpretation framework of a religion. They have found peace, purpose, and fulfillment in the organization. Rehabilitation support groups for addicts function similarly. The transition to a healthy plateau can be significant, and even lifesaving. Thus, altering our interpretation frameworks can help us proficiently contend with the variety of challenges that we face. When a healthy plateau is achieved, the "broken" state has been remedied. However, healthier plateaus may be possible. A choice to attempt to preserve that condition or to grow from that condition (raise the standard) is to be made. If growth is selected, it is very possible that the next step abandons, to some degree, a number of the elements of the supportive organization's interpretation framework. Should the organization's culture be intolerant of that growth, the organization may have simply served as part of the path to a better interpretation framework. Thus, the organization may need to be at least partially left behind to grow to a healthier plateau. It is clear that the culture of our organizations of choice play a very large role in our lives and in our relationships with others.

With this cultural emphasis, the members of an organization may be somewhat inclined to pursue status and identity within that culture in addition to the pursuit of the organization's mission. This observation leads to a hypothesis that an organization's culture results from blending of the organization's mission and the member's organizational aspirations. Let us call this the M-O continuum (Mission-Organization). If the culture is fully mission driven (M), the members tend to be selfless and operate on principles that guide the organization to accomplishing its mission. An example of this happens when a school teacher purchases supplies for the class with personal resources. The mission of education is the motivation behind this donor's act. In a more extreme case, a soldier's life might be forfeit for the benefit of a military mission. When the culture is organization based (O), a member emphasizes their standing within it and attempts to preserve the organization, which also protects their status. In this situation, high-achieving individuals in the organization's culture (i.e., by title and granted authority) may be mistakenly perceived as leaders. These individuals function as manipulators with characteristic actions supporting status preservation and political advancement as their priority. As with any continuum, a blending of these two extremes may be found in any given circumstance or in the actions of any given member of an organization. If this blending hypothesis holds, it will serve as an interpretation framework to help assess organizational behavior and its associated collective intelligence. Accordingly, it follows that an organization will have intelligent actions directed at its mission by true leaders and, by definition, unintelligent actions that are not necessarily well directed at the mission by manipulators that tend to serve organizational aspirations.

The distinction between leadership and manipulation in an organization is revealed in the action priorities and the values that are expressed. If the accomplishment of a goal or mission of the organization is the priority, the conventionality (cultural norms) of the means to address it is of little importance. If culture or status within the organization is the priority, it is not entirely acceptable to accomplish the goal in an unconventional way. In effect, the responses and interpretations need to be conventional to keep the manipulators comfortable and unthreatened. The threat to a manipulator's authority arises from a relative competition with anyone who might do a better job, which can only follow from doing something in a different way particularly when it is in good alignment with the organization's mission. In response to the threat, the manipulator may choose to abuse power and issue punishment for behaviors that actually improve the organization's condition. To illustrate, a colleague of mine was being considered for a promotion in a human-resource-department-led meeting. At the outset, a vice president declared that he will not allow this promotion because my colleague had circumvented one of his decisions. To my surprise, the conflict involved the orientation of a desk for one of my colleague's subordinates. This "offense" revealed my colleague's willingness to serve higher goals of employee retention and satisfaction rather than simply following convention. In this instance, the manipulator's "in control" self-interest was not adequately accounted for by my colleague. Years later, after that particular VP retired, my colleague was promoted. In another case, I witnessed a manipulator forming a plan for retaliation against a counterpart that did a better job serving the company's mission. This manipulator revealed a lack of interest in the mission of the company and was choosing to spend resources to damage it and a principled colleague.

This unhealthy mission-versus-organization dynamic has confronted humanity for a long time. Common historical knowledge suggests that Galileo was convicted and imprisoned for a strong suspicion of heresy for his belief that the sun is at the center of the solar system in the 1600s. This radical position was in direct conflict with an authoritarian organization's notion that Earth is at the center. At that time, the organization appeared to assert itself as the holder of all truth, and it provided the interpretation frameworks for all things for its members. This was certainly a noble mission for an organization. Yet, when an opportunity to gather truth presented itself (which supports the organization's mission), the organization reacted as if it was threatened through retaliation. If the leadership accepted Galileo's interpretation, it would be an admission of fallibility. This could cause the organization to lose standing with its membership and a weakening of the leader's authority. The authority in the organization was manipulator based with a strong organization allegiance as it displayed unintelligent behavior related to an important mission of the organization. It is easy to imagine that the political environment within that organization would not permit internal corrections to their "unquestioned truths," given the harsh treatment that they dispensed to outside objectors. This same influence was observed by business and quality consultant Dr. Deming in *Out of the Crisis* (1991). Although he did not recognize the organization's manipulators in his teachings, he saw the vested interests of the resident leadership as an obstacle to change. He suggested that most constructive change to an organization has its origin in outside influences.

It is not uncommon for an organization to begin with a mission-driven blend (M) position in the continuum when critical concerns are involved. At an organization's inception, the mission (purpose) is usually established when "over the cliff" circumstances are recognized. An organization's constructive leadership actions take these situations onto a healthy plateau in response to the concern or it completely resolves the concern. To refresh, there are mainly two mission or challenge types: First, a challenge that is renewed, ongoing, or open-ended. This type of challenge requires routine maintenance. Many such organizations are aimed at supporting well-being, and they defend against the certainty or chance of deterioration or damage for these challenges. A second type of challenge is called a close-ended challenge, which means that when these challenges are met, they are finished. The primary difference of the close-ended challenge type from an ongoing challenge type is that no residual maintenance process is required when it is addressed. In the close-ended case, the importance of the organization might be short lived, while the ongoing challenges inherently have sustained relevance for the organization.

Ongoing challenges that exist on a healthy plateau do not have a need for the organization's leadership to make corrective actions until a departure from it occurs. In this state, the organization's leaders become nearly irrelevant and unimportant. Further, the effectiveness of reaching the plateau can even trivialize the organization that achieved it. In the past, the United Auto Workers Union made great strides in improving working conditions and compensation for its members in manufacturing plants. The resultant improved practices became a new standard for doing business in the automotive industry through the years. Competition for workers helped secure the progress, since workers with a choice would gladly change companies for better wages and working conditions. Thus, this competition assumed the role of maintaining the healthy plateau, and intervention by the UAW leadership became unnecessary to sustain it. In general, the UAW Union had effectively addressed major concerns and only minor concerns remained—it achieved a healthy plateau. In this circumstance, the membership began to question paying union dues to support an organization that provided very little additional benefit to them. This lack of enthusiasm made the UAW organization weaker as workers in many new plants elected not to be members. In a related way, the American Dental Association effectively campaigned for prevention of tooth decay. As a result, the need for dentists has been significantly reduced by means of the effective preventative care that they encouraged. These are good examples of how effective organizations move to a diminished state by making real progress on their missions. This "reduction of relevance" effect applies when an individual or organization takes an "over the cliff" condition onto a healthy plateau. Further, when a close-ended challenge is permanently met, irrelevance naturally follows as the need for the organization has been erased.

From personal experience in an engineering research job, I inherited a process that was dominated by physical testing and laborious data processing that required a large test team and roughly seven months of effort per year. Further, this job was a large reason to utilize (build or rent) test facilities that supported the company's vehicle-development activities. Through a new process, a large portion of physical research activities was replaced with in-house mathematical simulation models; specialized, focused testing procedures; and novel computerized data-processing methods. With that approach, our team reduced a seven-month job down to around three weeks with a fraction of the staff. The "seven month" process that I inherited had considerable overtime compensation, and the company paid travel expenses for those that participated in the physical data-gathering phase. Thus, our improvement took away some of the personal benefits that the staff enjoyed. These changes established a new healthier plateau that did not consume excessive company resources and, in fact, added content that expanded on the research aspects of our job. These company-benefitting accomplishments led to recognition, for a short time. As time went on, our routine high achievement was assumed to be straightforward, ordinary, and not noteworthy. To combat this complacency, we developed innovative ideas with the time surplus we created; otherwise, we could have easily been downsized (diminished). This added focus led to some extraordinary contributions that kept our department relevant and visible to our upper management as well as garnering recognition outside of the company. Later, as an engineering manager, I wanted my department to deliver consistent excellent results and to improve our efficiency during the process. To that end, developing the capability of my staff and leveraging resources in creative ways to support our group's mission was our team's focus. At some point, a performance plateau was achieved that was stable and highly dependent on my team's very capable members and refined processes. Basically, together we fostered contributors that did not require "saving" who reliably delivered outcomes as they handled difficulties very well on their own. Although our contribution was critical to the commercial viability of our products, our proficiency seemed to dilute our importance. In this way, we evolved into a state of being part of the "assumed" sufficient conditions that enabled delivery of our product. (Recall the example of assuming the sufficient condition of electrical power availability to light a room when a switch is tripped.) Prior to fading into the background in this way, our issues were proximate causes that prevented us from delivering our products to the market. At that time, our "rescue missions" were highly visible, and our accomplishments were widely recognized and rewarded. However, in this new state, we did not require rescue missions, and our reward-recognition opportunities were reduced.

Further, this high-performing team no longer required a strong "leadership" presence or demonstration on my part. My role was becoming irrelevant. Our processes had largely achieved the aim of low maintenance. One could interpret the impact of these displays of competence and that of the UAW described earlier as follows: *The accomplishments of true and effective leadership involving organizations are destined for a perception of insignificance and being trivialized.*

For ongoing challenges, when the achievements of effective leadership are trivialized, it indicates that a healthy plateau has been attained. Those in positions of authority wish to preserve this condition and often shift their attention to organizational behaviors aimed at sustaining it (the *O* of the M-O continuum). When this happens, the leadership functionally appears to be afraid of disrupting the healthy plateau and has lost the courage to improve it. One could say, "If it isn't broken, don't fix it." In this way, the organization's operational interpretation framework resembles that of an entrenched symbolist that is not accepting of alternative viewpoints or approaches. This position in the continuum tends to replace the mission-aimed intelligence functions of its members with a strong passive-intelligence connection to the new "preservation" culture. Evidence of this occurs when the staff attempts to advance the company's mission (make an even better plateau) and finds that those actions (and related changes) are unwelcome. If effective leadership addresses a close-ended challenge, the mission is completed, and this trivializes the organization itself (i.e., it becomes suddenly obsolete). In such a case, the manipulators may attempt to create and exploit artificial relevance for the organization to preserve their status within it.

Artificial relevance can be created through the use of a variety of techniques. First, not achieving a healthy plateau or to postpone mission achievement for a close-ended challenge can sustain the need for the organization. A second technique exploits poor challenge interpretations. Basically, the organization's primary mission is underserved while a different agenda is being pursued. In the case of a close-ended challenge, it may be falsely interpreted as an ongoing challenge that sustains the organization. A third way is to create a bonding within the membership through association of the organization's mission with shared attributes. This bonding can sustain the organization as long as the shared attributes remain. A fourth technique, rather than not achieving the mission, is the suppression of progress information to take advantage of those that do not confirm (reinterpret) that the mission has been accomplished. Thus, the reasons for the organization to exist are still perceived to be relevant to its members. Each of these techniques comes with a cost because of the unnecessary nature of artificial relevance.

The first technique of not delivering a healthy plateau enables organizations to exploit those that the organization serves as a means to sustain itself. From a tangible product example, it has been said that light bulbs can be engineered to last almost indefinitely. If they were, the need for new light bulbs would be greatly diminished. Thus, designed-in (useful life) obsolescence for the light bulbs can be used to sustain the need for the industry by not delivering a near-permanent response to the challenge, making it an ongoing challenge. A variety of consumer products demonstrate this approach as is reflected in the comment that "they don't make them like they used to" by customers and service persons. By means of example, suppose a light-bulb vendor is very self-serving. Imagine that their light bulbs last only a few weeks. If this is the state of the industry, there will be a huge demand for replacement light bulbs, which is great for the vendors. In this example, the general public will suffer the inconvenience, costs, and pollution created by sustaining relevance in this way.

As an example of the second technique of poor challenge interpretations, consider that a higher learning institution is sustained by its reputation for education proficiency. When an institution excludes individuals that are most in need of education and only admits top students with proven aptitude, it is not serving an education mission comprehensively. The fact is that the top students will likely succeed even with poor instruction. As a result, because of the bias of their admission standards, the institution is able to graduate high-performing individuals. This enables the institution to pursue the "reputation" part of their mission. For instance, a professor may delegate teaching responsibilities to less-educated individuals in order to pursue valuable research that strengthens the reputation and the external influence of the institution. The poor challenge interpretation is to build reputation rather than to enhance education proficiency. As long as the top students continue to purchase reputation, the organization can be sustained. The conversion of a close-ended challenge to an ongoing challenge may also be part of the poor challenge interpretation in this technique. The alleged need for maintenance and prevention are good examples of this when a concern is resolved. When a person purchases a small appliance, for example, it can be checked for adjustments periodically, for a fee.

The functioning appliance meets a close-ended challenge as it serves its intent. This challenge is converted into the prevention of the loss of that function, which is an ongoing challenge. Similarly, a cosmetics company may have a product that heals a skin condition. It might be recommended to use this product routinely to prevent a future recurrence. The close-ended challenge was to repair the skin. The ongoing challenge is to maintain the cured condition, which helps sustain the relevance of the company. Unfortunately, with poor-challenge-interpretations, resources are not well directed. For example, it would serve the public better to have proficient education practices, dedicated research institutions, maintenance free appliances, and permanent cures for afflictions.

The third artificial relevance technique collects organization membership based on attributes, and those attributes are associated with the organization's mission. The shared attributes serve as a bonding agent for the organization. One unifying attribute class is to suggest an inadequacy on the part of those that the organization serves. When that perceived inadequacy (often, but not always, a thought poison) is accepted, the members or beneficiaries of an organization's services can be unified in their shared need to erase their shortfall in the care of the organization and its leadership. Thus, sustaining the perception of inadequacy is central to the efforts of the organization's manipulators, in order to retain relevance. Consider an overriding premise that you are human (unifying attribute) and flawed is used to form an organization: "Our organization has the answers to address your flaws." A reasonable expectation is that this organization will ideally resolve your imperfect condition. If they did correct the flaws, you wouldn't need them any longer—they would have accomplished their mission. However, a manipulative organization will not assess your improvement and will not graduate you to an unflawed status. Instead, the organization emphasizes and reminds you of your flawed state to sustain the inadequacy perception. Further, if progress is made, they will point out that you remain human, and therefore, you are flawed. Thus, logically, you must escape the "human" attribute to realize the organization's mission. In a similar manner, a generalized inadequate economic condition may be correlated in some way to an ethnic group by an organization. Correction of the causal factors that lead to prosperity for that group should be a supportive organization's actual mission. Yet the organization's relevance is sustained by maintaining that the reason for the group's economic status is due to being part of that ethnic group (an attribute). Just like in the "humans are flawed" example that requires an exit from humanity, the only logical means to meet the economic challenge is to change ethnic groups. It is the organization's fallacious attempt to persuade the membership that the associated attributes are causal factors of the mission that holds the organization together. In this state, these organizations tend to prioritize growing their membership and the organization itself. They rest near the organizational extreme of the M-O continuum primarily for their own benefit, fostered by a pretense of an actual mission that will not be achieved by intent. Clearly, these are dysfunctional organizations. Examples of this can be recognized in religious, public, charitable, and political organizations that primarily serve their cultural constructs and, upon examination, make little progress on a mission that would diminish their relevance. This inability to reduce relevance suggests that manipulators dominate the organization's positions of authority. When attributes of distinction are part of an organization's reason for existence, it is a red flag for detecting the service of an imitation mission. That mission is designed to deliver artificial relevance and member exploitation.

From the example of the United Auto Workers Union, we can see multiple techniques being used to promote artificial relevance as it progressed through the M-O continuum to the organizational extreme. The organization's mission came from widely recognized need to correct poor-compensation and working conditions to a fair and equitable state. This placed the organization firmly in mission mode (M). This organization did not succumb to the first technique of underachieving on the mission. However, with the mission of the organization being largely accomplished, previously well-intentioned and effective leaders in the mission part of the continuum could sensibly become stakeholders in the organization because of their meaningful successes. This climate is well suited to cause these leaders to evolve into manipulators as they begin to serve the organization part of the continuum. In order to sustain relevance, the manipulators may exploit the membership's quieted interpretive-intelligence genre. During mission completion, the culture of the organization developed an "us against them" mindset as many confrontations were required to resolve concerns. The embedding of this oppositional belief quieted the member's interpretive-intelligence genre, and this suspends any current condition reassessment. As a result, the sustaining premise of the organization became the passive-intelligence position that the membership is not being treated fairly and that they have an adversary. The "us against them" mindset is a bonding agent for the organization. To nurture this, it requires an irrelevant attribute of distinction to sustain it, since the mindset is largely no longer valid. The manipulators could cite the fact that the plant supervisors wear neckties: "They are different from us, and we will continue to protect you from them (so pay your dues)." It doesn't really matter if the supervisors are actually not against the members; they are simply different. In the absence of membership confirmation and reassessment, a manipulator can additionally perpetuate the over-the-cliff inadequacy story (the fourth technique). This could include squelching communication of progress assessments that would reflect the organization's achievements. With this, artificial relevance is created and the organization depends on it for survival. In this example, a "club" of similar people without a real mission is the essence of the organization. The close-ended challenge of compensation/condition fairness was altered to an ongoing persistent challenge of being different from plant supervisors, which is a poor challenge interpretation.

In some cases, delay in challenge resolution is a result of incompetence, which is not the first artificial relevance technique—the relevance is real. In general, the incompetence origin is genuine or inherited. Genuine incompetence simply means that the challenge is truly difficult for those attempting to address it. Inherited incompetence can be found in the inferior conventional practices that are being used. The resulting inability to proficiently address challenges not only rewards organizations by longevity extension via an unmet challenge, but this influence also enables recognition and rewards within organizations (i.e., recall the personal benefits that the "seven-month job" provided). From our earlier discussion, challenge mastery demonstration inspires a perception of triviality (it must be easy), and the apparent lack of proficiency (it must be difficult) creates an impression of importance. I noticed that managers who maintained their struggle with their over-the-cliff performance could regularly demonstrate leadership behaviors as they "saved the day" for their departments. These opportunities provided visibility to upper management by being the face of explaining the concerns that could prevent us from delivering product to the public. This spawned an impression of their high value to the company through routine-like recognition and rewards. Upon closer examination, the persisting over-the-cliff problems were simply being "managed" in a visible manner. For instance, we were building a test facility that could be used for vehicle development. An expert was in charge of making a special large paved area very flat for vehicle braking and handling testing. His frequent reports to our management revealed multiple failed attempts to smooth the irregularities in the surface. Finally, when he succeeded, he was given an award to reflect our gratitude for his effort. Had he been successful on the first try, this would have made the task appear to be easy and nothing special. Further, this task would not have had significant management visibility. As a consequence, this accomplishment would not have been nominated for the award. The difficulty that was demonstrated to complete the job not only generated an award from us, but we also rewarded the individual with extended compensation and associated overtime pay during the struggle to complete the task. In effect, the nature of the organization's culture is to reward actions that appear difficult and to ignore or dismiss functions that work well as if they are trivial. A side effect of this culture is that it discourages constructive behavior (i.e., getting it right the first time) because it forfeits opportunities for political exposure and its related rewards. One could interpret the impact of the display of incompetence as follows: The favorable exposure that arises from challenge-related incompetence can be leveraged for an individual's status growth and recognition within an organization. In addition, an organization that does not fully address its challenge(s) may be rewarded by continuing to exist.

This "struggle recognition and reward" within organizations is a counterproductive force that organization manipulators can use for their own benefit. The manipulator recognizes that if one wishes to rise in status with this organizational culture, the causal factor of exposure needs to be leveraged. Thus, rather than simple incompetence that sustains a manipulator's relevance, it is a choice by a manipulator to appear to struggle (it must be difficult) relative to the organization's mission as a means to generate exposure chances. Perhaps unknowingly, this deliberate incompetence is promoted by management training practices that encourage the top levels to focus on "what to do" and push the "how to do" of a job function to the lowest levels in the organization. At first, this seems reasonable since the "what to do" should come from contending with the high-level challenges at the heart of the organization's mission. Yet, when the M-O continuum is focused on the organization (O), the status quo of the organization is the priority of the leaders; and some level of mission neglect is only natural given that interpreting "what to do" differently from those in authority is politically risky. To make matters worse, the inadequacy of the "how to do" is typically why an organization falls into crisis, and this is arbitrarily out of scope for the leadership to address according to their training. For example, the "what to do" is to make an appealing product. An organization will utilize inferior research methods for product attributes and specifications, pay too much for components, and use outdated manufacturing processes to create it. The organization's vulnerability is not in the idea of making an appealing product; rather, it is in the shortcomings of "how" an appealing product is created. In a stark example of "how to do" neglect, a top executive responds to concerns regarding a department's function with, "We should fire those that complained." This manipulator's response has the effect of defending the conventional practices against any potential improvement and politically discourages others from coming forward with new growth opportunities. When the sustained incompetence exceeds the tolerance of the stakeholders in the organization, an executive manipulator can visibly punish the staff in the lower levels (for their failed "how to do") in an effort to impress their superiors. Since the "protected" approaches are generally at fault, those punishments are irrelevant, and the organization's incompetence is sustained. With no meaningful change, the inferior approaches continue to underperform. When those shortcomings threaten the organization or put it into a crisis, effective leadership is deployed to address the over-the-cliff condition. Their corrective actions are predominantly in the domain of "how to do" in as much as it has failed a typically credible "what to do" (as in the appealing product example). The most successful rescuers of organizations correct the "how to do" and may update the hindered "what to do" elements of the mission to better match the current business climate. As a result, a successful rescue establishes a new healthy plateau through true leadership that is disruptive to the status quo of the manipulator through intelligent action aimed at the mission of the organization.

Growth to a healthy plateau does not happen without change, and prudently controlling that change, is vital to avoid setbacks. Although the over-the-cliff crisis condition caused by a poor adjustment of causal factors is undesirable, the perspective and awareness concerning the sensitivity to these factors (the location of the cliffs) are essential to avoid creating a setback in the future. When the members of an organization have only experienced a reasonably healthy plateau, there is a risk of causal-factor ignorance. In such a case, the healthy plateau is taken for granted, and any change is assumed to be for the better. Uninformed opinion may cause methods, rules, or laws to be modified, discarded, or supplemented that alter how the causal factors are applied. These actions can pose a setback risk when an organization undoes some of the actions that were necessary to prevent a crisis. By means of example, a governmental organization needs to optimize compliance with behaviors that support the society. This is done through incentives and punishments. First, rules and laws are used to set the boundaries for some of the causal factors. The interpretation framework that the laws provide is linked through a passive-intelligence connection to a consequence, perhaps a fine or jail time. These artificial consequences replace the real consequence of everyone in society behaving accordingly. For example, if everyone looted all of our stores, we would no longer have any stores. On the side of incentives, some products are subsidized through financial support to encourage society's use of them. The artificial viability of fledgling technologies in the energy sector is a good example of guiding the society to a more environmentally friendly plateau without financial ruin. When an organization's behavior is based on principles and the causal factors of a healthy plateau, it is functioning intelligently. In this state, when a healthy plateau is achieved, a decision is to be made to attempt to preserve that condition or to grow from that condition. If preservation is chosen, the manipulators will assume residence in the organization, until the next crisis occurs.

As we have seen, manipulators are most likely found when the organization departs from the mission-driven limit of the M-O continuum. From an economic perspective, an organization's fundamental mission is to deliver a good or service to the public. However, the process of delivery presents an opportunity for exploitation for the financial benefit of the organization that arises from the motivation to maximize the return from of every sale. Thus, the salesperson, much like a manipulator, may attempt to overcharge or persuade a customer to purchase additional items that do not serve the person's best interests. Similarly, at a dental office following an oral cleaning, various recommendations might be made in order to manipulate the patient into getting more services that perhaps are not necessary (x-rays, etc.). The good news is that competition effectively limits the departure from the mission to the organization side in the M-O continuum. From the short-life light-bulb example, suppose a new vendor offers a much-longer-life light bulb, which quickly becomes the best choice in the marketplace. The original vendor will need to extend bulb life; otherwise, they cannot be sustained as all business shifts to the long-life bulb provider. The natural forces of fair competition have proven to be an effective means to reduce the manipulator's exploits. This fairness of competition may require governmental intervention to safeguard the public from exploitation. For example, regulation of monopolistic industries can take the form of dividing a consolidated industry to create separate entities to foster competition or to strictly control the industry. With the advent of artificial intelligence, we may have another means to keep manipulators in check and to leverage our resources more intelligently:

The role of artificial intelligence in an industry has potential to keep an organization focused on a clear mission and insulate it from the influence of potential manipulators. In effect, the AI serves only the mission side of the M-O continuum. Thus, competition in the marketplace is not essential to protect the public. Without competition, the redundancies of multiple organizations doing the same tasks can be eliminated. This liberates economic capacity that can be leveraged elsewhere. Now by means of example, let's consider intelligent mission-based management of the light-bulb industry with only one vendor. The challenge is to provide sustainable lighting solutions (light bulbs) to the public. Industry sustainability follows from the need for the product and the ongoing capacity of the vendor to provide product. First, let's make a product that will not fail under normal use. This means that the need for bulb replacement happens due to accidental damage or exposure to hazards. The second requirement is that the manufacturing system must be able to provide replacement light bulbs. Additionally, a growth of the light-bulb supply in the hands of the public will be needed to support new buildings, for example. A single manufacturing system can be sized and optimized for this circumstance as it is sustained by very limited product failures and a possible growth in the need for more lighting. Clearly, with these superior bulbs, the discarded light-bulb (waste) volume will be greatly reduced, and the pollution consequences of creating new light bulbs will be significantly reduced. This industrial configuration serves the mission and minimizes the disturbance of the planet's condition. Given that a healthy plateau is characterized by routine processes, an artificially intelligent device could be used in place of the principled (mission driven) leaders to maintain this healthy condition.

Unfortunately, with a shift to artificial intelligence control of an industry, the free-market economic forces that motivate improvement or movement to a healthier plateau for the industry are largely forfeit. This result is similar to what manipulators deliver in that the AI also continues with familiar stagnate approaches and resists change. In the absence of competition, there is no challenge to serve the public more effectively. This motivation can be artificially created through clever regulation by a government to challenge the industry to improve and, in effect, replace those forces. This is not an unfamiliar mechanism as successful Environmental Protection Agency mandates in the United States have reduced pollutants and have motivated improved transportation energy efficiency in the past. For the "single-vendor light-bulb industry," a mandate to make a healthier plateau could be issued to reduce production and material costs as well as to reduce lighting power consumption in future light bulbs through design and technology choices. In this circumstance, there is no economic consequence for not meeting these mandates since the industry is needed and will remain relevant regardless of progress. Thus, some sort of reward for meeting the mandated improvement requirements is needed.

One way to encourage improvement is to share the benefit of the improvement with the innovators that advance the industry to a healthier plateau—at least for a time. This concept was utilized when the seven-month job was dramatically reduced in an earlier example. When this improvement happened, the support staff was "losing" considerable overtime pay. This was a counterproductive force that caused them to resist change, since it took something away from them. In that case, I elected to grant pseudo overtime to them based on our efficiency gains. For example, at the peak of the core activity, a typical day would require around thirteen hours of tedious work per person. With the new processes, we trimmed those days to around nine hours and accomplished over twice the previous output. Recognizing this, I instructed the staff to claim two hours more than what they actually worked for those days. In effect, the company was receiving at least twenty-six hours' worth of "old" value from the staff at a cost of around eleven hours per day. The following year, the pseudo overtime was only one hour. After that, we emphasized that we didn't have to work so hard, and the pseudo overtime was discontinued. This compensation approach creatively connected the benefit of growing efficiency to the staff, and it was motivating for further improvement. At the same time, the company immediately benefitted from the reduced expenses that truly exceeded expectations since no reduction was expected at all. In a similar way, the economic value of mandated improvements in a controlled industry can be used to generate profit and revenue for the industry's innovators if the existing pricing structure is largely maintained for the public. The idea to slowly reduce the pricing partially shares the benefit with the public as these profits from the improvement are gathered for the innovators. Eventually, the new low-cost condition will be fully given to the public. This is one means to provide economic motivation for achieving a healthier plateau. The short-term benefit to the public is not maximized (the price could be reduced immediately), but the delay to get the full benefit is profoundly better than not having the improvement whatsoever.

Naturally, not all of our industries are mature and ready to be delegated to an artificially intelligent device or to be insulated from competitive market forces. These industries are dynamic and evolving to meet new needs that may be known or are perhaps anticipated. These organizations tend to reside near the mission side of the M-O continuum. Ideally, this forms an organization with a mission-based culture that the market rewards as proficiency improvement, and mission achievement occurs. Internally, new interpretations for the "how to do" and "what to do" aspects of the mission (or challenge) are welcomed and recognized from all levels of the organization. The growth of the interpretation framework of the organization to an exceptional condition is desirable since the interpretation of the challenge and pertinent resource recognition is central to intelligent responses. The interpretation frameworks held by experts will not be compromised by popular consensus, but will be challenged by alternative perspectives to foster learning and growth. The organization is expected to shrink and grow as a reflection of its relative proficiency and pertinence related to key elements of the challenge and mission. In essence, a healthy plateau is continually being adapted to be made even healthier. The perception of not being on a sufficiently healthy plateau (despite significant progress) can prevent the leadership's accomplishments from being trivialized. This can maintain the focus on the mission portion of the M-O continuum through a healthy respect for the "how to do" aspects of the mission. This falls in line with the "if it isn't broken, raise your standards" mindset. For challenges that are close-ended, when the challenge is met, the organization should either take on a new challenge or disband. Clearly, it is not very intelligent to contend with a challenge that no longer exists.

CHAPTER 11

DON'T LET AI EAT YOUR PIE

The passive-intelligence genre is the domain in which artificial intelligence can excel through rapid and repeatable recall of memorized information. An AI device with sufficient development time will have a response record for any challenge that has ever been experienced. A typical human being functions largely in the passive-intelligence genre as well. These persons respond to challenges with what has been trained and familiar or essentially they react by habit. This means that an AI device may directly compete with humans that function in this way, but it is its proficiency of recognition and response that can eclipse that of most human beings. The nature of the passive-intelligence genre operates well for familiar and confirmed experiences, but it is potentially foolish and harmful when an unsubstantiated response is delivered.

More sophisticated AI devices form their own interpretation frameworks through analysis of large data sets. A cognitive scientist might identify this approach as a heuristic (a reasoning shortcut) called *anchoring* (Sternberg & Sternberg 2012), which essentially secures a fixed reference as a starting point that serves as the basis for future reasoning. Ideally, this anchoring secures causal factor sensitivity recognition from the data set for future use. Unfortunately, this reasoning shortcut may generate a bias called *illusory correlation* (Sternberg & Sternberg 2012) that tends to link attributes together, even if they should not be. This bias is often produced by giving statistically invalid relationships, found in the anchoring data, credibility. Such a failure occurred when an AI tool was deployed to detect persons infected with COVID-19 (Heaven 2021). In this case, the training data set included patient scans that were standing or lying down. The AI learned that patients lying down were more likely to be sick (and infected). Thus, a key factor to determine infection status of a new patient depended on their physical position when scanned. Although the correlation in the limited data set is true, it is not statistically true that standing people are not infected, and the tool was deemed not valid for clinical use. Because of a lack of evidence that sick people can also stand in the data set, the AI essential formed a stereotype for this attribute. In a similar way, automotive market researchers reported a new trend in the United States to use locking gas caps. The researchers erroneously based their findings solely on the vehicles available to the public at the New York Auto Show (that had locks to avoid theft and contaminants in the fuel tanks). The data set itself was not comprehensive enough to infer properly and without bias.

In 2014, an AI-powered recruiting tool was trained with the intent to help the human resources department of a large company screen employment applications (Dastin 2018). Thus, the challenge is screening applications, rather than finding the best candidate match for open positions. (If the challenge is to match the position's requirements to the candidate's credentials, an inquisitive AI could work very well.) The company's historical screening behavior from ten years of employee population and resume information was used as the data set to train the tool. The AI learned and applied judgment criteria that led to typical candidate choices that would sustain the current employee population's attributes. Perhaps this seems reasonable, but if a specialist is needed, the AI may not consider this somewhat rare candidate as *typical* and reject them. In effect, the recruiting tool is acting to normalize the hiring practices of the company on its existing plateau. To make matters worse, the bulk of resumes received were from male candidates, which created an *illusory correlation* bias. As a result, the tool learned to become sexist in its recommendations and was scrapped by the company by 2018. The poor challenge interpretation and an improper AI approach selection resulted in missed opportunities. This behavior is similar to an organization's manipulator that holds an allegiance to past practices and will not welcome outliers that might deviate from them.

In general, when an AI device is required to respond outside of its training (experience contained in the data set), an assumption is made that the causal factor sensitivities are valid and can be applied to unproven circumstances. This can be dangerous when we reflect on the principle of plateaus and cliffs. AI applications (and people) that attempt to predict or forecast future results are extrapolating from an existing or historical plateau. For example, according to CNN in 2021, the company Zillow used an AI-powered software that recommends purchasing project houses that can be renovated and resold for profit. The software assumed typical renovation timing that did not account for labor shortages in a pandemic. This "cliff" caused delays that harmed the company's profitability. In product refinement research, one may have a taste test that includes sugar as a causal factor in the appeal of a pastry. A positive relationship emerges that reveals increasing sugar content results in a better tasting pastry. It would be a bit irresponsible to recommend a pastry with excessive levels of sugar without verification. Otherwise, the assumption that increasing sugar makes a better pastry could result in passing over a cliff of too much sugar. Thus, the unclear pertinence of projected assumptions regarding causal relationships creates risk of failure.

We cited an example of a child that has a mission to eat pie for dessert. If the child eats the entire pie, the objective is met. Yet the pie was supposed to be shared among the guests at a dinner party. The child did not consider the coexisting challenge to provide dessert to everyone. This type of neglect is an area that people fail and where an AI can readily fail to respond intelligently. Science fiction sometimes has an evil AI destroying all human life as it serves its selfish needs. It is the lack of a mature interpretation framework that is behind these failures. A mature interpretation framework will grasp all coexisting challenges and connect to a response that serves all concerns. Perhaps a more comprehensive interpretation framework is demonstrated by an autonomous vehicle that elects to crash into a guard rail to avoid hitting a pedestrian. Although safely completing a trip on time is the primary challenge interpretation, an interpretation framework that also includes minimizing human damage en route is a more comprehensive interpretation of the challenge. The ability to interpret challenges more suitably is a means to highly proficient responses for artificially intelligent devices and for humans.

With high proficiency as a very desirable condition, let us consider a new challenge to make genius-level proficiency in our intelligent devices and in ourselves. Our first step is to interpret this "genius" challenge statement. When we do so, we find that this challenge statement is not very good. It is a relative goal with a vague implied comparison to an arbitrary level of proficiency. Conventionally, correctness and proficiency have been strongly associated with high intelligence, having the highest level being genius. However, from countless historical examples, it is clear that "correctness" is an evolving condition that renders previously considered intelligent responses foolish. Similarly, as higher levels of proficiency are achieved, what was once believed to be exceptional becomes commonplace and not noteworthy. Perhaps it is speed, relative ease, complexity, or elegance of the response that influences our interpretation of an intelligent act that can make it noteworthy; but those criteria satisfy a subjective supplemental "style challenge" or a secondary requirement that is added to meeting the original primary challenge. The genius label is what we apply to entities that offer responses that not only meet a challenge but also are extraordinary. Thus, an exceptional proficiency demonstration by any or all of the three intelligence genres is where genius can be recognized.

The genius label from the passive-intelligence genre arises from recognition and response proficiency. It does not come from the novelty of the response. Passive intelligence has an almost seamless transition from recognition to response, and this blending makes for fast responses. The comprehensiveness of recognition and connected responses is one way to be perceived as exceptional. For example, a student that scores perfectly on a test is considered exceptional compared to those that do not. This might not necessarily earn the subjective label of genius, but certainly there is a tendency to label the student as smart. Trivia contests provide another chance to display the comprehensiveness of the passive-intelligence genre's resources with fast responses, and the winner is considered to be exceptional compared to the others. In effect, the valued proficiency is simply a mastery of the delivery process of known information. An expert that relies on their unique challenge recognition and specialized training similarly may be considered a genius due to the ability to translate what is recognized into uncommon responses that few others possess. The fact that the response is not widely known is what makes it appear to be exceptional—a false novelty. Thus, the conventional training of the passive-intelligence genre's resources can lead to high performance through the growth of the volume of information that can be accessed. It is the seamless flow from challenge recognition to a response that compels us to provide the label of genius, as long as the response is pertinent. However, some people may fake their expertise by providing quick or complicated responses. Others might perceive those imposters as intelligent without confirmation of the correctness of their responses. The passive-intelligence genre is vulnerable to providing incorrect responses, since the pertinence of those responses is assumed rather than confirmed. When the response is not pertinent, the genius label is certainly not applicable. Further, when there is no connected response to a given challenge, the genius label is not applied. Given that a genius must deliver pertinent responses, it is clear that any credible response may require confirmation through the use of the active-intelligence genre and not take a chance on a pertinence assumption.

Pertinence confirmation, by the active-intelligence genre, is another place where genius can be found. When Albert Einstein was refining his interpretation logic framework (relativity theory) for physics, he was contending with conventional understanding of causal factors and investigated their appropriateness, even to the point of questioning time itself. During the scientific process, various interpretation logic frameworks contain hypotheses of how to interpret the causal relationships. Einstein challenged his frameworks through thought experiments for unusual circumstances. When inconsistency was found, the interpretation logic framework required adjustment to make sense of the circumstance. Eventually, Einstein's genius was captured in his interpretation logic framework that emerged as the best fit for the laws of physics thus far. The refinement of truth found by the active-intelligence genre can be extraordinary.

With this, we have the ability to recognize high proficiency or extraordinary function in the passive-intelligence genre and in the active-intelligence genre. The interpretive-intelligence genre proficiency for passive intelligence has the simplest of demands on the interpretation function—recognition, which is not extraordinary. From many examples cited before, the confirmation activity by the active-intelligence genre can be used to correct and refine interpretation frameworks (i.e., not falling off the earth). Thus, the higher level proficiency in the interpretive-intelligence genre is a consequence of interacting with the active-intelligence genre. When the interpretive-intelligence genre incorporates verified causal factors into an interpretation logic framework, it is influenced by the active-intelligence genre. The following question can initiate that influence on the interpretation framework, what are the *controllable* causal factors related to the challenge? Since an intelligent action is not possible using uncontrollable factors, a challenge statement that relies on uncontrollable factors is of limited use. For example, a goalie for a sports team may have a challenge to be on a winning team. Another challenge is to be the best goalie in the league. These challenges have many factors that are not controllable. Thus, useful causal factors are not in sharp focus. A better challenge statement for the goalie is not to allow any goals. This statement leads to a high content of controllable causal factors that are pertinent in forming a goalie's response. If this challenge is accomplished, it will ensure that the goalie's contribution will not result in the team's loss. (Goal-keeping proficiency is the focus and not the performance of others.) For this reason, the highest-quality challenge statements are based on absolute and not relative goals. Thus, any kind of comparison to another's proficiency should be avoided. In business, a challenge is to deliver products without defects to the market place. The question becomes, "What are the causal factors and resources that enable delivering defect-free products?" This forms an interpretation logic framework that is sensitive to those factors rather than, "How can we deliver fewer defective products than a competitor?" In that case, study of the flawed competitor tends to be the focus rather than the mastery of the controllable factors. Let us begin the pursuit of high-intelligence proficiency by embedding a means to interpret challenges.

What follows is an attempt to coach a means to optimize each of the causal factors of intelligence and build them into an interpretation logic framework: At first, when we observe or receive a challenge, our interpretation logic framework should instantly look for better ways to interpret that challenge. As we have noted previously, interpretation frameworks can often be articulated through questions. These questions can be trained to be triggered by any challenge statement and eventually be embedded in the passive-intelligence genre, which means that they basically happen by reflex: What is the actual purpose that the current challenge statement is attempting to address? Additional questions that support this answer are: Does this challenge statement imply a specific solution or limit the responses in any way? Is there a more general way to express this challenge? Is this statement really the challenge, or is it something else? If this challenge is a relative challenge how can it be restated to be an absolute challenge? If this challenge is blended with other challenges, how can we separate and prioritize them? Is the challenge based on credible information (is it statistically meaningful)? Is this even a challenge at all?

These are only a few of the questions that can be practiced to train interpretation proficiency regarding challenges. It would be naïve to think that this collection of questions is exhaustive, but this list likely takes the place of doing essentially nothing with a given challenge statement. If so, this indicates that a nonfunctioning interpretive-intelligence genre has been activated and infused with active-intelligence genre causal factors for challenge interpretation. By means of example, a friend claims that they have a challenge to make a public presentation. They are worried about making a presentation due to being plagued by a thought poison. Specifically, the friend has habitually believed that they cannot speak publicly.

To them, the challenge is to speak in public, and that is distressing. However, the purpose of their presentation is not to present it publicly—that is not the challenge. Rather, the challenge is to share the content of their presentation. Why share that content? The answer is that the content can help people—and ideally as many as possible. So the challenge statement evolves into helping people with this presentation's content. The higher goal of helping people takes the place of the challenge of speaking publicly. What happened? The value of the true challenge reduces the thought poison to an obstacle in a bigger and more important challenge. Hopefully, the friend can be persuaded that the value they are bringing is far more important than any clumsiness that they may or may not have in bringing it. Perhaps an analogy of withholding food from hungry people only because of a risk of spilling a little when it is delivered would help refocus the friend on the true challenge.

The habitual use of an interpretation logic framework for the refinement of any challenge statement is useful to set the criteria of pertinent responses (inherited or otherwise) and will improve proficiency potential. The next step to high proficiency is to connect that challenge interpretation with the active-intelligence genre to refine it. The answers to the controllable causal factor question create an interpretation logic framework for responding to the challenge and other related challenges. If that framework is refined and validated, the response selection comes from well-known rigorously confirmed relationships. By function, the interpretive-intelligence genre has a built-in simulation mechanism that recognizes what responses will be successful or will not be successful regarding a challenge. On occasion, when creative persons operate with this connection, others may be amazed with the speed and effectiveness of the response. With the tendency to view this cause-based interpretation proficiency as unusual, the label of genius may be assigned to those that successfully combine their interpretive-intelligence genre with their active-intelligence genre. The example of the philosophy professor refining his grasp of trigonometry to see how far the eye could see was a slow process to get the correct answer. Yet the student with a mature awareness of trigonometry could instantly provide the correct answer.

If the challenge interpretation is connected to causal factors (blended genres), the causal factors are used to recognize pertinent resources. From the example of assembling a jigsaw puzzle, the causal factors (attributes) of shape and color combination are considered when selecting a piece to be fit into a vacant position. The natural questions follow for observed free puzzle pieces: Is this shape appropriate for the vacancy? Is this color appropriate for the vacancy? These are interpretation-framework questions that will screen for the most pertinent candidate pieces. For many of us, we approximate the shape and color attributes, and this lack of exact detail means that we will need to try fitting the candidate pieces into the vacancy with some being rejected (confirmation testing). A "genius" deeply knows the exact shape and exact colors of the missing puzzle piece and would recognize that single candidate piece accordingly. For more complex challenges, there may be several alternative responses that can meet the challenge. Even in this case, the causal factors can be altered to make questions and establish an interpretation logic framework. What is it about the observed resources that can influence a causal factor for the challenge? From experience, a good question to trigger the interpretive-intelligence genre for this is actually a negative question: What is it about this resource that renders it useless for this challenge? This approach enables an assessment of resources that would normally be ignored because of the purpose that those resources normally serve. When no good reason emerges that disqualifies the resource, it is a candidate. For example, suppose we are running low on firewood and have a challenge to keep warm. When we observe nearby objects, we see furniture and curtains among other things. A negative resource question is, Why cannot the curtains be helpful in keeping warm? To answer this, the challenge's causal relationships that include insulating yourself and generating heat (burning fuel) are considered: Can the curtains be burned? Can the curtains be used for insulation? In this way, the interpretation logic framework for a given challenge can have unique questions that are essentially restatements of the causal factors that are used to identify pertinent resources. The curtains could potentially be burned or used like a blanket. In this case, we have recognized a single resource that can be utilized in different ways.

The final response selection from the various pertinent candidate responses finishes an intelligent action. Generally, there are coexisting challenges that aid in the final selection. This means that the side effects of the candidate responses need to be considered. This gives rise to an interpretation framework that seeks the most appropriate choice (Kepner & Tregoe 1997): What do we lose by making this choice? What risk do we create by making this choice? What opportunities or functions are lost if we make this choice? Is this choice a long-term or short-term response? How timely is this response choice? How costly is this response choice? These are a few useful questions that can facilitate a decision. From the curtain example above, removing the curtain might expose a broken window that makes the room impossible to heat. The choice to use the curtain like a blanket provides a long-term resource for warmth and avoids the risks posed by burning it.

To summarize, the genius label may come from the demonstration of extraordinary ability in any intelligence genre function. It is the connection of the interpretive-intelligence genre with the active-intelligence genre that supports the aim of uncommon or extraordinary proficiency. This high proficiency is rooted in seamlessly interpreting a challenge and pertinent response resources by incorporating full recognition of the challenge's causal factors. Beyond that, the interpretive-intelligence genre considers coexisting challenges either in the reformation of the challenge statement or in making the final candidate response selection.

Typically, the extraordinary performance furnished by the passive-intelligence genre arises from rapid connected responses to recognized challenges. The diligence to assess the integrity of the challenge and to confirm the pertinence of the response is neglected. Thus, misdirected actions with assumed pertinence are a shared vulnerability for AI devices and persons that depend on the passive-intelligence genre. If that vulnerability is exposed, it will not result in the label of "genius" or even be considered intelligent. This helps us recognize real intelligence in action:

Real intelligence does not tolerate a superficial challenge interpretation or an assumption of response pertinence. Rather, it acts to comprehensively clarify all aspects of the challenge and to confirm the pertinence of the response to it. Thus, if the interpretive-intelligence genre is immature or impeded (i.e., poor challenges, thought poisons, paradigm allegiance, coexisting challenge neglect), it hampers the demonstration of real intelligence. In an extreme case, warmongers maliciously pursue their own interests. Their narrow challenge interpretation leads to an overall degradation of the human condition. To varying degrees, AI devices or persons acting with poor or hindered interpretive intelligence skills fail. Thus, perfecting interpretive intelligence skills may be our greatest challenge.

BIBLIOGRAPHY

Dastin, Jeffrey. "Insight—Amazon Scraps Secret AI Recruiting Tool That Showed Bias against Women." https://www.reuters.com/article/idUSL2N1WP1RO/.

Deming, W. E. *Out of the Crisis*. Massachusetts: MIT Press, 1991.

Domingos, P. *The Master Algorithm: How the Quest for the Ultimate Learning Machine Will Remake Our World*. New York: Basic Books, 2015.

Duhigg, C. *The Power of Habit*. New York: Random House Books, 2013.

Gardner, H. *Frames of Mind: The Theory of Multiple Intelligences*. New York: Basic Books, 1983.

Heaven, Will Douglas. "Hundreds of AI Tools Have Been Built to Catch COVID. None of Them Helped." *MIT Technology Review* (July 2021). https://www.technologyreview.com/2021/07/30/1030329/machine-learning-ai-failedcovid-hospital-diagnosis-pandemic/.

Hersey, P. and K. H. Blanchard. *Management of Organizational Behavior: Utilizing Human Resources*, 3rd ed. New Jersey: Prentice Hall, 1977.

Kepner, C. and B. Tregoe. *The New Rational Manager: An Updated Edition for a New World*. New Jersey: Princeton Research Press, 1997.

Köhler, W. *The Mentality of Apes*. Translated by E. Winter. Boston: Harcourt, 1925.

Munson, R. and D. Conway. *The Elements of Reasoning*. Indiana: Better World Books, 1996.

Sternberg, Robert J., and Karin Sternberg. *Cognitive Psychology*, 6th ed. Massachusetts: Cengage Learning, 2012.

ABOUT THE AUTHOR

The proliferation of *artificial intelligence* in our lives has generated apprehension or fear of AI on the part of the general public. Further, nontechnical decision-makers tend to lack an informed high-level perspective concerning AI, which compounds the fear. At its root, the fear of AI arises from the risk of unintelligent actions. In such a case, *real intelligence* is lacking. To address these fears, pursuing real intelligence for humans and machines was the motivation behind this book. The author leverages background as an inventor of over forty US patents and experience in developing automated systems (currently called artificial intelligence) that has been refined through a thirty-five year engineering and management career in an international setting. He has received the EPA's Climate Protection Award in addition to serving as a technical reviewer for the US Advanced Research Projects Agency.

www.ingramcontent.com/pod-product-compliance
Lightning Source LLC
LaVergne TN
LVHW090321210926
848480LV00001B/315
* 9 7 9 8 8 9 3 0 8 2 0 8 1 *